HEARST

Lord of San Simeon

HEARST
Lord of San Simeon

BY

*Oliver Carlson and
Ernest Sutherland Bates*

GREENWOOD PRESS, PUBLISHERS
WESTPORT, CONNECTICUT

Originally published in 1936
by The Viking Press

First Greenwood Reprinting 1970

SBN 8371-2847-1

PRINTED IN UNITED STATES OF AMERICA

CONTENTS

ILLUSTRATIONS

INTRODUCTION

BEFORE William Randolph Hearst shall pass into the limbo of forgotten things, he will doubtless be the subject of many biographies. An extraordinary person, with extraordinary energy even for an American, he has combined in one a number of careers each of which would have sufficed for lesser men. As a capitalist, creating—according to the authorized biography by Mrs. Fremont Older—the second largest fortune in the country, he and his methods would deserve special study as a significant part of the history of American Big Business; for this task, the ideal writer would be one familiar from the inside with such methods—in other words, an honest Big-Business man. As a journalist, creating the greatest chain of newspapers in the world, Hearst would again deserve a special treatise; and in this case, the ideal writer would be an independent journalist. Once more, as a politician, an incendiary force in American life for forty years, Hearst demands particular consideration, preferably by a disinterested politician. And even if all three such rarities could be found and their special tasks completed there would still remain the larger and more difficult problem of seeing the man as a whole and estimating the emotional and other drives underlying all these special activities.

There is, of course, no such thing as a "definitive biography," for the simple reason that biographers, like their subjects, are products of their times. The obstacles in the way of even a satisfactory biography of such a figure as Hearst are peculiarly evident because of the complexity of the issues involved and the lack of such material as that mentioned above. Rather, however, than wait for their great-grandchildren to write a more adequate life of Hearst—by which time, it is to be presumed, he will be as unimportant for American life as the medieval Fuggers—the authors have preferred to offer their interpretation today when it is needed. Not being Big-Business men, journalists, or politicians, they have been compelled to take their material where they found it, using the customary methods of biographical research which they have found ample to explode a number of widely propagated Hearst myths. They do not pretend to greater "objectivity" than is to be found in a scrupulous adherence to the facts and in giving credit where credit is due. Their primary interest has been in understanding rather than in condemning, but they know no way of avoiding the implications of such descriptive terms as "mendacity," "hypocrisy," "economic motivation," other than by avoiding interpretation altogether. The sole question would seem to be whether the interpretation is borne out by the facts.

It may be helpful to consider separately for a moment the three main phases of Hearst's life that in the subsequent account become interwoven with his personality. Governing the general pattern of his activities is his private fortune. That he inherited thirty million dollars, which in turn he built up to a fortune of probably ten times that amount in holdings or control, forms in itself a chapter in American finance. It is naturally tempting to dismiss other considerations forthwith and interpret Hearst's actions as always a product of this economic drive. But this would be too easy. While it would give us—and does give us—the general framework within which his career could take place, it fails to differentiate his achievements from those of others, such as the Rockefellers and the Morgans. Hearst as a capitalist like other capitalists would not be particularly interesting. But as a capitalist unlike other capitalists he presents a fascinating problem. From the socio-economic viewpoint the difference is a minor one; for the biographer, it is fundamental.

The peculiar characteristics of Hearst as a capitalist are that he has always sought tangible rather than intangible properties, that he has combined spending with accumulation as no one else has done, and that during at least the earlier part of his career he stood out as an avowed liberal in politics. These characteristics can be understood only in the light of his upbringing as a parvenu California millionaire, the son of George Hearst—whose shady business and political dealings the present authors seem to have been the first to study—and also the son of the sentimental idealist, Phebe Apperson. Against that background, it is possible to see how Hearst the capitalist could for so many years appear to himself and others as primarily an opponent of capitalists in the days when capitalists were still divided among themselves.

The potent figure of the burly George Hearst, transmogrified into a plaster saint by senatorial eulogists after his death, also stood behind William Randolph Hearst's beginnings as a journalist. That George Hearst bought and developed the San Francisco *Examiner* as an aid to his political ambitions, that his son was groomed for the management of it, and that the latter started out in his journalistic career as the owner of a paper with a definitely "liberal," anti-monopolistic policy—all this is a hitherto untold but highly important chapter in the life of Hearst the journalist. That he introduced the latest methods of "yellow journalism" to the Pacific Coast, and that there and in New York he sought and achieved a new low level of publicity appeal—with devastating effect upon the whole field of American journalism—has long been recognized, but there has been less realization of the fact that from the standpoint of inner life, editorial efficiency, and news-gathering Hearst's early papers were much better than his later ones. Though always personal organs, the San Francisco *Examiner*, the New York *Journal*, and the New York *American* in the first years of their existence made a genuine effort to get the news, however much they might sometimès distort it in the telling. With Hearst's growing absorption in politics, his increasing cynicism as a result of political defeat, he ceased even to insist upon getting the news, occasionally finding it easier, cheaper, and more satisfactory to employ second-rate correspondents or none at all than to trouble to get those widely known in their profession. Hearst the journalist became submerged first in Hearst the politician and then in Hearst the business man until today his twenty-nine so-called "news" papers are little more than a gigantic chain-store, selling political patent medicines and adulterated economics.

With regard to Hearst's political policies there are three specious but contrasting methods of interpretation possible. The first, in line with the limited view of economic determinism mentioned above, would regard all of his alleged "reform" movements as cloaks in each case for some specific business advantage sought behind the scenes. That there was such explicit advantage in many instances cannot be denied. It is therefore tempting, though hardly justified, to assume that it must have been present even when this cannot be proved. The second interpretation, analogous to the first but broader, would argue that all of Hearst's concern for "reform" was motivated by self-interest of some kind—if not by desire for wealth, then by desire for power, prestige, revenge, or other well-known personal drives. This popular method of argumentation, when dealing with an enemy, has the forensic advantage but biographical disadvantage that it can never be disproved by facts, since there is no conceivable human action that might not have some indirect personal advantage the hope of which may be taken, if one wishes, to have constituted the "real" motivation of the act.

Both of these supposedly hard-boiled and realistic attitudes suffer from the disadvantage of being psychologically naïve, deriving from the sheep-*or*-goat dichotomy of earlier centuries. They refuse to recognize the patent fact, verifiable in everyone's experience, that most of our actions are *both* self-interested and other-interested, and that the important question is one of degree, not kind. Following this initial error, they make of their subjects logical monsters, akin to the abstract "economic man" of the classical economists, thus simplifying the irrational complexity of human nature to the point where it is no longer recognizable.

Such bad psychology is particularly disastrous in the case of so exceptionally irrational a figure as that of Hearst, since it would substitute a Machiavellian demon of consistent craft and cunning, highly self-conscious, self-controlled, and integrated, for an actuality in which craft and cunning have alternated with their opposites, and self-consciousness, self-control, and integration have been exactly the qualities most lacking.

This would apparently leave us with the third and more kindly assumption that Hearst's earlier "radicalism" was sincere enough in its day but that it gradually withered in the increasing disillusionment of maturity and age. Hearst would then belong in the familiar class that includes men like Mussolini, Laval, and MacDonald in Europe, or such minor Americans as Walter Lippmann, Mark Sullivan, and George Creel. It is difficult, however, to make the facts fit this assumption.

Our approach needs to be adapted much more closely to the actual life before us. One perceives in it at once evidences of the mental attitude generally called megalomania or "the Messianic complex," which we know to be essentially an overcompensation for felt inferiority, often accompanied by arrested development along certain lines and a tendency toward split personality. Examples have naturally been especially frequent in America, in line with our lack of discipline and tradition, but they have usually been furnished, at least on the higher levels, by the religious fanatics whom we have produced in such superabundance. It is Hearst's distinction to be the first notable example among the great American capitalists. He is a religious fanatic without religion, or rather, he is, quite simply, a Hearst fanatic. Once this is understood, the man becomes comprehensible.

There is needed no technical knowledge of psychoanalysis or psychiatry to be able to trace the manifestations of this type of personality in Hearst's career. The setting will be found in his divided inheritance of temperament and ideals, his privileged upbringing, his California background of raucous wealth, crude force, and noisy demagoguery, and in his unhappy experience when western impudence first encountered eastern snobbishness. The story will tell how out of these beginnings grew the peculiar Hearstian anachronism of the resurrected feudal lord, the Childe Harold travels, the looting of European castles; how it was necessary for him to establish himself in his own eyes as different from other men, including other capitalists; how in his imaginary world such concepts as truth and sincerity came to have literally no meaning; how he went from masquerade to masquerade not so much to hide himself as to find himself, always finding another mask—from journalism to politics, and from politics on this side to politics on that; how he grew old and hardened until Hollywood revived him; how all the time old George Hearst worked within him piling up the wealth and Phebe Apperson was forever dead; and how at the end the Lord of San Simeon nearly reached a belated, if horrible honesty, in realizing himself as the ruthless Fascist capitalist toward whom he had been slowly traveling from the day of birth.

To the authors this seems in the light of the evidence a psychologically consistent and convincing story. However others may interpret it, the tale will stand as a significant part of the whole truth about Hearst. If not all of him is here—and of course not all of any man is caught in a biography—what is here, at any rate, is Hearst.

A last word as to the treatment of Hearst's "private" life. His flaunting in the face of the public his personal disregard for accepted conventions is doubtless merely a phase of his psychic compulsion to feel himself an exception to all rules. At the same time, his habit of delving into divorce-court scandals and backstairs gossip against his enemies, while believing that his wealth protected him against similar attacks, would almost excuse a biographer in over-emphasizing the whole subject. Such a treatment, aside from a natural preference of the authors for a cleaner deck of cards, would totally distort the picture. Hearst's true significance lies elsewhere. His "private" life will be treated frankly in the following pages in so far as it has affected his public life, his reputation, and his general development.

HEARST

Lord of San Simeon

CHAPTER I

"My Father Was a Great Man"

"My father was a great man, a very great man in his day."—
William Randolph Hearst.

"It was such men as George Hearst who converted the vast region
between the plains of the Missouri and the Pacific Ocean from what
was supposed to be an uninhabitable desert into prosperous and growing states."—*Senator William M. Stewart of Nevada in the United
States Senate, March 25, 1892.*

"Success such as is achieved by George Hearst is not a mere accident nor the result of chance or luck. It can only be attained by
those qualities which were his—industry, perseverance, good judgment, and truth."—*Senator Leland Stanford of California in the
United States Senate, March 25, 1892.*

"He has left to his country an unsullied name and the example of
a well-spent life, and his country in turn will embalm his memory as
one of her truest and noblest types of manhood."—*Senator Daniel
Wolsey Voorhees of Indiana in the United States Senate, March 25,
1892.*

"During all his long career in that state [California] no man ever
accused Senator Hearst of one dishonest act."—*Congressman
Thomas Jefferson Clunie of California in the United States House
of Representatives, February 28, 1891.*

THE name Hearst, according to the genealogists employed
by the family, is as old as the Anglo-Saxon language. Originally, it was spelled Hyrst. Prophetic of the far distant future,
the name signified "a thicket."

The family was Lowland Scotch, though some of them

3

strayed down into England as far as Salisbury. During the Reformation they became Presbyterians, and—according to the authorized biography, *The Life of George Hearst*, privately printed by his son—they were all "sternly moral." In the course of time, the spelling of the name was changed to Hurst.

John Hurst founded the American branch of the family. He was firmly planted on the soil of the New World before the Pilgrim Fathers had landed on Plymouth Rock, for he arrived in the colonies in 1608 and settled in what was to become Isle of Wight County in Virginia, where he is said to have acquired ten acres of land and nine Negro slaves. He begot a numerous progeny of sons and daughters; and the sons moved on into North Carolina. It was there, in the early eighteenth century, that the name was changed to Hearst.

Admiringly, the official biographer assures us that "the Hearsts were a clannish family." In one instance, three Hearst daughters married three brothers, all of them Presbyterian clergymen. Kirk and Covenant long remained the chief objects of the family's devotion. In line with this, the Hearsts apparently took no part in the American Revolution.

Early in the nineteenth century, the vast tract of land which Jefferson purchased from Napoleon in 1803 offered new opportunities to restless and ambitious souls. Such a one was William Hearst of Abbeville County, South Carolina. In 1808 he made the long trek out to Missouri and settled on a high ridge in Franklin County, where he raised wheat and corn, bred horses and cattle, and carried on a precarious trade with the pioneer city of St. Louis. In 1817 he married Elizabeth Collins, daughter of a neighboring southerner, and in 1820 was born their son George Hearst, the father of William Randolph Hearst.

George Hearst was brought up on his father's small plantation in the midst of a sparsely settled territory. The total formal schooling which he obtained was limited, according to his own testimony, to two years. His interests were from the first directed into other channels. Lead mines were discovered about fifteen miles from the Hearst homestead. The elder Hearst raised and sold hogs to the mine settlement, and it was George's task to drive the hogs thither. Mining seemed to him much more thrilling than hog-driving; his life career was settled. When he was fifteen, a lead mine was discovered within a mile of the Hearst homestead. George spent all his spare time there, sometimes making "from four to six bits a day," and gaining a real knowledge of the occupation. He soon developed an uncanny knack of mineral discovery and was called by the Indians of the neighborhood Boy-That-Earth-Talked-To.

When his father died in 1846, leaving three farms, four slaves, and a country store, as well as several thousand dollars' worth of debts, Boy-That-Earth-Talked-To took charge of the estate, but his heart was already given to mining. Through successful ventures in the latter field, he had paid off his father's indebtedness by the end of 1849 with some capital left over, and so was ready to join in the gold rush for California.

He set off on May 12, 1850, in a party of eight men and six women who met with the usual hardships, dangers, and Indian skirmishes during the six months' journey before they reached their destination in the Nevada and California mine fields. There George Hearst, at the age of thirty, found himself in an entirely new social order governed by the noose, the bowie knife, and the pistol. Its exuberance of life and death was symbolized in the names of the mining camps: Hell-Out-for-Noon City, Ground Hog Glory, Delerium Tremens, Poverty Flat, Red Dog, Jackass Gulch, Hangtown—settlements of dirty shacks and tents, their color given by the saloons, the gamblers, and the percentage ladies who followed in their wake.

Into this rough existence George Hearst, a strong fellow over six feet tall, entered with full zest. He went first to Hangtown and then to Jackass Gulch, trying placer mining but with small success; then on to Grass Valley and Nevada City, with the same meager results. Momentarily discouraged with mining, he opened a general store in partnership with Hamlet Davis (later to become the first mayor of Nevada City); a loft above the store was converted by the partners into a theater, Dramatic Hall, with a reading-room in connection. This complex venture prospered, and under the spell of its success George Hearst went down to Sacramento to set up a general merchandising establishment. Here, however, he did not do so well. His knowledge of the business was adequate for a crossroads store in the backwoods of Missouri or in one of the small mining camps, but he was unable to compete with the more adroit merchants of Sacramento—who included such shrewd traders as Leland Stanford, Collis P. Huntington, Mark Hopkins, and Charles Crocker. Fortunately, in the meantime he had located two profitable quartz mines and had organized a company to work them. So he returned to his first love.

In 1859 a turn of luck at last laid the foundation of the Hearst millions. In the spring of that year word came to Nevada City, where Hearst was again living, that a new gold strike had been made on the slopes of Mount Davidson near the Carson River in Nevada. Hearst was off to the scene with two partners to buy a half interest in the Gould and Curry mine from its owner, Alvah Gould, for $450. The latter, who believed the mine worthless, thought that he had put over a fast deal, and went galloping down Gold Canyon, shouting, "I've got away with the Californians!" A few years later, Alvah Gould was running a peanut stand and George Hearst was in the Senate. The mine that Gould so lightly parted with was indeed poor in gold, and what there was could not be got out because of the abundance of a blue-black ore that constantly impeded the miners' operations—but that blue-black ore contained silver, and the mine was a part of the now famous Comstock Lode, the richest silver deposit in the world.

By good fortune, Hearst and his partners had also bought

for a few hundred dollars a one-sixth interest in the Ophir mine, the most important in the whole lode.

During the summer of 1859 they mined forty-five tons of the silver-bearing ore, and in the fall, with a long pack-train of mules, they carried the entire amount over the wretched roads through the mountain passes and down the valleys all the way to San Francisco. Their forty-five tons proved to be worth $2200 a ton. And there were untold thousands, perhaps millions, of such tons owned by them on the sides of Mount Davidson! The story of their success ran up and down the streets of San Francisco. The gold craze of 1849 was succeeded by the silver craze of 1860.

Late in the fall of the latter year, George Hearst paid a visit to the county of his birth in Missouri. He had left it but ten years before to seek his fortune, and he now returned a millionaire, one of the kings of the Comstock Lode. According to the romantic version of the official biography, during the intervening years his dreams had been haunted by memories of a neighbor's child, pretty little Phebe Apperson, who had been eight years old at the time of his departure. She was the daughter of the richest farmer in the county, and her family had pretensions to culture beyond that of their primitive environment. At eighteen, Phebe Apperson was a school teacher, vivacious, beautiful, and romantic. And the social status of the Appersons had always been somewhat better than that of the Hearsts. So when the middle-aged George Hearst, illiterate and uncouth, came a-wooing, she and her family hesitated. But the career of a country school teacher, then as now, was not so attractive as to invite perpetual celibacy; beyond it, life as an annual child breeder to some farmer in the neighborhood offered a hardly more alluring prospect. George Hearst might be a rough diamond, but he symbolized adventure, travel, opportunity, the open road. He pressed the matter, and the Appersons finally consented to the match. In later years, when guests harped upon the virtues of his wife, George Hearst was heard to mutter, "I could a had a better one as her if I'd a wanted to." But such had not been his thoughts when, dazzled by her youth and beauty, he wooed and won her.

The bridegroom of forty-two and the bride of twenty were married on June 15, 1862. They immediately went on a wedding trip to New York City, whence they sailed to Panama and, after crossing the isthmus, sailed again to California. In San Francisco they leased a house on Taylor Street in the aristocratic Nob Hill section, high above the swirl of traffic, and there, on April 29, 1863, William Randolph Hearst was born.

Meanwhile, the returns from the Ophir continued to roll in. During its first four years alone, the mine yielded fifteen million dollars' worth of gold and silver. Hearst and his associates retained as their attorney William M. Stewart (later to be one of Hearst's eulogists in the United States Senate); he was a physical giant, ruthless in his methods. Like others of their day, the owners of the Ophir were none too scrupulous about the way in which they acquired claims. Their mine was involved in no less than thirty-seven lawsuits, Stewart's annual fees usually running to about $200,000. Judges, juries, and witnesses were bought and sold by the competing mines. In one case (Ophir vs. McCall) we are told that "the only shooting which attended the trial was directed at witnesses on their way to and from the scene." Even after titles were legally established, the battle between competing mines often continued. It was customary to hire gun thugs—at twice the wages of the miners—to raid opposition mines and hold them long enough for miners, under their protection, working frantically with pick and shovel, to get out the richest ores.

While George Hearst was engaged in these little wars of the West, the great Civil War was being fought in the East. As a Missourian and former slave owner, his sympathies were naturally with the Confederacy, and he aligned himself with the

"Lecompton Democrats" who had favored the secession of California. Elected as one of their representatives to the Democratic state convention, he there supported the following resolutions:

1. Our senators in Congress are instructed and our representatives requested to vote against and oppose any and all measures having for its or their object the conferring upon the negro the right of suffrage in the District of Columbia or any other territory belonging to the United States over which Congress has the exclusive power of legislation.
2. To vote against and oppose any measure in Congress fixing or attempting to fix the qualifications of voters in any of the states or territories in the United States.
3. To vote for admission to seats in Congress of all senators and representatives who have been elected by conventions or legislatures, or by the people of the states heretofore in rebellion.

These resolutions precipitated a miniature war in the convention itself. Inkstands and cuspidors were hurled, hickory canes were brought into play, chairs were broken and chair-legs used as bludgeons. When the excitement subsided sufficiently to allow a ballot to be taken, the Lecompton faction was defeated by the narrow margin of a forty-one to thirty-eight vote.

The pro-slavery group was nevertheless strong enough to elect George Hearst and some others to the sixteenth session of the California state legislature. There he served on the Committee of Mines and Mining Interests and helped to formulate the mining laws of the state with due regard for the rights of private property. But he introduced no bills and made no speeches. When the ratification of the Thirteenth Amendment abolishing slavery in the United States came up, he was one of the few who voted against it. This action terminated his political career for the time being. Recognizing that the state was hopelessly Unionist and Republican, he went back to his own garden.

There was a business depression in 1866–7. And the output of the Comstock mines had commenced to decrease. Hearst undertook new ventures which were not wholly satisfactory: although a mine in Kern County yielded him a handsome profit and speculation in San Francisco real estate netted $100,000, he lost $40,000 on another deal and $90,000 in an Idaho enterprise which he went into with James Fair, another of the Comstock kings. By 1874 his fortune was so jeopardized that the Hearsts sold their carriages and their horses, discharged their servants, and went to live in a modest boarding-house. But the reverse proved only temporary, as Hearst had now established a favorable connection with two new business associates, Lloyd Tevis and James Ben Ali Haggin.

Tevis was, like Hearst himself, big, bluff, and hearty—a seeming personification of simple honesty and friendliness toward all the world. In 1868 and again in 1870 he was a director of the Central Pacific Railroad in close touch with its real owners, those former Sacramento merchants, Leland Stanford, Collis P. Huntington, Mark Hopkins, and Charles Crocker, who had persuaded the government to finance an enterprise to which each of them contributed a capital of only $15,000, and from which they received dividends of $1,000,000 a year. Working with these business sharks, Lloyd Tevis arranged to put over a clever coup on the Wells-Fargo Express Company. That innocent organization was first induced to enter into an agreement with the Central Pacific to ship all goods to California over that line. The sequel may be told in the words of Charles Edward Russell in his *Stories of the Great Railroads* (1912):

The next year, however, 1870, the Wells-Fargo people were dismayed to learn that Messrs. Stanford, Huntington, Hopkins, and Crocker, with Mr. Lloyd Tevis, had organized the Pacific Express Company and purposed to compete for the express carrying trade. Competition with the men that owned the railroad and could do what they pleased with rates was no competition at all, but merely a game of stand and deliver.

The Pacific Express Company went no farther than to print some stationery and open an office, when Wells-Fargo surrendered. For a gift of one-third of the capital stock of Wells-Fargo and Company, the Pacific Express Company agreed to go out of business.

One-third of the Wells-Fargo, $3,333,333.33, was thus acquired for the cost of a bunch of stationery.

Lloyd Tevis was obviously a business associate worth having. So also was James Ben Ali Haggin. His mother was a Christian Turk, and from her he had derived a soft, suave, and gentle manner as deceptive, in its different way, as was that of Tevis. In the early seventies, Haggin, in partnership with W. D. Carr, another close friend of George Hearst, acquired at a nominal price hundreds of thousands of acres of so-called "desert land" in the Sacramento, San Joaquin, and Kern River valleys—land which they represented to the government as being almost absolutely useless. In point of fact, the soil, when irrigated, was extraordinarily rich. Soon Haggin and Carr were selling it at extortionate prices to resentful ranchers of the neighborhood who combined to bring suit against them. But the owners had the wherewithal to keep the case in the courts year after year until the ranchers were exhausted.

With two such associates as Tevis and Haggin, Hearst's fortunes began to look up again. He and Haggin in 1874 purchased the Ontario mine in Utah, called to their attention by Marcus Daly, a boss foreman of W. A. Clark, the Montana mining magnate. Through shrewd dealing and high-pressure methods, they were able to acquire the mine for a song—$27,000—and it was soon paying them dividends of nearly a million a year. With Daly's aid, they also secured another, smaller mine which yielded an income of about $30,000 a month.

Meanwhile, in company with William Compson, George D.

Roberts, and others, Hearst bought the Eureka mine in California and acquired large interests in the Richmond Consolidated and the Ruby Consolidated mines. Charges of theft and corruption in the acquisition of these mines led to many additional lawsuits. In fact, such charges and suits tended to become the habitual sequel to Hearst's appearance as a new owner of any mining properties. But the four million a year earned by these mines alone was ample to take care of all the lawsuits.

Having successfully weathered the depression of 1873–4, his fortune thereafter went up by leaps and bounds. For $80,000 he and Haggin were able to obtain a heavy interest in the largest gold mine in the United States, the Homestake, and within a year they had complete control of it, as well as of adjacent property totaling 2616 acres. The city of Lead, South Dakota, built to house the miners, was owned body and soul by Hearst and Haggin, who also secured water rights for many miles around and thus were able to collect tribute from all near-by towns. The Homestake ore brought an annual income of four million, the water rights added another $100,000.

From the Homestake in South Dakota on to the Anaconda in Montana, George Hearst's biggest strike. And again, as for the beginning of his fortune, he was indebted to chance. He and Haggin went into the venture on the advice of Marcus Daly, thinking they were getting a silver mine. Instead, they uncovered the world's richest copper vein, in one place thirty feet wide. By 1890 the Anaconda was producing sixty-seven million pounds of copper a year. It employed over five thousand men, and was alone responsible for one fifth of the world's annual copper supply. George Hearst was the largest single shareholder, having thirty shares to Haggin's twenty-seven and Daly's twenty-five.

He now reached out to foreign lands. Mines were acquired in Mexico, in Chile, in Peru. His San Luis mine in Mexico yielded a monthly profit of $25,000. And by this time his reputation for possession of the Midas touch enabled him in slack periods to earn extra thousands as a mining expert. His fees rose in proportion to his success until he was asking, and obtaining, fifty thousand dollars for his opinion on a single mine.

But the days of swift fortunes made in mines and mining stocks were almost over. The big money began to go into land and George Hearst went with the tide. In company with Haggin and A. E. Head, he bought the Victoria cattle ranch of 250,-000 acres in New Mexico, again securing the neighboring water rights, thus bringing the surrounding ranches into dependence. He next acquired over 25,000 acres of land near Phoenix, Arizona, and then bought a tract of 4500 acres in San Mateo County just south of San Francisco. He took title to extensive timber holdings in Shasta and Siskiyou counties and became one of the largest land-holders in Tulare, Fresno, Marin, and Butte counties. For his wife he purchased a charming five-hundred-acre tract near Pleasanton in Alameda County, where Mrs. Hearst was to reside after his death.

As with his mines, so with his land-holdings he found the confines of the United States too narrow. On frequent visits to Mexico he became a fast friend of President Porfirio Diaz, who was always willing to part with his country's property—for a consideration—to British, French, and American capitalists. Learning that Mexico did not have a public land surveyor, Hearst made a deal with the government whereby in return for doing the surveying himself he received full and complete title to a thousand square miles of land in the states of Vera Cruz, Campeche, and Yucatan.

There was another great tract of Mexican land upon which he had long cast covetous eyes—the Babicora ranch of 900,000 acres in the state of Chihuahua, only two hundred and forty miles from the Texas border. But the district was terrorized by Geronimo's Apache bands, and the ranch was looted again and again. In 1887, receiving through his friends in the Mexican government early information of Geronimo's capture, Hearst made haste to purchase the ranch from its absentee owners before they learned of the event. There are conflicting accounts as to just what he paid for it, but the highest figure mentioned is forty cents an acre.

Of all his holdings, the one that was to mean most in the history of the family was the Piedra Blanca ranch in California. It was a relatively modest tract of 40,000 acres, extending from San Simeon Bay on the Pacific back into the Santa Lucia mountains. Hearst bought it at a cost of seventy cents an acre, and immediately improved the harbor of San Simeon, erected ranch buildings, and began to import prize cattle. Within a few years Piedra Blanca was one of the great stock farms of the state. The Hearst family with their retinue of servants spent much time on its pleasant stretch of coast, loving the mild climate and attractive scenery.

As an avocation, George Hearst, like his friend Haggin, took up the breeding of race horses. But whereas Haggin's stables, both in California and near Lexington, Kentucky, turned out a continuous stream of favorites that captured trophy after trophy between 1880 and 1890, Hearst in this one field had little luck. His colors were indeed carried by the notable King Thomas, Gorgo, Ballarat, and Tournament, but these winners were offset by scores of pedigreed but slow-footed beasts. By and large, he lost more than a million dollars on his racing stables.

As an old forty-niner, George Hearst, of course, was fond of cards and liquor. Stakes had always run high in the gold and silver country, and in the set with whom he continued to play poker, white chips were rated at one hundred dollars, the red five hundred, and the blue a thousand.

The standards of pioneer California were entirely quantitative, and so were those of George Hearst. To control the largest and richest mines, to own vast tracts of land here, there, and everywhere, to be able to gamble heavily without feeling his losses, to be able to live as ostentatiously as possible with more servants than he could count—these things in his eyes, as in those of millions of his countrymen, constituted the whole of success. Or almost the whole of it. There was also the field of politics, from which he had been so rudely ejected in 1866. That, too, was a man's game, and he would re-enter it if the favorable moment came. As for books, art, and education, those were women's toys. He was glad that his beautiful wife was interested in them; he would always furnish her with a few thousands to send poor girls through college as she liked to do; and he was proud enough when she was made a regent of the University of California. It was quite fitting that she should be a philanthropist; he enjoyed being philanthropic himself in a small way: almost every noon, as he strolled down to the Palace Hotel for lunch, when he passed the "Sunshine Club," that group of derelict mine owners wont to gather at the corner of Montgomery and Market, he would stop and chat with them and would often unobtrusively slip a five or ten into the pocket of an old rival whom he had beaten out of millions. After all, life should have its ornamental moments. Business was business, but business was not everything.

Such was the pioneer philosophy of George Hearst, like himself a product of the period, differing not a whit from that of the men by whom he was surrounded.

CHAPTER II

California Background

"The images of his noble qualities, of his uncommon faculties, of his strong common sense, of his clear perceptions, of his unsurpassed judgment, of his incorruptible simplicity, of his unostentatious usefulness, of his delightful companionship, of his devotion to his friends, of his love for his country, of his justice to humanity, of his modest, kind, gentle life come thronging to our thoughts and fill our hearts with unspeakable emotion."—*Senator Matt Whitaker Ransom of North Carolina in the United States Senate, February 28, 1891.*

THE later career of George Hearst and the entire career of William Randolph Hearst cannot be understood unless they are seen in the light of the political and social conditions on the Pacific Coast out of which they sprang. It is therefore necessary, even at the cost of chronological regression, to give a brief sketch of that historical background.

Violence and bloodshed were as characteristic of the early cities of California as of the mining camps. Between 1849 and 1856 a thousand murders were reported in San Francisco alone, a town of less than forty thousand inhabitants—a thousand murders and but one conviction. Adventurers, gamblers, gangsters, and criminals from all the world poured in upon California, their numbers increasing with every boatload. The better classes, with the political laziness so characteristic of Americans, allowed things to go from bad to worse until conditions became intolerable. Then, roused to sudden frenzy, they did violence to civil government and law by taking these into their own hands through the organization of "vigilance committees" which would function for a brief period, then lapse until the same conditions reappeared, then revive for another brief period, then lapse again, then revive again—the intermediate stretches gradually becoming longer as the state slowly attained efficient government.

Vigilantes were organized in San Francisco in 1849, 1851, 1856, during the sixties, and once more in the late seventies. Their tradition still lingers in California, like that of the Ku-Klux Klan in the South, capable of revival for more sinister purposes, as was shown during the San Francisco general strike of 1934.

Meanwhile, in the early days the conditions of labor in California were, if anything, worse than in the East. Large numbers of Chinese coolies were brought into the state by the railroad, steamship, and construction interests with the result that there were lower wages and less work for the white men. The white workers, through mass meetings and riots, tried to intimidate the Chinese, but they were unable either to prevent their coming or to drive them out as long as there was work for them.

The nemesis of the common man in California was the Central Pacific Railroad. This instrument, which had been hailed with joy, and to which individuals, towns, and counties had given money and land to insure its completion, had become in the space of a few years a hydra-headed monster. Until 1883, when the Santa Fe Railroad opened its lines into southern California, the Central Pacific controlled all traffic with the East. It charged exorbitant freight rates, discriminated against certain sections and routes, and openly bought for itself such legislation from the state as it deemed necessary. It extorted, it corrupted, it exploited, and it crushed, while into the coffers of the four erstwhile shopkeepers of Sacramento poured an ever-increasing river of gold and silver. Not even the bonanza mines of the Comstock yielded such wealth as did this common carrier.

Then suddenly in October 1877 a movement was started which for a time threatened to engulf railroad magnates, mine owners, and Chinese coolies in a common ruin.

It had been a critical year for all but the biggest business. When the Consolidated Virginia mines of the Comstock Lode passed the customary monthly dividend in January 1877, stocks immediately crashed. The speculative and financial structure of a thousand mines and real estate ventures collapsed. The ranks of the unemployed, already swollen by the competition of coolie labor, grew at a terrifying rate as one business house after another went into bankruptcy. "All that was needed to unleash the pent-up wrath of the mob," writes Dr. Ira B. Cross of the University of California, "was a palpable excuse and a leader whom it might follow; both were not long in appearing. The leader was an uneducated Irish drayman, Dennis Kearney; the excuse was the Chinese." Kearney was uneducated, but he at least had the wit to trace the presence of the Chinese to its cause, and he mingled denunciations of the Central Pacific with threats against the coolies. He was also an organizer. Under his leadership the Workingmen's Party of California was formed, which gained thousands of adherents in San Francisco and soon spread throughout the state.

Until this time, the hundred-odd millionaires up on Nob Hill, where the Hearsts again were living, had not seriously felt the effects of the depression which washed away their lesser business brethren. They had continued their life of ostentatious splendor with its pseudo-culture of costly bric-a-brac, liveried servants, grandiose banquets, imported foods and liquors—while just a stone's throw below them were the brothels, the dingy saloons, the cheap rooming houses, and the sand lots where now the hungry unemployed of San Francisco were rallying to the Workingmen's Party.

There, at the foot of Nob Hill, Kearney addressed a monster mass meeting. "The Central Pacific men are thieves," he shouted, "and will soon feel the power of the workingmen. When I have thoroughly organized my party we will march through the city and compel the thieves to give up their plunder. I will lead you to the city hall, clear out the police force, hang the prosecuting attorney, burn every book that has a particle of law in it, and then enact new laws for the workingmen."

The crowd cheered their demagogue, and he continued:

"I will give the Central Pacific just three months to discharge their Chinamen, and if that is not done Stanford and his crowd will have to take the consequences. I will give Crocker until November twenty-ninth to take down the fence around Yung's house, and if he does not do it, I will lead the workingmen up there and tear it down, and give Crocker the worst beating with sticks that a man ever got."

The party issued a manifesto, reading:

We have made no secret of our intentions. We make none. Before you and the world, we declare that the Chinamen must leave our shores. We declare that white men, and women, and boys, and girls, cannot live as the people of this great republic should and compete with the single Chinese coolies in the labor market. We declare that we cannot hope to drive the Chinaman away by working cheaper than he does. None but an enemy would expect it of us; none but an idiot would hope for its success; none but a coward and a slave would make the effort. To an American, death is preferable to life on a par with the Chinaman. . . .

The workingmen know their rights, and know, also, how to maintain them, and mean to do it. The reign of the bloated knaves is over. The people are about to take their own affairs into their own hands, and they will not be stayed by . . . vigilantes, state militia, nor United States troops. The people made these things and can set them aside. The American citizen has a right to express himself as he please, as he thinks, and to arm himself as he will, and when organized and strong enough, who shall make him afraid? There is none.

The aristocrats of Nob Hill at last were worried. Vigilance

committees were formed, but they avoided open conflict with the workers who were now themselves well armed. Minor measures of relief were adopted. Charles Crocker offered employment to a thousand men at a dollar a day to fill in portions of Mission Creek. The feasts and revelry on Nob Hill ceased, partly because it was impossible to obtain the usual Chinese servants, and partly through fear of the rabble. Winifred Black Bonfils ("Annie Laurie") writes in her privately printed biography of Mrs. Phebe Apperson Hearst: "The great castles on Nob Hill built by the railroad princes stood—but those who lived in them had to give up their gorgeous entertainment for a while, and one fervid orator tried to get his followers to go up and tear down the lions that stood in front of the Hearst house because, he said, they were a threat and a menace to the freedom of the people below." Gentle Mrs. Hearst "was so hurt and astonished at the strange things that had come over the city that she loved so dearly that she would have been glad to go away and never return."

The first state convention of the Workingmen's Party took place on January 21, 1878. One hundred and forty delegates, representing groups from all parts of California, were on hand. They decided that the time had come for the formal organization of a labor party "to embrace within its ranks all those engaged in productive industry and its distribution." The platform demanded limitation of the private ownership of land to 640 acres, new systems of finance and taxation, establishment of the eight-hour day, free public education, abandonment of the practice of farming out convict labor, the popular election of the United States President, Vice-President, and Senate.

The Workingmen's Party entered the March elections of 1878 and elected mayors and other officials in Sacramento and Oakland. It then campaigned for a new state constitution and was again successful. In the constitutional convention of June 1878 there were fifty-one delegates from the Workingmen's

Party, eleven Republicans, ten Democrats, two Independents, and seventy-eight Non-partisans. The constitution adopted, and later ratified by a popular vote of 77,959 to 67,134, bore the plain imprint of the Workingmen's Party. The powers of the state legislature and of local authorities were marked out very definitely; the attempt to bribe a legislator was declared a felony; an income tax was authorized; the watering of stocks was forbidden; service rates of water, gas, and telegraph companies were limited by law; a railroad commission was established, with power to fix and adjust transportation rates and with authority to examine the books and accounts of all transportation companies operating within the state; the employment of Chinese workers by corporations or on public works projects was prohibited, and the Chinese were debarred from the right of suffrage; a legal day of eight hours was fixed for all public works projects.

The followers of the illiterate Dennis Kearney had framed a constitution which was (with exception of the anti-Chinese section) far more progressive than anything to be found elsewhere in the United States, containing provisions that were not to be included until decades later in the legislation of the national Congress or in that of even such a liberal state as Wisconsin.

In San Francisco, the W.P.C. entered the fall elections of 1879 with a complete ticket headed by the Reverend Isaac S. Kalloch, a Unitarian minister from Massachusetts. The campaign abounded in scurrility. The *Chronicle*, which formerly had supported the W.P.C., having been induced to change its policy, attacked Kalloch in front-page headlines: "Kalloch— The Record of a Misspent Life," "Infamous Career of W.P.C. Candidate for Mayor," "Driven Forth from Boston Like an Unclean Leper," "His Trial for the Crime of Adultery," "His Escapade With One of the Temple Choristers." San Francisco journalists did not have to wait for the *Examiner* to teach them the art of newspaper slander!

Kalloch might have been defeated by these tactics had not one of his political opponents resorted to an attempt at assassination. According to the account in the conservative *Argonaut*, "Charles De Young assaulted Mr. Kalloch with intent to murder him. It was done in a cowardly and dreadful manner. . . . He went in a closed carriage to his study and called him to his death by a messenger boy with a lying message. Kalloch came to his carriage window; unarmed and innocent of danger, he thrust his head and shoulders into the vehicle and received the unexpected shot full in the breast. Withdrawing, he received another; then fell and was carried bleeding to his office."

Kalloch recovered, and, partly as a result of the general indignation over this attack, he was elected. And, incidentally, in the following April his son shot and killed De Young—and was acquitted by a jury for his action.

Meanwhile, however, outside of San Francisco and soon within the city also, the Workingmen's Party began to disintegrate. With the easy-going trust of Americans in paper constitutions, its members assumed that victory was won and that no further effort was necessary. Factional fights for the party leadership disgusted the rank and file. Business improved, jobs became plentiful, and the workers lost their interest in politics.

Not so the opposition. The corporations, the land-barons, the railroad magnates, the speculators, and the reactionary politicians pooled their forces in a mighty effort to interpret, modify, or have declared unconstitutional all those features of the new constitution that were objectionable to them. In this they were to be largely successful; year after year would see the constitution slowly whittled to pieces. The San Francisco victory of a fusion ticket of Democrats and Republicans in 1881 heralded the return of the old parties to power. Machine politics were once more to be the order of the day. It was at this auspicious moment that George Hearst re-entered the arena.

His motivation in doing so is not difficult to understand. High political office was regarded in the West as the natural culmination of a successful business career. He had before him the example of his mining friends in Nevada. An editorial in a captious San Francisco journal of 1881 described the situation in that state as follows:

Speaking of a moneyed and political aristocracy, we must almost of necessity refer to our neighbor over the hill. Nevada has always, we believe, since the election of Nye, sold her Senatorial positions to the highest bidder, or, in gratitude given them to her richest men. Let us recall her illustrious sons. As colleague to the story-telling Nye was William M. Stewart, then the most prosperous and money-making of her money-making lawyers. How much money it cost him to go to Washington we do not know, because we do not know how rich he was when he began his Senatorial career, nor how poor he is now. Then came John P. Jones, whilom King of the Comstock. If he does not own Nevada, he ought to, for he bought it, and paid for it, and bought it again, and paid for it again, and now he talks about it and bargains over it as if he owned it, and we think he does. And then the Comstock had another King, and Sharon, deeming the Senatorial position a part of the regalia of the throne, reached out and snatched it, and although he did not choose to wear the bauble very much, he kept it about his royal person and, when it suited him to visit the national capital, availed himself of his royal prerogative to wear the Senatorial toga. Nevada is above politics and scorns the filthy pool; so when Mr. James G. Fair would not accommodate his party feeling to the State, the State accommodated itself to him; for Fair was King of the Comstock, crowned by an obedient legislature with the Senatorial crown, and clad in the Senatorial toga. And now there is another King of the Comstock, Mr. Mackay; and, because he is the richest man in the State, he must be Senator from Nevada. So Jones will bargain himself into the Cabinet, and bargain Mr. Mackay into the Senate, and reserve to himself the privilege of swapping himself back when Mr. Fair or Mr. Mackay shall have tired of the pretty plaything which rich men may own in Nevada.

Amid so many Comstock kings, should not George Hearst

have a place? But California differed from Nevada in having a metropolis, San Francisco, and both parties in San Francisco had powerful bosses. It was necessary for Hearst, a Democrat, to make a deal with the Democratic boss, Christopher Buckley.

Chris ("Blind Boss") Buckley, who ran a popular saloon on Bush Street, had come to San Francisco in the seventies. Though almost totally blind, he compensated for this defect by an uncanny memory for voices and names which enabled him to greet cordially and familiarly men whom he had met, perhaps, but once, years earlier. With this mighty asset, aided by the power of liquor, he was soon able to make his saloon a center of ward politics. Effecting an alliance with the underworld, while careful not to antagonize the Workingmen's Party, he, in company with Sam Rainey, organized the Yosemite Club on the model of Tammany, and this more efficiently corrupt institution took the political leadership away from the comparatively amateurish Manhattan Club of the older Democratic bosses, Mannix and Brady. According to one historian, of all the bosses who have dominated San Francisco, "the most notorious and shameless was Blind Boss Buckley. . . . All of them, and Buckley in particular, were experts in every form of human extortion, oppression, and demoralization of their army of human tools." The term "Buckleyism" is used even today in San Francisco as a one-word description of all that is lowest and vilest in municipal politics.

It did not take long for George Hearst and Buckley to come to terms. Hearst wanted political office, and the road to office lay through Buckley's saloon. Buckley wanted money and a newspaper organ which he sadly needed. Hearst was able to supply both.

The *Evening Examiner*, which George Hearst bought in October 1880, had been founded by Captain William Moss, a southern Democrat, on December 12, 1865. It was the direct successor to the *Democratic Press*, also owned by Captain Moss, a pro-slavery journal the office of which had been wrecked by a

Unionist mob on receipt of the news of Lincoln's assassination. As his first editor Moss secured the services of B. F. Washington, distantly related to George Washington; later B. F. Washington was replaced by George Pen Johnson; but neither of these men could make the paper pay. Moss himself had little money, and was unable to hire a first-class staff; eventually he sold the paper, which passed from one unsuccessful owner to another until it came into the hands of George Hearst.

He at once reorganized it, enlarging and improving the staff. One of the well-established articles of faith which he was to hand on to his son was that money can always buy brains. Since he wished to use the paper, not for financial profit but for political power, he did not object to losing a few thousands in it. Accordingly, he gathered together a journalistic staff as good as any in the city.

Clarence Greathouse, editor-in-chief and also Hearst's private attorney, affected an awe-inspiring manner which had real ability behind it; the Duke de Clarence, as he was nicknamed, was politically astute, a brilliant talker, and a forceful though arrogant writer. George Palmer, his secretary, was a clever journalist who wrote many of the editorials; Joseph M. Ward was city editor, John Coryland telegraph editor, and John Timmons night editor; others on the staff were Al ("Blinker") Murphy, Andrew M. Lawrence, Wallace F. Diss, and James Donahue. William T. Baggett was publisher and William Bogart business manager. A number of the members of the staff were to continue to work on the paper under William Randolph Hearst until dismissed by old age or death.

The *Evening Examiner* became the *Examiner*, issued in the morning. The new four-page paper began to attract attention at once, and within two years it became the outstanding Democratic organ in the state. Its original quarters at 538 Sacramento Street were now too narrow, and more spacious accommodations were obtained on Market Street. As early as February 17, 1882, the *Wasp*, a satirical weekly opposed to Hearst, admitted that his paper was "a bold and spicy sheet," and continued with even greater concessions to the enemy:

The *Examiner* is really the best morning paper in the city. Its telegraphic news is really superior to the *Chronicle*. Its editorial column, despite its strong Democratic bias, is honest and vigorous, while in general news and their preparation it ranks first. The public appreciation of these facts is made evident by a rapid yet healthy growth, and when the new building on Market Street is occupied, *Examiner* stock will boom.

The "strong Democratic bias" of the paper had, on the other hand, already earned the approval of the *Argonaut*, willing to overlook the *Examiner's* "spiciness" because of the lofty moral tone in which Greathouse set forth the Jeffersonian principles of individual liberty and universal justice. An editorial in the *Argonaut* of August 20, 1881, expressed a commendation which Pixley, who was guilty of it, was soon to retract:

The course of the *Examiner* quite astonishes us. It is a new departure in Democratic journalism in this state. It is the first instance where an avowed Democratic paper has undertaken political leadership; the first one that has dared express opinions in opposition to the Party; the only one that has undertaken to wag the Democratic dog. It has *dared*; and it has in a great measure succeeded. It has seized the helm of the Democratic ship after it had become an almost total wreck. It had gone upon the rocks and was sinking; Republicans were standing on the beach stoning the rats as they swam ashore. The gentlemen who own and edit the *Examiner* deserve great credit; not because they are gentlemen and have plenty of money to run the paper in a manly and independent way, but because, being gentlemen, they have preferred to be independent rather than be run over by the unwashed and alien mob that compose the rank and file and working majority of the Democratic party.

Pixley was over-hasty in assuming that Hearst and Great-house would have nothing to do with "the unwashed and alien mob." The majority of the voters in San Francisco were foreign-born, the largest group being Irish. Of the 37,915 registered voters in January 1879, 10,000 were natives of Ireland, 5630 of Germany, 1399 of England, with an additional 2000 from other countries. Buckley's men were drawn from these elements, and as soon as the *Examiner* had established a sufficient reputation for integrity and independence to make the move safe, it was swung toward Buckley and the Irish vote.

It now openly supported "Honest Tom" Desmond for Sheriff, "not so much because he was honest as because he was Irish." Changing his tone, Pixley of the *Argonaut* waxed sarcastic. "George Hearst," he commented, "is very fond of the Irish. He contemplates going to Ireland as soon as his gubernatorial term shall end." Then he pointed with glee to the paper's change of front since the days of the old *Examiner*:

Frank Washington, who founded the *Examiner*, was a Know-Nothing [the popular name for the anti-Catholic American Party of the fifties]. George Pen Johnson, for many years its editor, was a Know-Nothing. . . . The Southern Confederacy was Know-Nothing. Yet the *Examiner* people hate the very name. They love the Irish. They want all the Irish to vote for Desmond for Sheriff, and they don't want any native-born American to vote for him. They inform native-born Southern men—who compose nearly all that there is of respectability in the Democratic Party—that John Sedgwick [Desmond's opponent] had the misfortune to be born on American soil; that his parents were Americans; that he has woefully and maliciously refused to forswear his allegiance to the United States and persistently remains an American. Sedgwick pleads that he could not help being born in America, and that the fault was that of his parents. But the *Examiner* is unrelenting; it will not forgive him the offense; it persists in hounding him with this stain of an accidental birth; it makes him share the disgrace of his unfortunate nationality; and calls upon all good Irishmen—all who love St. Patrick and adore the Pope—to cast their votes against John Sedgwick because he was born on American soil.

In the light of William Randolph Hearst's later career it is rather amusing to find his father thus pilloried as un-American by the vigorous jingoism of the *Argonaut*.

The reviving Democratic Party now profited from internal dissensions among the San Francisco Republicans. The Higgins-Gannon-Chute faction, being beaten by the Green-Bigley combination, came over, bag and baggage, to the Democrats. This increased the oddity of the Democratic complexion, already odd enough. Under the banners of the Democracy marched a strange assortment of people. There were the old-time southern Democrats, still loyal in their hearts to the ideals of the Confederacy. There were the former Workingmen's Party leaders who in southern California had gone into the Democratic Party for the purpose of capturing its machinery and turning it leftward (a tactic revived by Upton Sinclair in 1934). There were the disgruntled ex-Republicans, with their following of "Short-Hairs." There were the new Democratic bosses with Christopher Buckley at their head. And there was amiable "Uncle George," financial pillar of the resurrected party in San Francisco. The unique federation was referred to as "a sort of Democratic happy family, like we see in the prairie-dog villages, where owls, rattlesnakes, prairie-dogs, and lizards all live in the same hole."

In the Democratic convention of 1882 Hearst was the candidate of the Buckley machine for governor. But he did not have the united support of the San Francisco delegates, a part of whom were pledged to James J. Johnson, representing the railroad interests (for the Central Pacific, now the Southern Pacific, followed the usual strategy of corporations in trying to secure control of both the Republican and Democratic parties at the same time). Opposed to both Hearst and Johnson was the southern California contingent lined up behind George Stoneman, a former member of the Workingmen's Party, whose floor manager was Stephen White, also a former member of the

same party but now the leading Democrat of Los Angeles. It
was a tricky situation which invited bargaining.

Hearst's first effort was to try to unite the San Francisco delegation behind him. The *Examiner* had rather conspicuously refrained from attacking the Southern Pacific, and there was nothing in Hearst's record to cause the railroads to fear him. On the
eve of the convention—at least, so it was openly charged by
J. H. Wise two years later, and the accusation was never denied
—Clarence Greathouse went into conference with W. W. Stow,
political manager of the Southern Pacific, and a verbal agreement was reached that Johnson's votes should be thrown at the
right moment to Hearst, in return for which the latter would
give his support to W. H. Humphries, the Southern Pacific's
candidate for Railroad Commissioner.

There was the usual buying of votes at the beginning of the
convention. To and fro among the delegates circulated Buckley,
Hearst's old friend Carr, and W. W. Stow. In its issue of June
21, 1882, the San Francisco *Call* remarked: "Tonight it was
commonly reported that three country delegates coming from
within the shadow of the Sierra had been purchased within the
previous twenty-four hours for $2000; and the consequence was
that street quotations for delegates advanced from $300 to $500
apiece."

Hearst, of course, did not wish to be presented openly as the
candidate of either the Buckley machine or the Southern Pacific.
His managers arranged that Buckley's Irishmen should be kept
in the background and their votes given to Hearst in driblets so
as to create the impression of constantly growing strength, while
the Johnson betrayal should be postponed until the last minute
when it could be represented simply as part of a general stampede. Meanwhile, every effort was made to allay the suspicions
of the embattled farmers from southern California. Judge
Flournoy of San Francisco, who made the nominating speech
for Hearst, stressed the poverty of the candidate's early life;

Judge Searles of Nevada City, who seconded the nomination, spoke touchingly of the by-gone days when he and other miners had suffered untold hardships by Hearst's side; the candidate himself was so moved by these early recollections that he burst into tears, and in his speech accepting the nomination he proclaimed that he, too, was an anti-monopoly man, opposed to the railroads and devoted to the common people who "have finally concluded to take the management of the affairs of government into their own hands."

Everything had been well arranged by Hearst's managers; yet everything went wrong. His speech was interrupted by hoots and jeers from the southern Californians. Buckley's Irishmen, angered at this treatment of their candidate and little accustomed to staying in the background, came out too strongly for Hearst in the beginning; the Irish brogue was so prominent among Hearst's supporters that the farmers imitated it in their answering votes, "thus making the occasion altogether joyful." Hearst led on the first ballot by 126 to Stoneman's 117. His lead increased, but less decisively than his managers had expected, up to the twelfth ballot, when he reached his maximum strength of 174. Now was the moment for the Southern Pacific swing. But the railroad's forces had either intended from the beginning to double-cross the mining magnate or had been led by the anti-monopolistic sentiments of his speech to fear that he intended to double-cross them; at any rate, they made no move in his direction. His strength rapidly declined, and on the fourteenth ballot Stoneman was nominated by 243 votes to Hearst's 170.

Hearst returned to San Francisco very much disgruntled with the Southern Pacific. The *Examiner* at the end of June 1882 began a furious attack on the railroad, initiating a verbal warfare which it was to keep up for many years. Otherwise, it took little direct part in the immediate campaign. Stoneman and a Democratic legislature were overwhelmingly elected. But when this Democratic legislature was called in extra session by the governor to enact anti-railroad legislation it turned out that the Southern Pacific had not been idle in the meantime. The proposed regulatory measures were defeated in the state Senate.

This gave the *Examiner* a demagogic opportunity of which it took full advantage. Day after day, it thundered in italics against the recreant members of the Senate. "Every Senator took an anti-monopoly pledge," began its leading editorial of February 3, 1883. "Every one took an oath to oppose railroads. We will print your names and hold you up in the EXAMINER as men who have forfeited their honors and falsified their oaths, and *you shall not be again elected to office*. There can be no betrayal of the people, no bartering of their rights, and you, who by this vote *admit your venality and corruption, will act wisely to withdraw at once from our party*. The time is now at hand when treachery will no longer be tolerated. *The* EXAMINER *will not excuse or palliate any offenses of this kind. . . .*"

"Your conduct is not that of statesmen," the *Examiner* repeated on February 5, 1883. "*You are corrupt and mercenary.* . . . Your Committee on Federal Relations and Railroads is stacked. *The only punishment that can be inflicted upon you is to cut you off from all further chance of election, and this is the course the* EXAMINER *will try its best to have the people take. . . .*"

These and other editorials of like tenor drew a stinging rebuke from Editor Pixley of the *Argonaut*, who wrote:

The *Examiner* uses the birch rather freely for a new schoolmaster who has not as yet fully got the hang of the new schoolhouse. The *Examiner* was bought and newly capitalized, baptized, and born again, for the purpose of carrying out certain business projects. The first step was to make George Hearst Governor. The scheme failed —in fact, badly FAILED. The *Examiner* did not discover Stoneman, nor nominate him, nor help to nominate him; nor did it elect him. . . . The *Examiner* did not nominate anybody, nor elect anybody now in the legislature. The fact is, the *Examiner* sulked after the State Convention. Like Achilles, it went to its tent. It grumbled like a small boy with a bruised heel. . . .

The *Examiner* had been bought by a wealthy miner as a private speculation, through which he might acquire political honor and attain the gubernatorial office. He bought it as he would purchase a mining implement, and he hired men to use it as he would hire a foreman and practical miners to work the shifts. . . .

We would not object to an honest party issue framed upon the subject of fares and freights, but we do object . . . to remaining silent when Mr. Hearst and his business associates purchase a respectable party newspaper and run it as an anti-monopoly organ, under the direction of Mr. Clarence Greathouse, in the interests of a syndicate of moneyed men and monopolists. . . .

Popular disgust with the failure of the Democratic legislature to redeem the party pledges led to a Republican victory in 1884. The vacant senatorial office on which Hearst had now set his mind—as was indicated by the vehemence of the *Examiner's* denials that he would under any circumstances accept such a position—went to Leland Stanford of the Southern Pacific. But the senior senator, John T. Miller, was known to be seriously ill, and in view of his possible demise Buckley rounded up the Democratic delegates at their first party caucus and induced them to recognize George Hearst as the party's candidate for the next senatorial opening. So when Miller died in the middle of March, Governor Stoneman, on March 23, 1885, appointed Hearst to fill the vacancy. Luck had returned at last to the old miner.

California, like Nevada, was now represented at Washington by two of the richest men in the state. Leland Stanford, already installed there, wishing to indicate to his new colleague that he had never taken the latter's denunciations of the Southern Pacific too seriously, instructed the railroad lobbyist, Tom Ochiltree of Texas, to welcome the new senator from the West with a suitable supply of liquor. Ochiltree, who was an inveterate humorist, accordingly sent around to Hearst's house, with Senator Stanford's compliments, two truckloads of whisky, cognac, liqueurs, champagne, and a variety of other wines. With his cellar thus well stocked and with a charming wife to act as hostess, Senator Hearst's entertainments soon became the talk of Washington—entertainments always graced by the presence of Senator Leland Stanford, now the late anti-monopolist's close friend.

In the Senate itself George Hearst was much less prominent. As a new member he was expected to keep quiet and he did, delivering only a single short speech in eulogy of the departed Miller. His sole legislative accomplishment during the session consisted in having struck from the Rivers and Harbors Bill a clause directing the Secretary of War to prosecute persons guilty of filling up navigable streams with the débris of hydraulic mines—and even this lone achievement was not permanent, as the clause was later restored to the bill.

After this brief experience of three months, Senator Hearst was replaced by a Republican, Senator Abram T. Williams. But in 1887 the Democrats once more returned to power in California, and this time Hearst was elected for the full term of six years, beginning on March 4, 1887.

The Senator and his wife now built for themselves, at 1400 New Hampshire Avenue, one of the largest and finest mansions in Washington. There they resumed their former round of entertainments on a still more lavish scale. The Senator became a close personal friend of President Grover Cleveland, and Mark Twain, Bret Harte, Bill Nye, and other famous westerners frequently enjoyed the hospitality of 1400 New Hampshire Avenue.

He also resumed his inconspicuous rôle in legislation, often referring to himself as "the silent man" of the Senate. During his three years in office he served on the Pacific Railroad Commission, the Committee on Indian Affairs, and the Committee on Mines and Mining, but he introduced few bills and made few speeches. The only measure which he supported with any fervor was a bill drawn by himself to give San Diego a $300,-000 federal building (though he admitted to his fellow-senators that he would be satisfied with one costing $100,000). California, he said, had been treated like a stepchild by the rest of the Union; this must not and should not continue; as soon as he could get around to it, he proposed to introduce bills for new federal post offices in San Francisco, San Jose, Stockton, "and several other places."

But death intervened to check these larger enterprises. Senator Hearst died at the age of seventy-one on February 28, 1891, and his mantle fell to his old enemy, Stephen White of Los Angeles.

Elaborate funeral ceremonies were held in San Francisco on March fifteenth. According to the sympathetic report in the San Francisco *Bulletin* of March sixteenth, "Such funeral honors as those which were bestowed yesterday upon the distinguished dead have rarely been witnessed in the city before. Nearly 2000 people took part in this bestowal . . . at the Grace Episcopal Church. A splendid tribute from the *Examiner* stood before the coffin. It represented the front page of that paper in white flowers. The columns, rules, and headings were in blue violets."

Though violets hardly seem appropriate for George Hearst it was fitting enough that his last rites should include a bit of publicity for the *Examiner*, managed at this time by his beloved son, William Randolph—certainly much more appropriate than any of the lying eulogies delivered in Congress by Leland Stanford, William M. Stewart, and their ilk, stressing the "honesty," "justice," and "incorruptible simplicity" of the departed.

George Hearst had none of these qualities. He was simply a typical robber baron of his period, who acquired great wealth and high political position by the usual crooked means, aided by good luck. He never had an original idea and never initiated anything of importance in either business or politics. In every way he was a creature of time, place, and opportunity. His significance for American history lies in the fact that he left to his wife an estate of between thirty and forty millions which could be manipulated for great good or great ill by their son, William Randolph Hearst.

CHAPTER III

The Early Life of "Willie Hearst"

"THE fates at his birth gave him a twisted and partial vision, left something out of him, blinded him to values and proportions that move even the mob when it turns thumbs up or down," wrote George P. West in his searching article, "Hearst: a Psychological Note," in the *American Mercury* of November 1930. But it was not the niggardliness of the fates that was at fault; rather, it was their too indiscriminate generosity; not something left out, but the warring abundance that was put in.

A psychologist might have prophesied that any child of two such opposed characters as George Hearst and Phebe Apperson would be likely to have a strange divided personality. The father, loud, flamboyant, outwardly genial, inwardly acquisitive and ruthless with a turn for knavish practices; the mother quiet, gentle, and refined, loving art and sweet charity; Chaucer's Miller and Chaucer's Prioress absurdly wedded; what could come from their loins save some incongruous combination of fairy prince and werewolf? William Randolph Hearst was predestined when George Hearst and Phebe Apperson met at the altar on that June day of 1862.

From his mother he derived, by inheritance or early influence, his soft voice and courteous manner, his strain of romantic idealism and his taste for art—both sadly vulgarized by the George Hearst within him. The father's physical characteristics were reproduced in the son's tall stature and large nose, while father and son had in common their enormous energy, their love of sports, and their yearning for unlimited power. That lofty devotion to humanity to which George Hearst paid lip service was genuine in Phebe Apperson, who labored through long years to transmit it to the boy whom she adored—and succeeded so far that in his after life there would always be two ghostly voices in his ears, one pleading gently, "You must do this for the sake of the common people," the other adding sardonically, "Yes, and it will be good business, too." Gradually, Phebe Apperson's voice was to grow more faint and George Hearst's deep tones were to be heard more constantly, ever muttering, "Good business—good business—good business."

The son's inheritance, however, was not entirely a divided one. The families of both his father and mother had owned slaves; and of the two, it was Phebe Apperson from the larger plantation whose outlook was even more feudalistic than George Hearst's. A kindly and benevolent feudalism, full of pity for the hard lot of the lower orders and striving earnestly to ameliorate it, but never questioning the necessity of there being lower orders; generosity, rather than justice; these, in the light of her formative years, were inevitably her ideals. Generosity, rather than justice, was an ideal which George Hearst too could appreciate in his less romantic manner. Thus re-enforced from both sides, the plantation standards of the Old South would be carried on by their son into the twentieth century. "Never just— Mr. Hearst is always generous," Ambrose Bierce was to write of his employer.

There was a third element in his inheritance to be reckoned with. From neither father nor mother came the son's mysterious eyes that were his most striking physical feature, large pale-blue eyes peculiarly his own, cold as steel, inhuman, remote, revealing nothing. Not Hearst eyes, not Apperson eyes; one might fancy in mystical moods that they came by some magic transubstantiation from those metallic godparents of the child, the Comstock Lode, the Ontario, the Homestake, and the Anaconda.

Certain it is that these godparents were as important in the formation of his character as either father or mother. His by right of birth were the wealth and lands that it took George Hearst a lifetime to acquire. His cradle was surrounded by servants; his faintest baby cries met with instant attention; the first lesson he learned was that whatever he wanted would be his for the asking.

Not until he was ten years old did this modern Prince Siddhartha realize that there are such things in the world as poverty and suffering, and when he did encounter them his outraged feelings prompted a quite Buddhistic gesture. He had been taken on a trip to Europe by his mother; it was in Dublin that the incident occurred. Mrs. Hearst wrote from there to her husband: "The poorer classes are so *terribly* poor. Willie wanted to give away all his money and clothes, too. . . ." Trivial incidents often have profound results. Who can tell how the history of the United States might have been altered had Willie's childish impulse not been inhibited by his charitable but conventional mother? Had he been allowed to return to his hotel, naked like St. Francis, would he have developed into another St. Francis? It hardly seems very probable, one must admit; and anyway, had his mother not checked him the first cop on the corner would have done so. The twentieth century is not the thirteenth. Yet it was to those far feudal times of arbitrary action when men were killed or clothed in ermine according to the caprice of the moment that a considerable part of the anachronistic spirit of Willie Hearst always would belong.

Much of his boyhood was spent at the Hearsts' summer home at Sausalito on San Francisco Bay. As a youth, he loved best the Santa Rosa and Piedra Blanca ranches. There he learned to play the banjo and to sing melancholy cowboy ballads, there he swam and fished in the coves and hunted on the hills, becoming a skilled horseman and a crack shot with rifle and revolver. Like

Lord Byron, he developed an inordinate and life-long love of animals. Always his association was with his inferiors, whether brute or human. Even when he accompanied his father to Mexico City and met Porfirio Diaz, the heir of George Hearst knew that the ruler of Mexico was in his father's pocket.

His academic education was mainly intrusted to private tutors, although in San Francisco he attended intermittently the North Cosmopolitan Grammar School, the Washington Grammar School, the Lincoln Grammar School, and the Geary Street Grammar School. These frequent changes may indicate some trouble with the authorities, for Willie was never a docile child, but all official records of those distant schooldays were destroyed in the San Francisco fire of 1906. There is a legend, however, that he was weak in mathematics but strong in geography and history—which would seem likely enough in view of his wide travels.

When he was fifteen, he was again taken to Europe, in company with a private tutor, by his mother. The party spent a full year on the Continent, where Mrs. Hearst reveled in the joys of European art galleries and initiated her son into the mysteries of the old masters. In August 1879 he was brought back to America by his tutor to enter the aristocratic St. Paul's School in Concord, New Hampshire, rooming with Will Tevis of the San Francisco Tevises.

Mrs. Hearst returned to the United States in November, visited her son at the school, and brought him down to New York for the Christmas holidays. When she went back to California, he was left behind to finish his preparation for college. The statement is made by James Casey in his pamphlet *Hearst—Labor's Enemy No. 1* (1935) that Hearst was dismissed from St. Paul's School, hardly an insurmountable disgrace, if true. A request for information addressed to the rector of the institution brought the following reply:

Concord, N. H.
January 25, 1936.

My dear Mr. Bates,

Thank you for your letter of January 20th. I doubt if any good
purpose could be served by our examining ancient records as to the
standing of an alumnus. Save in the case of younger alumni applying
for the Bar, or some other scholastic rating, I should not disclose the
record of a pupil.

In the Directory of the Alumni of St. Paul's School there is this
mentioned of the subject of your letter: "Hearst, William Randolph,
'79–'80–'81." This indicates that the pupil in question was here but
for one year.

Believe me,   Faithfully yours,

[Signed] S. S. Drury

Whatever the reason, Hearst at some time during 1881 returned to California to resume his studies under private tutors
and to become engaged, momentarily, to Sybil Sanderson, who
later had a meteoric career as an opera singer in Paris and New
York. In the fall of 1882 he entered Harvard.

Now for the first time alone and completely his own master,
with unlimited ready cash supplied by his fond parents, he
strove to atone for an inveterate personal shyness by tossing
money about in a lordly, lavish manner calculated to annoy
many of his less fortunate fellow-students. The scions of old
Massachusetts families established on the soil for generations
and accustomed to regard Harvard as their own resented the
presence of the upstart westerner and excluded him from the
"best clubs." The rising aristocracy of athletes found him, for all
his height, deficient in muscle and unwilling to compete in
the rougher sports to which they were addicted, while his own
polite accomplishments of horsemanship and pistol-shooting had
no opportunity for exercise in Cambridge. And the "grinds," of
course, would have none of him, or he of them.

A foppish taste for English clothes that he affected at this period, a faint trace of British accent—which always sounds effeminate to American ears—a light-colored mustache nursed too obviously and carefully, and a general air of æsthetic superiority considered especially unbecoming in a native of San Francisco Bay, all combined to earn for him in hostile quarters the unkind nickname of "Lily-Livered Willie."

Still, he had friends and even followers, both among the parasites ready to cluster about any generous spender and also among those rebels who resented in a blind way the dullness of academic life and were ready to follow a colorful leader whose very waywardness attracted them. Behind the affectations and the prodigality, alike indicating the uneasy inferiority sense of a westerner trying to make himself over into an easterner, one could sense a deeper restlessness not to be appeased by such small aims.

At the beginning of his junior year Willie Hearst obtained the important position of business manager of the *Lampoon*, Harvard's comic paper.

At that time the *Lampoon* had a rather extraordinary staff, including George Santayana, poet and philosopher, often to be mentioned in later years as America's foremost prose stylist; Hammond Lamont, later editor of the New York *Evening Post*; Ervin Wardman, later editor of the New York *Press*; Grover Flint, later war correspondent of the New York *American*; F. T. Cooper, later a professor in New York University; William W. Baldwin, later Third Assistant Secretary of State under Grover Cleveland; Samuel E. Winslow, later member of the House of Representatives.

Willie Hearst, of course, had nothing to do with the stream of wit and wisdom that flowed from these young pens. But indirectly he made it possible by his efficient management of the *Lampoon's* circulation and finances. So efficient indeed was he that there appeared unwonted monthly surpluses for the editors to spend joyously in Boston's most luxurious saloons.

In that primitive era when Old Heidelberg was still the ideal of American universities, the students' main drink was beer. Even a beer fest, however, if sufficiently prolonged, could be productive of much noise, hilarity, and broken furniture. And too large a combination of beer and filial devotion interrupted the connection of Willie Hearst with the *Lampoon* in the fall of 1884.

The occasion was the victory of the Democratic Party, his father's party, in the closely contested election that swept Grover Cleveland into his first term as president. To honor the event fittingly, Willie Hearst bought wagon loads of beer and fireworks, hired several brass bands, and with the aid of these and a noisy crowd of revelers managed to keep the sober denizens of Cambridge awake till daylight. The authorities of Harvard College did not appreciate his efforts in the cause of the Democracy. As ringleader of the too ardent demonstration he was rusticated for several months.

This interval was spent in Washington, D.C., with his mother who was then residing there, during which period he witnessed the inauguration of the President whose election he had so exuberantly celebrated, and also became engaged momentarily a second time. The recipient of his impetuous devotion was a California girl, Eleanor Calhoun, a protégée of the Haggins and the Tevises; but she was on her way to London to study for the stage, and Mrs. Phebe Hearst disapproved of her son's marrying an actress! Eleanor Calhoun, like Sybil Sanderson, later became a famous star and eventually she married (as Mrs. Fremont Older mentions with due reverence in her official life of Hearst) Prince Stephen Lazar Eugene Lazarovich-Herbelianovich of the royal house of Serbia.

Willie Hearst returned to Harvard with a dare-devil reputation which it was necessary to maintain. He attended every "tough show" that came to town, managed to be seen frequently in the company of chorus girls, and led in the throwing of custard pies, with which Harvard students greeted those ladies of the stage whose performance did not happen to satisfy the æsthetic requirements of their cultured audience.

As a devotee of the theater, Willie Hearst in his senior year was taken into Hasty Pudding and appeared in one of its shows, *Joan of Arc, or the Old Maid of New Orleans,* in which he assumed the rôle of "Pretzel, the German valet of Philip of Burgundy, an interesting cuss with a penchant for legerdemain." But then his theatrical and indeed his entire academic career were abruptly terminated by another contretemps with the collegiate authorities.

The occasion this time was not a national issue but a decidedly local one, namely, his unmitigated contempt for all of his professors. Harvard at that time had probably the most distinguished faculty in America, including such men as William James, Josiah Royce, Charles Eliot Norton, and Barrett Wendell. There is no evidence that Willie Hearst was influenced by any of these men, or, indeed, had the slightest respect for their intellectual attainments. He had been taught by his father that brains were articles of merchandise, and these professors sold theirs very cheaply, inferior in this even to the miserable tradesmen whose inconvenient duns the San Francisco youth who had caught a distant whiff of Oxford most cordially despised. Examinations were merely another kind of dun more loathsome than the merchants'. According to the adolescent philosophy which Willie Hearst was never to outgrow, professors were the natural enemies of the students and the natural enemies of man. So in the Christmas season of 1885 he determined to put them in their place in a right regal manner. To each of his instructors he sent, elaborately done up as a Christmas gift, a large chamber pot with the recipient's name ornamentally inscribed in the bottom. The perpetrator of the lordly jest was easily discovered, and Willie Hearst's connection with Harvard ended forever.

His years there had not been entirely wasted. The experience on the *Lampoon* had been of considerable value to the destined inheritor of the *Examiner,* and he had supplemented it by a systematic study of the great eastern newspapers, devoting much more time to this than to his academic courses. He had also obtained a letter of introduction to Colonel Taylor, owner of the Boston *Globe,* which brought him entree to that paper's office of which he made continual use until he was familiar with every detail of newspaper production from the first assignments to reporters on through all the processes of editing and the mechanics of printing to the final distribution of the paper. The wastrel of the campus was as assiduous as his father had ever been in preparing himself for his chosen line of business.

For a newspaper was simply a form of business; that fundamental fact of the modern world was clear to Willie Hearst from the first. "I didn't want to go into any business that would take a long, dull preparation," he said to Huntington Archer of *Printer's Ink* some years later. "The newspaper business seemed to offer more attractions than any other—more immediate attractions, and as many ultimate rewards." Besides, he was already *in posse* the owner of a paper, the *Examiner* being destined for him as soon as his father should obtain his cherished desire of a full term in the Senate.

From the first, also, Willie Hearst was clear as to the peculiar nature of the newspaper business. A newspaper's success depended upon its advertising now that retail business was more and more concentrating in the department stores; advertising depended upon circulation; circulation depended upon the owner's ability to satisfy the public taste. But there were, at least, two publics: the small public of the educated and the indefinitely larger public just literate enough to read newspapers and nothing else. Success obviously meant the capture of the larger public whose pennies were as good as those of the smaller public and much more numerous. The thoughtful editor of the old days was a back number; Edwin Lawrence Godkin of the *Eve-*

ning Post was the best thinker among the New York editors, and his paper had the smallest circulation; therefore, in the cool logic of Willie Hearst, Godkin must be written down a failure. After all, the function of a newspaper was to provide news, not learned editorials. And the larger public wanted not only news but a certain type of news; the good editor was one who would give them what they wanted. From this point of view the one thoroughly successful editor in New York was Joseph Pulitzer of the *World*, who had adopted and carried vastly further the sensational methods of James Gordon Bennett's *Herald*—and had thereby in three years raised the *World's* circulation from 15,000 to 250,000.

During his course of newspaper reading at Harvard, Willie Hearst had at once been attracted by the *World*. "Do you know who's running the best paper in the country?" he asked his colleagues on the *Lampoon*. "It's a man named Pulitzer down in New York. I have been studying his methods and I think I have caught on to what he is trying to do. Maybe I'll start a paper and give you fellows jobs."

Not taking his expulsion from college much to heart, Willie Hearst went happily down to New York for a fuller investigation of Pulitzer's methods on the spot. He did not get to know Pulitzer, but he became well acquainted with a man equally versed in sensational journalism, Sam Chamberlain, formerly James Gordon Bennett's secretary and the founder of the Paris *Matin*. Debonair, alert, and witty, Chamberlain was an individual after Willie Hearst's own heart, and the two knocked around New York together endlessly discussing the latest tricks of the journalistic trade.

Carefully and systematically, Pulitzer's admirer catalogued the *World's* ways of treating the news and compared its methods with those of the other New York papers: he noted the superior vividness of its crime stories and its copious use of diagrams—indicating the door by which the murderer entered, the chair in which his victim sat, the window through which the killer escaped, and so forth; he observed the hesitant appeal to sex and thought that it could well be made less hesitant; he counted the woodcut illustrations; he read the vituperative attacks on public characters and saw that the *Examiner* already had little to learn from the *World* on that point; he summed up Pulitzer's technique as consisting in a constant appeal to the fundamental emotions of love, hate, sympathy, and gain. Pulitzer's program, he decided, was the one that he would follow, and he would go as far beyond Pulitzer as Pulitzer had gone beyond James Gordon Bennett.

In all this, what had happened to the idealism inherited from Phebe Apperson Hearst? Nothing had happened to it. No more than his father or mother did Willie Hearst recognize any conflict between idealism and "legitimate" business with its claim to a "just" profit. And catering to the masses did not imply any neglect of the interests of the masses. Rather, the direct opposite, as Pulitzer had shown. Was not the *World* the most liberal paper in New York, fearless in its opposition to monopolies, foremost in tireless exposure of corruption and exploitation? Was there not need for a similar paper on the Pacific Coast, and was not the anti-monopolist *Examiner* already on the way to be that paper?

True, Pulitzer had one advantage in this campaign that Willie Hearst could never have—the advantage of having sprung directly from the people. Before entering journalism he had been a coachman, a waiter, a common laborer, a grave-digger during the cholera epidemic in St. Louis; his bitterness against capitalists was born in that earlier period of poverty; the issues he supported were bone of his bone, flesh of his life. Still, Willie Hearst at least had a miner for a father; he knew what all the issues were and on which side to stand; he had, he believed, more intelligence than Pulitzer and sooner or later he would have more money at his disposal than Pulitzer had even now. Yes, he would do better than Pulitzer as soon as he had the opportunity.

The opportunity, or its beginning, arrived when George Hearst was elected senator in the spring of 1887. Willie Hearst was recalled to California. And March 4, 1887, was marked by two events of importance in the history of the family: the father took his seat in the United States Senate, and the son became the owner of the San Francisco *Examiner*.

CHAPTER IV

Owner of the San Francisco Examiner

A LEGEND calculated to enhance the glory of William Randolph Hearst has long been generally accepted to the effect that the paper which he inherited from his father was, when he took it over, a poor and worthless sheet. Thus even John K. Winkler in his *W. R. Hearst: An American Phenomenon* (1928) says that George Hearst first accepted the paper merely in payment "of a bad debt" and adds: "When young Hearst took over the *Examiner* on March 4, 1887, the paper was easily the worst daily in San Francisco." On the contrary, as we have seen, George Hearst secured the *Examiner* as a part of his political campaign for governor and built it up until it was the most powerful Democratic paper in the state. In six years its circulation was almost quadrupled, rising from 8000 to 30,000, a very creditable figure in the California of that period. The *Examiner* was already a well-established enterprise when young Will Hearst, with little experience but with his father's millions behind him, assumed control at the age of twenty-four.

It soon appeared that money was now going to be put into the paper in a large way. The new owner had not been in charge more than six weeks when one morning word came to San Francisco that the renowned Hotel del Monte at Monterey was on fire. Hearst at once chartered a special train, filled it with staff artists and reporters, and rushed down the coast to be in at the death. The next day the *Examiner* published a fourteen-page extra giving the complete details of the disaster, with zinc etchings and banner headlines mostly written by Hearst himself.

GEORGE AND
PHEBE HEARST

The parents of
William Randolph Hearst.

The other papers having contented themselves with the usual meager telegraphic reports, three editions of the Hearst extra were called for during the day.

This spectacular success was followed by equally spectacular forays into San Francisco politics. The *Examiner* fought a proposed city charter, suggested a better one, and won its case; it demanded lower water rates for the city and got them; it led a campaign to compel the electric companies to run their wires underground in the suburban district, and was successful; it forced the reluctant streetcar companies to put fenders on their cars. For a novice, Pulitzer's disciple was certainly beginning well.

Meanwhile, during the first year and indeed for several years there was constant reorganization and enlargement of the staff. Clarence Greathouse had already been provided for by George Hearst, who had secured for him the consul-generalship at Tokyo, whence Greathouse subsequently went to Korea where he managed to become the confidential adviser of the king until in 1898 his intrigues against Russia on behalf of American capitalists caused him to be dismissed at the request of the Russian embassy, after which he disappears from history. His old place in the editorial office was taken by Arthur McEwen, second only to Arthur Brisbane as a popular editorial writer. McEwen described his policy on the *Examiner* as a search for the "gee-whiz emotion," elucidating thus: "We run our paper so that when the reader opens it he says 'Gee-whiz!' An issue is a failure which doesn't make him say that." McEwen's cynical pen was aided by Sam Moffitt's milder one. T. T. Williams was city editor. Sam Chamberlain was brought out from New York in 1888 to take what became under his management the most important position on the paper, that of news editor. "Cosy" Noble of the old *Lampoon* was Sunday editor, Charles Barnes real estate editor, Jack Christian dramatic editor. Al ("Blinker") Murphy stayed on as the paper's contact man with the bosses, and Edward ("Pop") Hamilton was the star political reporter. Pugilism was handled by "Big Bill" Naughton, baseball by Jake Dressler and Charley Dryden, the turf by Charles Trevathan, author of a popular ditty called "The 'Bully' Song." Billy Hart covered the waterfront. Ambrose Bierce, poet and short-story writer, contributed a daily column of caustic "Prattle," and Eddie Morphy, from the University of Dublin and formerly on the New York *Sun,* wrote special features. There was a host of excellent reporters: Harry ("Petey") Bigelow, Allen Kelly, Charles Michelson (now chief press agent for the Democratic National Committee), Dave Williamson, Charles Frazier, and Andrew, Joe, and Frederick Lawrence. "Phinny" Thayer of the *Lampoon* was on the staff for a short time during which he wrote his well-known "Casey at the Bat."

To the business office were added Edward M. Townsend, creator of Chimmie Fadden, and Charles M. Palmer.

The greatest improvement of all was in the art department, which included at various times under Charles Tebbs, the art editor, such men as Homer Davenport, recently escaped from a job as brakeman on the Northern Pacific; Jimmy Swinnerton; "Bud" Fisher; Harrison Fisher; Fred Briggs; Robert Carter; T. A. ("Tad") Dorgan; Theo Hampe; Haydon Jones. More famous than any of these, the great cartoonist Thomas Nast worked on the staff in 1888, giving potent assistance in the campaign against the streetcar companies.

Hearst also had a keen eye for special contributors, securing, among others, Mark Twain, Max O'Rell, Gertrude Atherton, Joaquin Miller, and Edwin Markham, who was to contribute to the *Examiner* in 1899 one of the most popular if not one of the greatest American poems, "The Man with the Hoe."

Within two years Hearst had unquestionably built up the best staff of any daily paper west of the Rocky Mountains. The youth of twenty-six, with a free and intelligent use of his father's money in paying large salaries, had proved himself a prodigy in getting able men to work for him.

Ambrose Bierce, whose caustic column, "Prattle," was one of the attractions of the *Examiner*, wrote long afterward an amusing account of his first meeting with his employer. A tall and innocent-looking young man called one evening at Bierce's lodgings in Oakland, and muttered bashfully something about the *Examiner*. "You come from Mr. Hearst?" Bierce asked. And then:

That unearthly child lifted its blue eyes and cooed, "I am Mr. Hearst," in a voice like the fragrance of violets made audible, and backed a little away. Twenty years of what his newspapers call "wage slavery" ensued, and although I had many a fight with his editors for my right to my self-respect, I cannot say that I ever found Mr. Hearst's chain a very heavy burden.

Bierce related other incidents of the early days on the *Examiner*. Once he expressed his surprise to Hearst that he had reappointed a manager who had been caught stealing and was discharged. "Oh, that's all right," his chief explained. "I have a new understanding with him. He is to steal only small sums hereafter; the largest are to come to me."

"It was customary when a reporter had a disagreeable assignment," Bierce tells us, "for him to go away for a few days and plead intoxication." The staff connived at this until one day Hearst happened to meet a reporter perfectly sober who was supposed to be off on a wild spree. "On the scamp's assurance that he had honestly intended to get drunk, but lacked the price, Mr. Hearst gave him enough money to re-establish his character for veracity and passed on."

The *Examiner* was, as John K. Winkler says, in many ways "Hearst's plaything." In fact, life itself seemed his plaything at this period. Young, flushed with success, his spirits high, with unlimited wealth at his command, he could afford, now as always, to override the puritanic scruples of those less able to indulge their own desires. The citizens of San Francisco listened, agog, and with some secret envy, to tales of wild doings in Hearst's home at Sausalito, where a certain Tessy Powers, better known under her nicknames of "the Harvard widow" and "Dirty Drawers," was said to be installed as hostess. Though Hearst's $60,000 yacht, the *Vamoose*, built for him in the East, proved unable to make the trip from New York to San Francisco, he built another, the *Aquila*, which was more serviceable and almost equally luxurious. On it he would take the favorite members of his staff for weekend hunting and fishing trips to the Piedra Blanca, while any slack afternoon might find them jaunting about San Francisco Bay in a steam launch. Minor frivolities which the owner of the *Examiner* shared with his staff were the setting off of fireworks and the flying of kites and toy balloons on the strong breezes that blew in from the Pacific.

In the *Examiner* office at this time there was a spirit of camaraderie unknown in the later days of the Hearst papers. The members of the staff would run in and out of Sam Chamberlain's room at will for conference or conversation, and the owner of the paper would sometimes preface his remarks to his editors by dancing a clog or jig, always with a solemn face as if it were a part of some strange journalistic ritual. However informal his manners, there was always a limit to familiarity. The skipper might make merry with his jolly tars but he never allowed the crew to forget who was the master of the ship. He danced only to his own piping. And he had a way of appearing unexpectedly in the office at any hour of the day or night, sometimes most inconveniently for members of the staff.

Eddie Morphy still remembers one such occasion.

I had been on the *Examiner* only a few weeks when Senator Hearst died. His body was brought back to San Francisco, and a tremendous funeral was staged. All the feature writers on the staff were assigned to the job except myself. Funerals were funerals in those days. There was plenty to eat and even more to drink. The procession was ended —and copy was badly needed for the big front page stories about the funeral. Chamberlain was frantic. The reporters who had been sent to cover the affair had imbibed so heavily that not one was able to write a line. Chamberlain called for me. "Ed, can you do a good feature lead on the Senator's funeral? The boys who covered it are drunk. We need a stirring yet dignified account. Can you do it, Ed?" "Sure thing," I replied. "I'll do a masterpiece for you. But tell me something about the length of the procession, and what the old man looked like. Did he have pink whiskers? Was he tall and thin or short and fat?" At this point Chamberlain was giving me signs to shut up. Some one had just come into the room and stood behind the chair on which I was sitting. "By the way," said Chamberlain, "meet your boss, Mr. Hearst." I was unable to say anything for just a moment. We shook hands. Mr. Hearst said he hoped I would do a good story —and I did.

In another instance the hero of Senator Hearst's funeral did not come off so happily. He had dodged an assignment on California wild flowers and was thoroughly enjoying himself in a crab-seller's place on the Sausalito waterfront when he observed outside the establishment a dog-cart with an ominously solemn-looking young man in it. The fugitive from duty was captured and locked up in an empty room until he completed the article on California's wild flowers.

Though likely to be drunk and disorderly when such tame topics as funerals or wild flowers were assigned to them, Hearst's men rarely fell down if given tasks of daring or excitement. While sheriff's posses were vainly seeking the train robbers, Sonntag and Evans, Petey Bigelow managed to track them through the mountains and bring back an interview. When, during a storm, word came that a solitary fisherman was marooned on a rock at the entrance of the bay, Hearst sent out a tug from which H. R. Haxton swam with a life-line to rescue the man before the life-saving crew from the near-by Cliff House station arrived upon the scene—this making a good opening for a violent attack in the *Examiner* upon the general incompetence of the life-saving service. Then directing his attention to the ferry boats, Hearst had the same Haxton jump overboard and note the time taken to rescue him, which, Haxton being an expert at submerging and coming up in odd places, was considerable. When a train was snowbound in the Sierras, and out of food, Hearst chartered a special engine equipped with a snowplow to rescue the passengers. When Golden Gate Park announced that it desired a specimen of the almost extinct California grizzly, he sent out a party of hunters headed by Allen Kelly, who brought back "Monarch, the *Examiner's* Grizzly." A bear was adopted as the *Examiner's* trademark, and Jimmy Swinnerton, according to Will Irwin, "drew bears for a year, until people tired of the feature."

A rumor reached Chamberlain that the City Receiving Hospital in the Hall of Justice Building at Kearny and Washington Streets was wretchedly managed. The so-called emergency ambulances of the institution were merely antiquated express wagons, and it was said that the internes were young rowdies who insulted the women patients. Chamberlain got hold of a winsome "little slip of a girl" (destined under the names of "Annie Laurie," "Winifred Sweet," and "Winifred Black" —her own name being Winifred Sweet Black Bonfils—to continue as a life-long contributor of sob stories to the Hearst papers), and she "fainted" on Market Street with such versimilitude that she was carried in one of the express wagons to the hospital where she was insulted by the internes to heart's content. Her story of this experience, "with a sob in every line," started the "woman's appeal" stuff which Hearst was to feature ever afterward. Incidentally, the exposé is said actually to have led to great improvement in the management of the hospital.

In all these instances the *Examiner* played the rôle of knight-errant with distinguished success. But there was more in it than that. Hearst and Chamberlain had introduced an innovation in western journalism—the innovation in connection with getting the news of creating news at the same time. Unfortunately, the line between making news and faking news was somewhat difficult to draw, and it became increasingly obscure as time went on. One of the *Examiner's* biggest hits, the sad story of "The Last of the McGintys" was as arrant a piece of pure fancy as journalism had ever seen. Again the fertile imagination of the incorrigible Eddie Morphy was responsible.

On one occasion [Morphy recalls], when I was doing feature stuff for the Sunday edition, Mr. Hearst dashed in with a "brain-wave." He wanted an entire page devoted to interesting San Francisco personalities—a column for each person. He suggested two or three personalities. I had to decide upon the remaining three or four. A few days later, he came in to see if the stories were completed. I had done all but one. Somehow I couldn't think of another colorful person to write about—but I didn't dare tell that to Hearst. I said I was going to have the last story completed in a few hours. Since there was no time to pick out a real character, I had to resort to my imagination. I wrote a touching story called "The Last of the McGintys" in which I pictured a small newsboy, by the name of McGinty, who had been left to care for his younger brothers and sisters. The story made a tremendous hit with Mrs. Phebe Hearst. She felt so sorry for the plight of the orphaned kids that she sent me a letter with five twenty-dollar bills in it, to be used to buy food and clothing for the youngsters.

I was in a dilemma. There *were* no McGintys. When I told the city editor about the problem, he suggested, "We'd better go over to the Mint [a neighboring saloon] to break one of those twenties, and think things over." This we did. Other reporters joined us. By the time we had spent the greater part of a twenty-dollar bill we found a solution to the problem. Some of the boys rounded up five or six dirty, ragged kids from the street. We photographed and sketched them in all their dirtiness. Then we took them out, bought new clothes for them, and cleaned them up. Once more we photographed them. For several Sundays thereafter we ran feature stories about the young McGintys. It was great stuff for the *Examiner*. But some young reporter of the San Francisco *News Letter* had heard the real story and told the truth in his paper.

For many weeks thereafter, I made it my business to keep out of sight whenever Mrs. Phebe Hearst was around. One such day she caught me. "Oh, Mr. Morphy," she said, "how could you do such a thing!" I didn't know what to reply and was trying to develop an adequate apology when she added, "Well, anyway, Mr. Morphy, that was a wonderful story you wrote about the McGintys. It had me weeping for several hours."

The owner of the *Examiner* also felt that a good story was its own excuse for being. Morphy became the chief "hot-air" writer on the staff. "And believe me," he adds to the above account, "we did lots of 'hot-air' writing for the *Examiner* in those days. Both Hearst and Chamberlain liked my style. Many the time when Jimmy Swinnerton and I would go down Kearny Street making up stories that were to appear in the next day's *Examiner*. Jimmy would draw the sketches, and I would write the fake."

Less mythical than "The Last of the McGintys" was the hero of Annie Laurie's sob stories, "Little Jim," a crippled child born to a drunken prostitute in the City Prison Hospital. "Every day for weeks," writes Will Irwin, "the women of San Francisco exchanged tears across the back fences over 'Little Jim.'" The *Examiner* started a "Little Jim" Fund on behalf of the infant and had raised $20,000 when the child died. This sum, however, was used as the basis of a campaign to build a hospital for crippled children which eventually became a reality.

In all these enterprises there was the same curious mixture of reality and unreality, fact and fakery, social service and personal profit. The causes were always good, the means were always sensational, the ends were always twofold: some improvement in social conditions and great improvement in the circulation of the *Examiner*.

On larger political and social issues the policy of the paper remained what it had been under George Hearst. It was still stoutly Democratic. In fact, at the beginning of the political campaign of 1888 Hearst for a moment attracted national attention by the vigor with which the *Examiner* supported the claims of San Francisco to be the seat of the Democratic national convention. He took half his staff with him to Washington where he published an anniversary edition of the *Examiner* during his first year of management. The other San Francisco papers fell into line behind the *Examiner* in the effort to capture the convention for their city, but ultimately the movement failed. Hearst's part in it cost him about $80,000; he claimed, however, that the money was well spent in view of the publicity it brought.

The *Examiner* employed only union labor, and it continued its early plan of supporting the residue of policies left over from the Workingmen's Party movement of the seventies. On the occasion of a new anti-Chinese agitation in 1889 it took a strong stand against the hated orientals and aided in the establishment of free employment bureaus for white labor. It even went so far as to support the workers in local strikes. And this, too, was profitable. Fremont Older, then working on the *Bulletin*, told, in *My Own Story*, of one typical instance—a teamsters' strike in which every paper in the city except the *Examiner* took the side of the employers. Feeling ran so high that the San Francisco business men boycotted the Hearst paper by withdrawing their advertising, while on the other hand organized labor rallied to its defense so heartily that its circulation boomed. When the strike was over, the *Bulletin* and the other conservative papers expected increases of advertising from the merchants and the manufacturers whose interests they had so loyally supported. Instead, the business men returned to the enemy. The city's biggest advertiser, who had withdrawn all advertising from the *Examiner* during the strike, not only gave it back, but increased the space, at the same time cutting down his space in the

Bulletin. "When our advertising manager remonstrated," so Older said, "he was told: 'Business is business; we are advertising strictly on a proposition of circulation, and your circulation has gone down.'"

The attack on the Southern Pacific begun by George Hearst in 1882 was continued by his son year after year almost as part of the family tradition. Almost alone, the *Examiner* fought the railroad's system of rebates and was instrumental in killing them. This fidelity to its old policy involved a break with George Hearst's initial backer, Chris Buckley, who had managed to get on to the Southern Pacific's payroll. But Blind Boss Buckley was now on the down grade. When he ventured to give the shelter of his saloon to Jimmy Hope, the notorious bank robber, public opinion was at last so roused that the boss, with an indictment over his head, deemed it wise to leave the city for the country.

Hearst's attack upon another boss, a Republican, Martin Kelly the fire commissioner, nearly involved the publisher in serious difficulties. The *Examiner* charged that Kelly had sold a second-hand fire engine to the City of Chihuahua in Mexico and had kept the proceeds for himself; Kelly immediately brought a $100,000 libel suit, and when the case came to court he clearly proved that the charge was false. Hearst's attorney, W. W. Foote, a humorous Tennesseean, admitted this, but waved the question aside with a jest.

"It is true," he said, "that Kelly didn't steal this particular fire engine. But, gentlemen of the jury, no matter what is said about the plaintiff Kelly, true or false, we hold that it is impossible to libel him."

The jury laughed, and found for the defendant. The case was ordered retried by a higher court, and the same farce was repeated. A trial jury, under explicit instructions from the court, found for the plaintiff, and awarded him damages of one dollar.

In 1893 the *Examiner* published a special World's Fair edition of 120 pages—the largest paper ever seen up to that time in America. Its foreign news had greatly expanded since Hearst took it over. In 1889 he had sent a special correspondent to China to cover the famine and in 1891 another to Japan to send back full details of the earthquake. Chamberlain had gone to Honolulu and obtained an exclusive interview with Queen Liliuokalani, and later the *Examiner* was the first paper to carry an account of her overthrow. Since 1889 it had flown at its masthead the proud banner, "The Monarch of the Dailies." In less than ten years' time, "Wasteful Willie," as the San Franciscans called him, had increased its circulation from 30,000 to 80,000.

But during the nineties there were signs that Hearst was beginning to tire of his plaything. He frequently ran off to Europe with George E. Pancoast, his private secretary since 1888, who communicated to his chief his own enthusiasm for the camera. The two photographed everything in sight from the battlefields of France to the bats beneath the Pyramids. The results were sent back to the *Examiner,* and Chamberlain found or faked the suitable stories to go with them.

While Hearst was abroad, he received a cablegram from his editorial manager, A. B. Henderson, a somewhat stiff individual who had never entirely sympathized with the mad doings in the office. It read: "Chamberlain drunk again. May I dismiss him?" Hearst replied: "If he is sober one day in thirty that is all that I require." He would rather have lost his right hand than Chamberlain, who fully as much as Hearst himself had been responsible for the *Examiner's* success.

His European itineraries followed the caprice of the moment. Once, after he had decided to return to America and had sent Pancoast on ahead of him, he suddenly changed his mind and cabled to San Francisco, requesting his secretary, who had barely arrived there, to come back at once to Paris. He calmly declined to recognize time and space, as he declined to recognize any other fetters on his will. Wherever he happened to be was made by that fact the center of the world. Winkler relates a delightful story of a sudden craving for American food which overcame the wanderer on the eve of a trip to Alexandria. Hearst cabled to Allen, the *Examiner's* New York representative, "Rush dozen cans Boston beans dozen cans clam chowder two codfish Alexandria Egypt." Allen, perplexed, unable to decipher the message by the *Examiner's* code book, cabled back simply, "What code are you using?" and received the irate answer, "No code. Want beans chowder codfish."

Hearst was already developing the habit, which was to grow upon him, of treating his newspaper employees as a part of his personal retinue; in addition to being journalists they must also be ready to act at a moment's notice as stewards, purchasing agents, or messenger boys.

The owner of the *Examiner* now had his mind set upon a paper in New York where he would at last be able to cross swords with the mighty Pulitzer himself. When his interest began to shift from California to the East, the local campaigns of the *Examiner* on behalf of righteousness and mercy flattened out. The paper still spoke with the same earnestness, but the causes it championed were hardly worthy of its zeal. During 1895 it devoted a great deal of space to what it called "the bicycle menace," excoriating the speed demons of that innocent machine with more indignation than is shown today toward the ravages of the automobile. "One of the reforms most imperatively needed," it shouted, "is a check on the 'scorchers' whose reckless disregard for the safety of others, as well as of themselves, puts every bicycle under suspicion and gives the tack fiend his only excuse for existence. . . . The trees and the park drives should be protected from the incursions of human catapults." Day after day the *Examiner* returned to the subject, running feature stories, drawings, and many editorials on this trivial topic. When the *Examiner* could find nothing worse in San

Francisco than the reckless bicycle riding of a few speedsters, it was a sign that the oil was running low.

To be sure, there always remained the Southern Pacific. But Hearst's last campaign against that corporation, before he left California, was singularly unfortunate. It was on behalf of the so-called "people's railroad" which was to free San Francisco Bay forever from the exorbitant rates of the Southern Pacific. The new enterprise, legally known as the San Francisco & San Joaquin Valley Railroad Company, was headed by Claus Spreckels, a German immigrant who had come to California in the early days and had prospered exceedingly until he was now popularly called "the sugar king of the West." For many months the *Examiner* featured stories and sketches of the new railroad and of its high-minded owners; subscription blanks for stock in the public-spirited undertaking appeared daily in its columns, and the names of all who subscribed were prominently listed. Great was the public rejoicing when the road was completed. And then the Southern Pacific quietly bought a controlling interest in it, and the rates went up higher than before.

In the fall of 1895 Hearst moved to New York to take charge of the New York *Journal*. Not long after his departure, the *Examiner*, to the surprise of many of its readers, seemed to change its policy in regard to the Southern Pacific. For nine months strange silence weighed upon its office concerning the iniquities of the railroad. Two years later Grove L. Johnson, father of Hiram Johnson and representative from California in the United States Congress, gave his explanation of this silence.

It would be too strong to say that Hearst left California under a cloud. Not a cloud, exactly; rather, a sort of cold mist shot with rays of sunlight enveloped him. Many Californians felt outraged by the contempt for conventional morality shown in his private life, while even among those who most approved of his public policies there were persistent doubts of his sincerity.

Both of these attitudes, too, would in the fullness of time find ample expression through Grove L. Johnson in the Halls of Congress.

Since Johnson's accusations dealt entirely with Hearst's California career, it seems appropriate to proceed with them at this point.

CHAPTER V

The Accusations of Grove L. Johnson

IN JANUARY 1897 there was a bill before the House of Representatives to fund the thirty-five-year-old debt owed by the Central Pacific to the United States Government. The bill proposed to extend the second mortgage held by the government, since the railroad alleged that it could not possibly meet the full amount of its indebtedness of 120 millions, but the measure also provided that the railroad should thenceforward make payments every six months toward reduction of the principal as well as to cover the interest. And the Southern Pacific promised, if the bill were passed, to extend its lines into southern California on the south and Oregon on the north.

Was the railroad bluffing when it said it couldn't pay? If not, the only alternative to the funding bill seemed to be for the government to foreclose at a loss and take over itself the ownership and management of the road—a measure that few congressmen had the hardihood to favor, though it was supported by Mayor Sutro of San Francisco, by the *Examiner*, which had resumed its anti-railroad stand, and by a petition to which that newspaper had obtained 150,000 signatures on the Pacific Coast.

On January 8, 1897, Grove L. Johnson of California delivered a long speech in defense of the funding bill. At its close he appended a few uncomplimentary remarks on Mayor Sutro and then turned the full force of his eloquence on Hearst. He was by no means as disinterested as he pretended since he had just been defeated for re-election largely through Hearst's influence. But amid the tarnished rhetorical gems of his speech were

63

some rough nuggets of accusation disastrous, if true, to the publisher's claims as a reformer. After dismissing Sutro, Johnson proceeded:

Of the other of this precious pair of literary coyotes, William R. Hearst, much could be said.

He is a young man, rich not by his own exertions, but by inheritance from his honored father and gifts from his honored mother. He became possessed of the idea that he wanted to run a newspaper. Like the child in the song, he wanted a bow-wow, and his indulgent parents gave him the *Examiner*. By the reckless expenditure of large sums of money he has built up a great paper.

The *Examiner* has a very large circulation. It did have a great influence in California.

It has done great good in California. It has exposed corruption, denounced villainy, unearthed wickedness, pursued criminals, and rewarded virtue.

At first, we Californians were suspicious of "Our Willie," as Hearst is called on the Pacific Coast. We did not know what he meant. But we came to believe in him and his oft-repeated boasts of independence and honesty. Daily editorials, written by "Our Willie," hired men praising his motives and proclaiming his honesty, had their effect. Besides, "Our Willie" through his paper was doing some good.

We knew him to be a debauchee, a dude in dress, an Anglomaniac in language and manners, but we thought he was honest.

We knew him to be licentious in his tastes, regal in his dissipations, unfit to associate with pure women or decent men, but we thought "Our Willie" was honest.

We knew he was erotic in his tastes, erratic in his moods, of small understanding and smaller views of men and measures, but we thought "Our Willie," in his English plaids, his cockney accent, and his middle-parted hair, was honest. . . .

We knew he was debarred from society in San Francisco because of his delight in flaunting his wickedness, but we believed him honest, though tattooed with sin.

We knew he was ungrateful to his friends, unkind to his employ-

HEARST AS "THE YELLOW KID"

Satirical cartoon published in the *Bee* at the time of the Spanish-
American War.

ees, unfaithful to his business associates, but we believed he was trying to publish an honest paper. . . .

We knew he had money, not earned by himself (for we knew he was unable to earn any money save as a statue for a cigar store), but given him by honored and indulgent parents; we knew he needed no bribes with which to pay his way, hence, while we knew all these things, we did believe "Our Willie" to be honest.

We thought that he was running an independent newspaper on a plane far above the ordinary altitude of newspapers, with a sincere desire to do good to the world, with an honest wish to expose shams, to speak the truth, and to establish a paper that, while it might be a personal organ, would still be an honest one. We came finally to admire "Our Willie" and to speak well of him and his paper.

When William R. Hearst commenced his abusive tirades against C. P. Huntington and the Southern Pacific Company and the Central Pacific Railroad Company and all who were friendly to them, and to denounce the funding bill and all who favored it as thieves and robbers, we thought his course was wrong, his methods bad, and his attacks brutal, but we believed "Our Willie" to be honest.

When C. P. Huntington told the truth about "Our Willie" and showed that he was simply fighting the railroad funding bill because he could get no more blackmail from the Southern Pacific Company, we were dazed with the charge, and as Californians we were humiliated.

We looked eagerly for "Our Willie's" denial, but it came not. On the contrary he admitted that he had blackmailed the Southern Pacific Company into a contract whereby they were to pay him $30,000 to let them alone, and that he had received $22,000 of his blackmail, and that C. P. Huntington had cut it off as soon as he knew of it, and that he was getting even now on Huntington and the railroad company because he had not received the other $8,000 of his bribe. He admitted by silence that the Southern Pacific Company was financially responsible, but that he dared not sue it for the $8,000 he claimed to be due because of fear that his blackmail would be exposed in court.

With brazen effrontery only equaled by the lowest denizen of the haunts of vice "Our Willie" knows so well in every city of the globe, he unblushingly admitted he had blackmailed the railroad company, but pleaded in extenuation that he did not keep his contract, but swindled them out of their money.

He showed himself to be the correct exponent of a scoundrel, as defined by Bill Tweed, namely, "A man who wouldn't stay bought." I cannot tell how sad I felt to learn of this phase of Hearst's life. I had been his attorney. I had regarded Hearst as honest. I had praised his *Examiner* for its course, because I believed it to be dictated by honest, although at times mistaken, ideas.

To learn "Our Willie" was nothing but a common, ordinary, everyday blackmailer—a low highwayman of the newspaper world—grieved the people of California, myself included.

I regret it. For the honor of California I wish this exposé had never been necessary; but it is true, sadly true.

We have lost on the Pacific Coast an idol. We mourn a leader. We grieve over a dead and wicked newspaper.

People read the paper because it gives the news in large type but they say while reading it, "Isn't it too bad Hearst should have sold himself. We did not expect it. He must be wicked at heart, for he didn't need the money."

If it be given to spirits of the departed to know the actions of those left behind them on this earth, the honored and respected father of "Our Willie" is suffering now from the blackmailing conduct of his son.

At this point in the speech there shamelessly appears in the *Congressional Record* the notation "[laughter]"—for there were still men in Congress who remembered the actual character of Senator George Hearst. Grove Johnson continued:

And that is the man who has created all this furor in California. He has intimidated men. He has intimidated people. You do not know the terrorism that he has exercised in California with his paper. It is a paper that has a large circulation. You know how it has abused and caricatured people in this House, the honored chairman of our committee [Mr. Powers] and other members of our committee, and our honored Speaker [Thomas B. Reed]. I will not speak of myself, because I do not know but what I can get reasonably even with this man before I get through with him. [Laughter.] But he has carried it on for years. While we knew all these things about him, we believed he was honest because he said he was, because he had his newspaper; but he has debauched the public mind in California by terrorism, he has terrorized over every one, he has issued his edicts that any man who dares to favor this funding bill shall be driven from public life, shall be ruined in private life, and shall be disgraced before the people and before the gods. But for one, knowing that I am right, knowing that this is a business settlement of the question, I am willing to stand for what I believe to be right, even if this blackmailing paper does continue to assault me.

The speech was obviously in large part a rhetorical appeal to prejudice, its lapses in logic were terrific, and it contained several minor inaccuracies such as the reference to "editorials written by 'Our Willie'" (Hearst himself writing no editorials on the *Examiner*). Nevertheless, its ringing charges of a deal between Hearst and the Southern Pacific demanded refutation, if the publisher were to retain any credit for political sincerity.

Hearst had a friend at court, Congressman James G. Maguire of San Francisco, who was devoted to the Hearst interests. But Maguire did not rise and answer Johnson on the floor of the House. Instead, he availed himself of his privilege to have his speech printed in the *Congressional Record* without delivering it. He also sent a copy of it to the *Examiner* which immediately published it as a genuine utterance on the floor of Congress. In it, Maguire, without answering the charges against Hearst, attempted to carry the war into the enemy's territory by insinuating that Johnson had first come to California under an assumed name in order to escape an indictment and arrest in the state of New York. This gave occasion to another speech by Johnson, in which he not only defended himself but indulged in further comments on William R. Hearst's methods of political warfare.

Rising to a question of personal privilege on January 12, 1897, he first referred to Maguire's attack and then went on:

It is true, sir, that thirty-four years ago I was in trouble in the State of New York. It is true, sir, that thirty-four years ago I was indicted. It is true, sir, that thirty-four years ago I did go to the State of California to endeavor to rear a new home for myself. It is untrue that I went there under any name except that of Grove L. Johnson, as the gentleman from Syracuse [Mr. Poole], who has known me from boyhood, knows. I went to Sacramento. I settled there in 1865, as Grove L. Johnson, well knowing the charge against me, the people in Syracuse well knowing it and my residence in Sacramento. I worked in Sacramento day in and day out, and by the blessing of God and the help of my wife and through my own labor I was able to pay back every dollar of indebtedness that I owed in the city of Syracuse, in the State of New York. [Loud applause.] Every charge against me was dismissed. The very men that had suffered pecuniary loss at my hands were the first ones to congratulate me upon my success. And I visited Syracuse in 1870, and nearly every year since—always as Grove L. Johnson. . . .

In 1877 I was a candidate for a member of the assembly in Sacramento County. I went before that convention, and I said to the members of the convention, "Gentlemen, I will tell you my history." I told them the truth about these charges. I said I had been indicted, but that I had paid off every dollar of my indebtedness. I said to them, "I do not want any member of this body to vote for me and after he has cast his vote be permitted to say that had he known of these things he would have voted against me."

After that statement these men of Sacramento, with a knowledge of all of these charges, gave me the nomination by a three-fourths majority, and I was elected by an overwhelming majority in my own county. Afterwards I served my term as an assemblyman, and was nominated unanimously to the State Senate and elected, receiving the highest vote of any candidate. That was the condition of affairs then, although every man in that county knew of my life and the circumstances connected with my going to California. . . .

In 1896 I was renominated for Congress, and the bitterest fight against me was made that was ever made against any man on earth. You, Mr. Speaker, yourself have knowledge of that fact, because you were present in California and took part in that campaign; the honorable gentleman from Maine [Mr. Boutelle] knows of the fact, for he was present and participated in the campaign, as also did the honorable gentlemen from Massachusetts [Mr. McCall and Mr. Apsley]. They can all testify to the condition of affairs existing when they were present in my district. And yet, Mr. Speaker, in view of those facts, despite the bitter fight made against me personally, and although Sacramento County gave 300 majority for Bryan, I carried every election district in the city of Sacramento, my home, receiving nearly 1,200 majority in the county. [Applause.] The district is Democratic; it gave Bryan over 2,000 majority.

I refer to this, sir, to show that the people of Sacramento, who know me well, and who knew of the charges made against me, regarded them as they would the rattle in the tail of a toothless snake, which is heard without exciting alarm. But during the entire campaign, from the very beginning to the end of it, I was the recipient of the vilest abuse from the paper conducted by this man Hearst— the vilest abuse that was ever heaped on a man. That paper was filled with the bitterest slanders and the vilest caricatures of myself. Every man here has received a copy of it. You gentlemen who were present in our State during that canvass know the facts of which I speak. You know how our honored Speaker was caricatured by that paper during the campaign because you were present and saw it. You know how bitter were the assaults that were made upon him. The gentleman from Maine [Mr. Boutelle] knows how he was assailed by that infamous paper; but the bitterness and the assaults upon our honored Speaker were but as drops of water compared to the roar of the cataract of Niagara to the assaults that were made on me. I am a man, with all the sentiments and feelings of a man, and can stand a reasonable amount of punishment, although I am not invulnerable to every shaft. But in addition, when my wife lay sick upon her bed during the campaign, from which sickness the doctors said she might not perhaps recover, this infamous wretch sent the editorials and the caricatures from his paper, put them in envelopes, sealed them, and sent them to her as correspondence, until the doctor directed my daughters never to give my wife a letter until they had first read it themselves to know what was in it.

Is it wonderful that, having been assailed in this manner, I struck back when the opportunity came? Is there a man here who would do less, except this gentleman from the Fourth District, James G. Maguire? Is there any man here who would not protect himself? I have no newspaper. I did what I did boldly. I knew the attacks would be made upon me. I knew I would be assailed in the columns of this paper. I knew I would be assailed by others, but I did not expect to be assailed in this cowardly, this unmanly, this underhanded method of printing in the RECORD a speech that never was delivered in the House. There is a race of men in Ireland called "informers." There is a race of men in Italy called "bravos." There is a race of men in Russia called "paid police spies." Either one of those would have scorned to do what the gentleman from California [Mr. Maguire] did with reference to me. . . .

Every charge that I made against Hearst is capable of proof. I do not shelter myself behind my constitutional privilege. Whatever I say as a Congressman I am responsible for personally and pecuniarily as a man. . . .

For thirty-four years I have tried to make a living for myself, my children, and my grandchildren who have been born unto me (and I have taken good care of them); and now, in my old age, when I can only look backward and not forward in life; when but few more years are given to me; when I ought to be permitted to enjoy a few years of peace, is it right that a man should go back thirty-four years and unlock the doors of the secret recesses of the past to bring up the skeleton of my youthful conduct before you and exhibit it to the people of the United States, especially in this sneaking, cowardly manner? Is it right? Ought not there to be a statute of limitations to the past of a man? Is it right that a man should be thus cowardly assailed? If I should say what I was going to say, it would not be proper. I say, is it right, is it proper to go back thirty-four years in the life of a man and bring out the follies and crimes of his youth and forever throw them at him? . . .

This time Maguire did reply. He disavowed any intention in

his speech to make a "direct assault upon the gentleman from California" and then proceeded:

Any member of the House might read the speech from beginning to end without discovering any unparliamentary reference to the gentleman. [Expressions of dissent.] It was only because his knowledge enabled him to identify the man described in the picture I had drawn of the author of the most malicious, malignant charge relating to the early life, to the boyhood of an absent man whom he had so cowardly assailed, that he felt so outraged. . . .

The gentleman whines about what he calls the attack upon himself. He thinks only of himself—his own self-loving self. He thinks not of grief, thinks not of trouble, thinks not of anguish, until it strikes the only man on earth he cares about—himself. Why did he not think of these things before making an assault on Mr. Hearst? Why did he not think of what the people of the southern States, and the people of the northern States, and the people of the western States, would think of such a cowardly assault? The man who has made this whining, weeping, tearful speech before you this morning, pleading with you to believe that I should not have replied to him as I did, used this language concerning an absent man, whose character or whose life, either in boyhood or in manhood, was not in question here.

Maguire here quoted extensively from Johnson's first speech and then continued:

The gentleman from California said these things of an absent man. They are false, and it ill becomes him, after using that language, to whine about my answers to his charges. [Applause.] . . .

He states, by way of justification of his attack on Mr. Hearst on Friday last, that Mr. Hearst during the last campaign had sent editorials and caricatures denouncing him and holding him up to ridicule to his wife while she was sick. Mr. Hearst has not been in California for over a year, except perhaps for two or three days on business, when he had no time to think of the gentleman from California or his concerns. He has been living in New York for more than a year, conducting one of the greatest newspapers printed in the English language, [laughter and applause]—the greatest newspaper printed on this continent. [Renewed laughter and applause.]

The laughter came from the Republican side of the house, the applause from the Democratic side. Mr. Poole, Republican from Syracuse, corroborated Johnson's account of his own life and demanded that Maguire's undelivered speech be stricken from the *Congressional Record*. This was done, and the House then turned its attention to other matters.

An interesting angle of the case was Huntington's willingness not merely to admit but to proclaim the Southern Pacific's share in the bribery. Why should he not? It was an open secret on the Pacific Coast that the Southern Pacific had most of the papers in California on its payroll. Fremont Older tells us that the monthly subsidy of the San Francisco *Bulletin*, for instance, was $175, increased in 1898 to $375—much more than was offered the *Examiner*, whose silence was purchased very cheaply. The man who had almost openly bribed a United States Congress saw no reason to deny that his railroad had bribed a few newspapers now and then. All this was a necessary and recognized part of the game that capitalists played. Bribe givers had never been held in any dishonor in the United States.

But it was different with the bribe taker. Had Hearst bribed Huntington, the glory would have gone to Hearst, the shame to Huntington. And the case of the *Examiner* was a little different from that of the *Bulletin* and the other conservative papers which might be held to have supported the Southern Pacific from conviction as well as from the profit motive. The *Examiner* had been from its very beginning the sworn foe of monopoly as typified in the Southern Pacific. If it could not be trusted here, it could not be trusted anywhere. It was a test case as to the sincerity of Hearst's political principles, and if Grove L. Johnson's charges were true, the answer was decisive.

With regard to the funding bill, Congress decided, rightly

enough, that the railroad was bluffing. The bill was defeated and another passed in its stead, requiring immediate payment of the principal and interest. For this, though it was not at all the measure he had recommended, Hearst took all the credit so loudly and continuously that his readers were convinced.

CHAPTER VI

Owner of the New York Journal

HEARST is said to have sunk nearly half a million dollars in the *Examiner* before he finally got the paper on an adequately paying basis. He knew that he would need much more than that amount for the conquest of New York. It was his mother who had made the ultimate success of the *Examiner* possible, and she now financed his invasion of the east by supplying him with truly Napoleonic resources. Through the sale of the Hearst interests in the Anaconda mine, she was able to turn over to her son for his new undertaking the sum of seven million five hundred thousand dollars. No other American publisher had ever started a paper with such financial backing.

Strictly speaking, Hearst, of course, was not starting a new paper. The *Morning Journal,* located in the Tribune Building at 154 Nassau Street, had been founded by Albert Pulitzer, brother of the great Joseph, as a sheet of backstairs gossip, a kind of daily *Town Topics,* featuring with salacious overtones and undertones the more sensational doings of the American aristocracy. It was sufficiently successful to enable its owner after a few years to retire to Paris, the paper being sold early in 1895 to John R. McLean, owner of the Cincinnati *Enquirer.* McLean endeavored to make a more respectable sheet out of it on the model of his middle-western paper, but to do so he was obliged to raise the price from one to two cents—and this proved his undoing. The circulation dropped from 100,000 to 77,000, and by September 1895 he was glad to sell the paper to Charles

M. Palmer, Hearst's representative, for $180,000. Thrown in with it was a paper in German, *Das Morgen Journal*. Hearst became the owner on September twenty-fifth, but formal announcement was deferred until November eighth.

To his new enterprise Hearst brought the best of his San Francisco staff—Chamberlain, McEwen, Tebbs, "Cosy" Noble, Winifred Black, and a number of his star reporters. The size and format of the *World* were reproduced, and its technique and contents were imitated more closely than local conditions had ever permitted on the *Examiner*. At the same time the price of the *Journal* was put back at a penny where its only competitors were the *Press*, the *Recorder*, the *Morning Advertiser*, and the *Sunday Mercury*—none of them strong papers. Hearst, of course, had bigger game in mind than these weaklings; his program was to give the public something as good as the *World* at half the price; and he prepared to watch Joseph Pulitzer tremble.

During the last three months of 1895 Hearst put into the *Journal* more than twice as much as it had cost him, but the returns were hardly commensurate with the outlay. The circulation did, indeed, go up to about 100,000, restoring the paper to the position it had been in when McLean had taken it. But the gains of the *Journal* were entirely at the expense of its penny rivals; Joseph Pulitzer, with his circulation of more than half a million, was untouched; he remained serenely unconscious that any competition with the *World* was even intended.

Hearst's San Francisco staff, excellent though it was, had difficulty in adapting itself to the new environment. The frontier cynicism of California had been only skin-deep, covering an underlying sentimentality and moral idealism, so that it had been easy to tap all three sources at once; furthermore, San Francisco was, relatively speaking, a small town where individual personalities stood out or could be made to stand out with little effort. New York, on the other hand, was a world metropolis, experienced, sophisticated, and disillusioned, needing much stronger stimuli to arouse its jaded emotions.

The readers of McEwen's editorials in New York did not say "Gee-whiz!" New York was too well stocked with Little Jims for Annie Laurie to be able to cook up a sensation on such a score. Even Sam Chamberlain had been away from the city for so long that he had lost his contacts there. The *Journal* was ignominiously forced to steal its news from the *World*. According to Don Seitz, "it used to be asserted that when the first edition of the *World* reached the *Journal* news-room, a grateful copy desk would set up this refrain:

> Sound the cymbals, beat the drum!
> The *World* is here, the news has come!"

Hearst decided that the time had come for drastic action. Hitherto, his relations with Pulitzer had been most amiable: the *World* had a telegraphic exchange with the *Examiner* for Pacific Coast news, and Hearst had long since rented an office in the Pulitzer Building for his California paper's New York representative. Nevertheless, Hearst now made up his mind to utilize his mother's money in a raid on Pulitzer's staff.

The center of the *World's* success had been its Sunday edition embellished with large type and profuse illustrations. Its editor, Morrill Goddard, was an erstwhile Bowdoin student, who had been expelled for hazing, had finished at Dartmouth, and had then obtained a job as a space-rate reporter for the *World*. In that capacity he had selected the City Morgue down on the East River as a congenial field of observation and had been so successful in depicting its blood-curdling horrors that Pulitzer soon gave him a staff position and then within a year made him Sunday editor. His specialties were said to be "crime and underwear." No one else could tell a murder story with such gusto for all the gory details, no one else had quite such a nose for the neurotic elements in sex. Pulitzer personally disliked these features of his paper, but, recognizing their commercial value, he compromised by rewarding his editor's achievements while at the same time he tried to keep them within the bounds of outward decency. And it is only fair to Goddard to point out that he had other important assets—unbounded energy, a lively imagination, considerable humor, and endless ability to "jazz up" any topic that he took in hand.

Goddard's formula for a Sunday supplement page ran as follows: "Suppose it's Halley's comet. Well, first you have a half-page of decoration showing the comet, with historical pictures of previous appearances thrown in. If you can work a pretty girl into the decoration, so much the better. If not, get some good nightmare idea like the inhabitants of Mars watching it pass. Then you want a quarter of a page of big-type heads—snappy. Then four inches of story, written off the bat. Then a picture of Professor Halley down here and another of Professor Lowell up there, and a two-column boxed freak containing a scientific opinion, which nobody will understand, just to give it class."

Goddard was indirectly responsible for the name "yellow journalism." As Frank Palmer tells the story, "Heating his brain for an idea one day, he happened to look over his shoulder at an artist, who was also seeking an idea and was absently drawing a fantastic face with a spot for a nose and two spots for eyes on his board. 'That's a good kid,' Goddard said. 'We'll dress him in a yellow shirt and call him the Yellow Kid and have funny things printed on his shirt, we'll put him through all kinds of stunts and he'll go." Don Seitz, on the other hand, gives the story somewhat differently, and more plausibly, that the original draughtsman, R. F. Outcault, drew the Kid deliberately as one of a tenement group in an illustration called "Hogan's Alley" and that the idea of making him all yellow originated with Charles W. Saalberg, the *World's* colorist. At any rate, the Yellow Kid, whatever the precise circumstances of his birth, was "put through all kinds of stunts" and soon became the favorite feature of the *World's* comic supplement. Then Outcault was bought by Hearst to draw Yellow Kids for the *Journal*, while George B. Luks now drew them for the *World*. The New York public at last grew tired of so many Yellow Kids, and the term "yellow journalism" came into use as a descriptive term for all that the two papers represented.

But Hearst wanted more than Outcault from the *World*. His eye was on Morrill Goddard himself. Secret negotiations were carried on in the *Examiner's* convenient office in the Pulitzer Building. In January 1896, yielding to an offer of $35,000, Goddard went over to the enemy, taking the entire staff of the Sunday paper with him. Pulitzer at once sent Solomon Carvalho, his business manager, to lure them back with a higher offer, and for twenty-four hours the recreants returned. Then Hearst went still higher, and they again left Pulitzer—this time forever.

The owner of the *World* was deeply incensed by what he regarded as Hearst's trickery, and demanded that the *Examiner's* office in his building be given up. This, of course, was immediately done. But Hearst's raid was by no means over. In the reorganization of the *World* necessitated by the desertion of the Sunday staff, Pulitzer advanced the city editor, Richard A. Farrelly, who had been with him seventeen years, to the headship of the morning edition. A banquet was arranged by Pulitzer for Farrelly; it was to be held on a Monday evening; on Sunday came the news that he, too, had joined the Hearst forces.

To meet the now dangerous rivalry of the *Journal*, Pulitzer cut the price of the *World* to one cent. But since he was paying for losses out of the paper's earnings instead of out of his mother's millions, this necessitated a raising of advertising rates which caused much resentment among the merchants, the brunt of which fell on Carvalho as business manager. A quarrel ensued between him and his chief, and in April 1896 Carvalho followed Goddard and Farrelly into the Hearst ranks.

Pulitzer was fortunate in having a man to put into Goddard's place who was fully as well versed as the former editor in the art of mass appeal. His name was Arthur Brisbane. The son of Albert Brisbane, who had been one of the most ardent Utopian Socialists of the fifties, author of *The Social Destiny of Man* (1840) and a reputable journalist, Arthur Brisbane knew all the patter of liberalism even better than Hearst himself. He had been educated mainly in France, where he had been influenced by his reading of Montesquieu, d'Alembert, Rousseau, and Voltaire—especially Voltaire. And he had been in newspaper work ever since he was eighteen. Starting as a cub reporter on the New York *Sun*, he had leaped into Dana's attention by covering a prize-fight of John L. Sullivan one night when the sporting editor was drunk. In the philosophy of journalism it was obvious that a man who could write up a prize-fight well was fitted to understand diplomacy and politics (one recalls the present instance of Westbrook Pegler). Brisbane was sent to London where he covered both Houses of Parliament and Jack the Ripper with equal satisfaction to his editor. He became an intimate friend of Gladstone's son and sat at the feet of the old religionist, learning from him all the tricks of moral and political hypocrisy. Soon he won positive fame by the amount of sentiment he infused into his account of the great prize-fight between John L. Sullivan and Charley Mitchell, representing Mitchell as inspired by his seconds to contend on behalf of "the dear little kids at home" (in spite of which, fate unjustly allowed him to be defeated). On his return Brisbane was made managing editor of the *Evening Sun*, but in 1890 he joined the *World* where he soon became, next to William H. Merrill, Pulitzer's most trusted subordinate.

His mind was fully as fertile as Goddard's. He had practically invented the big-type headline which was the best means yet discovered for attracting attention to a paper. Headlines were a perfect medium of expression for him. As Frank Palmer wrote, "The sum of his genius is his art of stating a part so that it will seem a whole," and for this nothing could be so suitable as the headline. His political and social views formed, in the words of Will Irwin, a mass of "insincere sincerities"; no one so well as he knew how "to talk politics and philosophy in the language of truckmen" and, in apparently identifying his interests with theirs, in reality to identify their interests with his. As a good newspaperman, he shared Goddard's cold passion for crime and underwear. The two combatants were well matched, but Pulitzer felt that he could safely count upon Brisbane's broader equipment to give him the victory in the long run.

With the battle now engaged on all fronts, Hearst poured out his wealth like water. Every available means of publicity was impounded. He put huge advertisements in the regular papers and in trade organs; billboards were erected in every vacant lot, spreading the legend of the *Journal's* merits; sandwich men paraded the streets in its honor. Hearst is estimated to have spent within several months at least two million dollars on a publicity campaign whose like had never been seen in America before.

By the clever device of enclosing the *Journal* within the comic supplement he converted each reader, as Frank Palmer expresses it, into "an involuntary sandwich man," garishly advertising the *Journal* by merely carrying it beneath his arm.

Meanwhile, Morrill Goddard was outdoing himself. Released from Pulitzer's restraining influence and told by his new chief to "go the limit," he soon showed that there was no limit so far as he was concerned. Using streamer headlines and splashing pen-and-ink drawings all over the page, he now went in for crime and underwear on a scale to which even New York was wholly unaccustomed. He sent Alan Dale, the dramatic critic, a minor acquisition from the *World*, to interview

Anna Held, the French comedienne, and the carefully staged meeting was reported under the heading: "MLLE. ANNA HELD RECEIVED ALAN DALE, ATTIRED IN A 'NIGHTIE'." Under Goddard's inspiration, Dale's dramatic criticism became largely a comparative study of shoulders, bosoms, and legs. To introduce a saving romanticism in the midst of the salacity, Winifred Bonfils wrote articles under such heads as "WHY YOUNG GIRLS KILL THEMSELVES" or "STRANGE THINGS WOMEN DO FOR LOVE." And the whole enterprise was sanctified by Goddard's frequent use of Biblical references—the origin of the Hearst custom of running Bible texts at the top of the editorial page—while the paper ran riot with pseudo-science, "just to give it class"—stories such as the marvelous tale about "THE JUMPING LAELAPS OF 50,000 YEARS AGO."

The circulation of the *Journal* leaped and bounded. By Easter 1896 it was treble or quadruple what it was when Hearst assumed command. But meanwhile Brisbane by similar methods had brought that of the *World* up to 600,000. The gap between the two papers was slowly narrowing but the *World* still had a comfortable lead.

Then came the presidential campaign of 1896. At first, the dying *Recorder* was the only New York paper to come out for Bryan. To do so was generally considered in New York journalistic circles to be equivalent to suicide. Hearst hesitated. He sensed that a large proportion of his special audience would be for Bryan before the campaign was over, and he had his own private reasons for desiring Bryan's success. The reader will not have forgotten George Hearst's investments in silver mines.

Following the repeal of the Sherman Purchasing Act in 1893, the silver-mine owners had organized under the leadership of George Hearst's old friend, Marcus Daly, in a mighty effort to obtain control of one or both of the old parties at the next election. Their efforts were checked in the Republican convention by the American Bankers' Association which sent $85,000 to the

New York boss, Thomas C. Platt, to be used discreetly in promoting a "sound money" platform. The $85,000 was certainly sound, and although McKinley, a mild free-silver advocate, was nominated, an out-and-out gold platform was adopted. The silver-mine owners then redoubled their endeavors to capture the Democratic convention. No less a sum than $289,000, as Daly's books showed when examined after his death, was expended by the mine owners in securing the right delegates to the convention and in keeping them secure. Under these circumstances, the delegates were in a mood to respond readily to Bryan's "Cross of Gold" speech with its fervent appeal not to press a "crown of thorns" upon "the brow of labor."

In July 1896 Hearst called a conference of his editorial and business managers and, after listening to their arguments, which were all in favor of "sound money," he announced firmly that the *Journal* was going to come out for Bryan on the following day. It did so, and the editors bent themselves to follow the unwelcome policy of "the boss" as best they could. Hearst announced his public reasons for lending Bryan his support, which ran as follows:

I am supporting Mr. Bryan because he is his own man. No syndicate controls him. He came to his nomination by no tricks or dark methods. Slanders and abuse showered upon him after his nomination hastened and heated my judgment to support him. Bryan is not an anarchist, not a public menace. The convention which selected him was not moved by lunacy nor made up of Satan-inspired traitors seeking the overthrow of American institutions.

Certainly the nominating convention had not been "inspired by lunacy" nor did it desire "the overthrow of American institutions"—especially not the institution of capitalism—but otherwise Hearst's statements were in doubtful conformity with facts. Needless to say, he made no mention of his private reasons.

Once Hearst had taken his stand, he made up for his long

delay by the savagery with which he attacked McKinley, and McKinley's financial general, Mark Hanna. The members of the *Journal's* staff denounced those exponents of their own convictions the more furiously because the Republicans represented the side which they themselves would have chosen had they been free men. Though McKinley was not spared, the attacks were centered upon Hanna as the more vulnerable of the two. Thomas Beer, in his life of the Ohio magnate, gives an accurate summary of Hearst's campaign of vilification:

Marcus Alonzo Hanna [was] revealed in the newspapers owned by William Randolph Hearst as an amalgam of all sins. He was foulness compact. He was the red boss of Cleveland's city politics. The town council trembled when he sent minions to address it. He had stolen a theatre from poor John Ellsler, foreclosing a cruel mortgage and rejecting the man's plea for time. He ruled Cleveland from his office, terrorizing unions and ruining rival street railways. He sent poor sailors, forced on his ships by bestial labor masters, out to sea on the wintry lakes, cold and starving, unpaid and mutinous.

There was little misrepresentation or exaggeration to which the *Journal* did not descend in its accounts of the great exponent of class collaboration who was wedded to a scheme of "benevolent" autocracy and who in a few years would be receiving the unofficial support of organized labor in his tentative efforts for the presidency. The abusive editorials and news stories in the *Journal* were supported by the famous "dollar mark" cartoons of Homer Davenport representing Hanna as a typical fat boss, clad in a suit covered with dollar signs, smoking the inevitable cigar, and usually dandling a doll-like McKinley on his knee. Davenport, though strong in execution, was weak in ideas, and these were generally supplied by Hearst himself or by Sam Chamberlain. It may be admitted that these cartoons, however personally unfair to Hanna, nonetheless dramatized the essential situation in the Republican Party, but for the picture of contemporary politics to have been complete there should also have been shown on the opposite page cartoons of Marcus Daly arm-in-arm with Hearst.

During the heat of the campaign in September 1896 Hearst enlarged his output by establishing an evening edition of the *Journal* in competition with the *Evening World*. At about the same time, after his secretary, George Pancoast, who had an inventive mind, had smashed three presses in an attempt to improve upon them, Hearst purchased from R. Hoe & Co. a special color press able to print from four to sixteen pages in all colors. As a result, the Sunday *Journal* blossomed forth with an enlarged comic supplement described as "eight pages of iridescent polychromous effulgence that makes the rainbow look like a lead pipe," enabling the *Journal* to laugh to scorn the "desolate waste of black" in the *World's* "weak, wishy-washy" four-page comic. Soon a sixteen-page addition to the Sunday *Journal* appeared, called the *American Magazine*, forerunner of the later thirty-two page *American Weekly*.

On the day before election the *Journal* featured a telegram from Bryan in which the candidate declared, "The *Journal* deserves great credit for its splendid fight in behalf of bi-metallism and popular government." Although that fight was lost on the following day, all was not lost. The three Hearst papers in New York ran off election extras up to a grand total of 1,506,-634 copies—an unprecedented journalistic feat—and chartered special trains to carry them to Boston, Washington, and Buffalo. Four months later, the inauguration of Bryan's successful rival gave Hearst the opportunity to send another special train from Washington to New York which broke all speed records between the two cities in his zeal to give the metropolis its first news of just how McKinley looked and what he said and how gallantly the Hearst reporters carried on their labors in a train that rocked along at a mile a minute. Incidentally, but of significance in connection with his later career, Hearst made use of the newly invented vitascope motion-picture machines in catching the inaugural procession.

The outcome of the election left Pulitzer in a better position than his competitor, but the owner of the *World* now began to have trouble with his right-hand man, Arthur Brisbane. Off for a European cruise, he made Brisbane editor of the *Evening World*, which certainly seemed a good appointment. But Brisbane took advantage of his chief's absence to execute a project which he had long cherished but which Pulitzer had always refused to permit, namely, that of running in either the morning or the evening edition a special editorial column of his own. Europe was a long way off, and Brisbane reckoned that his chief might not learn of the development until his return when it would be sanctioned by use and wont. All went well for several weeks. Then arrived a wrathful cable: "Stop that column at once. I don't want the *Evening World* to have an editorial policy. If you want good editorials, rewrite those in the morning *World*."

Brisbane, checked in this innovation, hatched another in his fertile brain. This was the bizarre idea of incorporating Morrill Goddard's type of Sunday "freak" stories into the daily news, thus converting the whole paper into a glorified magazine section with Jumping Laelaps and half-naked actresses performing on every page. As soon as Brisbane started this, the Hearst papers immediately followed suit, and then the *Sun* and the *Post* attempted the same vein. American journalism had touched a new low.

The reaction in general circulation was favorable, but the more reputable and influential readers were highly indignant. They had been able to throw away the magazine section without reading it, but when the "freaks" dominated the news page there was no escape. A strong movement to boycott all the "yellow journals" was begun. Librarians refused to keep them on file, clergymen preached against them. By December 1896 a moral crusade against the offending papers was well under way.

It was an opportune moment for Hearst to resume an old rôle that had been somewhat neglected by him since coming to New York. The Board of Aldermen was about to make a gift to the local gas companies of a franchise estimated to be worth ten millions. Hearst went into court and secured an injunction, and three days later the application for the franchise was withdrawn.

The incident furnished Hearst with a new slogan of his own coinage: "WHILE OTHERS TALK THE JOURNAL ACTS." Developing this idea, the paper proclaimed itself to be an exponent of "the new journalism," distinguished from the old by the fact that in addition to strict accuracy in reporting the news it would strive to improve the social and political conditions which the news revealed. "WHAT IS EVERYBODY'S BUSINESS IS THE JOURNAL'S BUSINESS," the paper boldly proclaimed.

All this considerably bettered the *Journal's* moral standing in the eyes of the community. The crusade of righteousness against it was definitely halted. And in line with its new policy it went on to support other local reforms that were successfully carried through—prevention of further franchise grabs by various corporations and improvement of the scandalous conditions at the terminal of the Brooklyn Bridge. It did not, however, discontinue the circulation-getting "freaks" which, on Pulitzer's return, were summarily eliminated from the *World*.

In April 1897, through the purchase of the dying *Morning Advertiser*, Hearst secured an Associated Press franchise, the lack of which had hitherto seriously hampered the development of his news service. Knowing, or believing, or affecting to believe, that Pulitzer had been responsible for his previous inability to obtain this franchise, he accused his enemy of underhanded plotting to that end and characterized the owner of what he had once considered "the best paper in America" as "a journalist who makes his money by pandering to the worst tastes of the prurient and horror-loving, by dealing in bogus news, such as forged cablegrams from eminent personages, and by affecting a devotion to the interests of the people while never really hurting those of its enemies, and sedulously looking out for his own." The *World* replied with a precisely similar characterization of Hearst, and henceforward personal invective was added to the other weapons used by both men in the long duel between their papers.

There could be no doubt, however, that Hearst's star was again in the ascendant. Five editions of the *Evening Journal* were called for when it came out with the first page in color to celebrate the dedication of Grant's Tomb on Riverside Drive. Hearst obtained the exclusive rights to all interviews with the principals in the Corbett-Fitzsimmons fight at Carson City. (His papers were much opposed to prize-fighting, as well as later to horse-racing and dog-racing, but this of course did not prevent their featuring such events.) He organized and equipped two expeditions to the Klondike, and their adventures were reported in detail. When war threatened between Greece and Turkey he sent James Creelman to obtain a special cable message to the *Journal* from King George, and when the war broke out he sent over seven correspondents—among them Julian Ralph and Stephen Crane. The coronation of the czar was reported exclusively for the *Journal* by Richard Harding Davis, the jubilee of Queen Victoria by Mark Twain. Alfred Henry Lewis, Edward W. Townsend, and Rudolph Block contributed to the magazine section. The *Journal* now had, as John K. Winkler asserts, "the greatest staff of reporters and special writers ever assembled on an American newspaper," including, among others who have been mentioned, Bob Davis, later editor of *Munsey's Magazine*, Edgar Saltus, Julian Hawthorne, Murat Halstead, Henry W. Fischer, Julius Chambers, W. J. Henderson, James L. Ford, and A. C. Wheeler ("Nym Crinkle").

Better known than any of these, at least to the mass of femi-
nine readers, were the Beatrice Fairfax and Dorothy Dix who
supplied saccharine answers to the sentimental missives that
blossomed in Hearst's column, "Letters from the Lovelorn."
This column, which was an outgrowth of Annie Laurie's sob
stuff, was even more popular, since it allowed moronic readers
to be actors as well as audience; eventually it led to similar columns in papers all over the country. Equally popular with such
wishful readers were the elaborate accounts of society events,
the Gould, Astor, and Vanderbilt balls, etc.

Nor was crime ever forgotten. A special "murder squad" of
Journal reporters was formed to help the blundering investigations of the police; it was under the special direction of none
other than William R. Hearst himself. With all the ardor of a
schoolboy, he threw himself into this new pastime. He offered
liberal rewards for the apprehension of criminals, he studied
clues and devised solutions, he sent his reporters here, there,
and everywhere, to the infinite annoyance of the police—and
occasionally they did turn up a criminal.

Hearst's greatest success as an amateur detective was in the
solution of the "Guldensuppe mystery" in the summer of 1897.
Guldensuppe was a corpse, or rather, he was bits of a corpse,
which were found scattered around the East Side, each piece
carefully wrapped in oilcloth. Hearst printed the pattern of the
oilcloth in its own colors, and put thirty men on the job to find
the purchaser. One of these, George W. Arnold, was successful,
and the crime was traced to an East Side midwife and an accom-
plice who had helped in the dismembering of Guldensuppe.
The corpse, before it became a corpse, had been one of the lovers
of the midwife, and she had quarreled with it. The whole case
was made to the *Journal's* hand.

In September 1897 Arthur Brisbane, Hearst's greatest acquisition, came over from the *World*. Pulitzer had alienated him,
not only by killing his editorial column and junking his

"freaks," but by refusing to allow him to run headlines a foot deep. This was the last straw. Brisbane met Hearst in the Hoffman House and made him a sporting offer: to work for him at $200 a week, plus one dollar for every thousand readers he should add to the circulation of the *Evening Journal*—all provided he could have his headlines. Hearst readily agreed. During the next two years, with the help of the Spanish-American War, Brisbane's salary went up to $50,000 a year. As the *Journal* was then at what was obviously the top point of its circulation, Hearst generously consented to scrap the verbal contract and give Brisbane a regular salary of $70,000 a year. This seemed enormous at the time, but finally the ever-rising salary would go beyond $250,000.

There was at least this much of genuineness in Hearst's ostensible anti-capitalist attitude: personally he had little in common with those Shylockian captains of industry, the Daniel Drews, Jay Goulds, and Rockefellers who believed in Franklin's motto that "A penny saved is a penny earned." His contempt for such grasping methods was real enough. Always he was the lord of the manor whose code insisted upon the utmost generosity to the knights, squires, and pages who surrounded him. That he could afford such generosity also increased his sense of power and was a subtle form of self-flattery.

The high salaries Hearst paid his headliners, much higher than had been previously offered anywhere, undoubtedly raised the wage-scale of the top-notchers in the profession although the effects were less evident the further down in the ranks one went. But this was almost inevitable. The serfs on a feudal estate could hardly expect to profit as much from its owner's success as did the knights and ladies of his entourage.

Much of the free-and-easy atmosphere of the *Examiner* was carried over to the *Journal* office. Chamberlain could still be "drunk again" as often as he pleased, and every now and then he and McEwen would run off to Europe without warning to be patiently reclaimed by their employer whenever he could establish cable contacts with them. Or if that failed, Hearst knew that they would return as soon as their money was exhausted, and when that happened he reinstated them without a word. If ill-luck came to members of his staff, he was invariably responsive to their needs. He fitted out the spendthrift Davenport with clothes; he brought a Pasteur specialist from France to care for the cancer-stricken Bill Hart; when a stenographer in the office had a stroke of paralysis he sent her to a sanitarium and when on her recovery she married a cripple whom she met there he found a job for the husband and fitted up an apartment for the two of them.

And yet all during 1896 and 1897, as will be related in the next chapter, this man, so tenderly sympathetic toward the suffering of personal acquaintances, was working with might and main to bring upon his country the infinitely greater suffering of a foreign war. This was the supreme instance of the mass of contradictions that Hearst had now become. Still bashful in personal conversation and the most blatant of self-advertisers in public; courteous in speech and given to billingsgate in print; a reformer when reform seemed "good business"; a capitalist who hated capitalists; and editor of a paper which was the embodiment of his own contradictions, a paper which would go to endless pains to obtain the news and was utterly conscienceless in its handling thereof, a paper which supported the political interests of the common people and at the same time played the pander to their lowest vices.

What did Phebe Hearst out in San Francisco think about the way in which her seven millions had been spent? Possibly she thought little about it; she was busy with her own work in financing the competition for plans to be submitted for new buildings at the University of California and then in financing the buildings themselves, Hearst Hall and the Mines and Mining Building; in arranging for the seven scholarships she gave the university; in her tasks as vice-regent of the Mount Vernon Ladies' Association. She had little time to read the New York *Journal;* if she did so at all, the woman who had sobbed over the "Last of the McGintys" certainly approved of her friend Annie Laurie and may even have been able to read the "Letters from the Lovelorn" without a smile. When she heard of Grove Johnson's speech, as she doubtless did, she probably dismissed his accusations as so many lies. "Willie Hearst" was still her "Willie" who had wanted to give away his clothes to the Dublin urchins. And when now he rushed, full-panoplied, to war, she probably, like many Americans, saw in him a noble patriot.

CHAPTER VII

Owner of the Spanish-American War

IN THE complex modern world it is impossible for a single individual to start a major war. Small groups of bankers and munition makers have frequently, if not always, played an important part in initiating wars, but they have acted as groups, not as individuals. William R. Hearst, however, in 1898, almost solely for the private profit of William R. Hearst, succeeded in prodding this country into a wholly unnecessary war which resulted in riveting upon the nation the imperialistic policy that has been followed ever since. It was the first instance of that effective use of newspaper propaganda on a large scale which has become one of the most familiar features of the twentieth century, an outgrowth of democracy perhaps destined to destroy democracy, presenting the sinister paradox of the chief means for the dissemination of the truth being turned against the truth and, at least temporarily, destroying it.

It would, of course, be absurd to assign the whole responsibility for the Spanish-American War to Hearst. The jingoistic propaganda which directly brought about the war was initiated by him, but it was, though reluctantly, taken up by Pulitzer, and eventually many excitable congressmen joined in. And behind them was half a century of expansionist enthusiasm occasionally solidifying into the definite policies of Henry Clay, Polk, Grant, Seward, and Blaine. All of these men, from Clay to Hearst, were more or less unconscious agents of capitalist destiny moving on to its imperialistic end. But as late as 1898 American capitalists, never very intelligent in world affairs, were still for the most part quite unaware of this destiny. Although the American sugar owners in Cuba were eager for the intervention of the United States in the affairs of the island, big business as a whole, under the leadership of Mark Hanna, was definitely opposed to it, and the representative of big business in the White House, President McKinley, took every step to prevent it that his congenitally weak nature permitted. Finally, he yielded to the pressure of Congress; but that pressure was caused by the demands of a public inflamed by two years of misinformation from the "yellow press" and chiefly from the New York *Journal*. The conclusion seems justified that without W. R. Hearst there would have been no Spanish-American War.

There is little reason to accuse Hearst of deliberate insincerity in the beginning. His California background was excessively jingoistic; as we have seen, the Workingmen's Party marched under the banner of "Americanism," the vigilantes used the same slogan in attacking the Workingmen's Party, the *Argonaut* adopted it in assailing George Hearst, and George Hearst's son resorted to it in assailing the Chinese. Furthermore, that background reeked with memories of violence; like other Californians of his day, W. R. Hearst was brought up in the vigilante tradition. As has so frequently happened in the chaotic culture of America, while his mind had become extraordinarily expert in mastering the methodology of acquisitiveness, in other ways it remained incurably adolescent. Just as he always retained the schoolboy's attitude toward teachers, so he always kept the schoolboy's attitude toward war.

When the perennial troubles in Cuba under Spanish misgovernment broke out anew in 1893 and 1894, the *Examiner* at once advocated American intervention as a natural solution. Had Hearst remained, however, on the Pacific Coast, far removed from the scene of conflict, it is doubtful whether he would have developed more than an academic interest in the question. But by the time he reached New York, a scant two days' journey from the island, an armed rebellion had been going on for six months and the insurgents had established in the American metropolis the Cuban *Junta* which was already hard at work on a whispering campaign against the Spanish government. Hearst was quick to see the circulation possibilities in making this a shouting campaign. It was not the first time that jingoistic convictions and the profit motive coincided. Of course, there is also a possibility that Hearst had some direct tie-up with Cuban investments—though this has never been shown. Even this, however, would not affect the question of the initial genuineness of his jingoism.

Curiously, soon after Hearst's arrival in New York the Spanish troops in Cuba apparently began to resort to the most inhuman methods of warfare. All through the fall of 1895 the *Journal* reported an increasing list of atrocities, its knowledge of which was derived, not from newspaper correspondents in the island but from mysterious "letters" and statements of "recently arrived Cubans," much of this material coming directly from the Junta. Thus the American public learned through the *Journal* that it was "the daily practice of the Spanish jailers to take several prisoners from the forts and prisons and shoot them," that Spanish troops had a habit "of beating Cuban prisoners to death," and that they specialized in attacks upon unarmed peasants, women, and children. All this, strangely enough, during the régime of the humane General Campos, who was recalled precisely because of his too great leniency toward the insurgents. The stories, nonetheless, especially those relating to the outraging of women, aroused too much pleasant moral indignation in the readers of the *Journal* not to be believed.

Pulitzer did not like war; his experiences as a cavalryman for a short time during the Civil War had left him with a permanent disgust for this primitive method of settling differences. Nevertheless, as the *Journal's* circulation mounted he felt it necessary to take the same tone, and when his own circulation mounted in turn he became as enthusiastic as Hearst himself in the search for Spanish outrages.

Not once, however, during the next three years did Hearst relinquish his position as the foremost American jingoist. In January 1896 when the other papers were asking merely that the insurgents be accorded the rights of belligerents, the *Journal* clamored loudly for the complete recognition of Cuban independence. It made no pretense of impartiality. According to it, the outrages, which were doubtless frequent, as in any war, were all on one side. General Weyler, the much more ruthless successor of Campos, was almost immediately dubbed by the *Journal* "Butcher Weyler." When Gomez issued his famous order to the insurgent troops, "You will proceed immediately to destroy all towns and villages within your jurisdiction," the *Journal* saw no inconsistency in highly approving his methods. When a force led by Maceo was ambushed by Weyler's troops and Maceo was killed in the battle, the *Journal* insisted and continued to insist that "the Spanish entrapped General Maceo and murdered him."

At first, Hearst counted on the support of President Cleveland. The *Journal* opined that "this administration is ambitious to leave a brilliant record as a patron of American foreign trade" and would therefore respond to "the almost universal demand of the American people"; when, instead, the administration offered to Spain its friendly assistance toward a compromise with the insurgents, the effort was characterized by the *Journal* as a "conspiracy with the Spanish government whereby the United States becomes its efficient ally," and all Spanish measures of conciliation were condemned in advance.

A year after Hearst took over the *Journal* the paper was able to announce an increase in circulation for the daily from 77,239 to 430,410 and for the Sunday edition from 54,308 to 408,779. But this still left the hated *World* a lead of 200,000. And

Pulitzer had sent to Cuba his ablest correspondents, William Shaw Bowen and Sylvester Scovel, who were much better known than any of the men his rival had as yet sent there.

Hearst saw that it was necessary to increase his efforts. He dispatched his star correspondent, Richard Harding Davis, and the artist Frederick Remington to Cuba, the services of Senator-Elect Hernando de Soto Money were secured for a trip to the island as "Special *Journal* Commissioner" to interview Weyler and Fitzhugh Lee, the United States Consul-General in Havana, and James Creelman was sent to Madrid to report the progress of events at the Spanish court. These achievements led the *Journal* to proclaim in no uncertain terms its superiority to the *Herald* and the *World:*

No matter of international discussion interests the people of the United States more than the struggle of the Cubans for liberty. . . . Recognizing the existence of this universal interest, the *Journal* has spared no pains and no expense in its effort to gather and publish every piece of trustworthy information on the subject. It has sent to Cuba from time to time correspondents who represent the highest journalistic, military, political, literary, or artistic attainments. It despatched to Madrid Mr. James Creelman, who antedated by sixteen days the *Herald's* instructive "news" of yesterday. To those eminent exponents of the old journalism, the *Herald,* which copies after sixteen days the news the *Journal* obtained from headquarters at Madrid, and the *World,* which positively contradicted statements of fact which the *Herald* now affirms, the *Journal* presents its compliments and promises to leave them to the uninterrupted practice of their style of newspaper making. The new journalism prints what is new and prints it first.

The *World* retorted in kind, pointing out that Money's latest "news" had been reported much earlier by Scovel and continuing: "The difference in the date of news is not more important than the difference in quality. The *World's* correspondent reported what he saw and knew. The amateur visitor to Weyler and Lee tells only what he heard and believed." Week after week the boasting of the *Journal* was matched by the bragging of the *World*.

If Senator-Elect Hernando de Soto Money proved a disappointment as a journalist, the same could not be said of Davis and Remington, whose combined reports were as full of thrills as could be desired. Davis was an excellent war correspondent with an actual respect for facts, though he well understood that he was to present the facts on one side only; Remington went much further: as an illustrator with an artist's poetic license, he was expected to embellish Davis's facts by a liberal use of fancy. Hearst's oft-quoted instructions to him: "You make the pictures, and I'll make the war," were probably never uttered in exactly that form, but unquestionably this was the substance of his commission. His high-water mark of accomplishment was a picture showing a half-naked Cuban girl being stripped by lustful Spanish officers—which was based on Davis's simple account of the examination by women searchers of a girl suspected of carrying secret messages through the lines to the insurgents. The New York office of the *Journal* altered Davis's story to conform with Remington's illustration, only to be confounded by the girl's indignant denial—to the unholy glee of Joseph Pulitzer. But by that time the desired effect upon the chivalrous American public had already been created.

Meanwhile, the *World* was enjoying a series of "scoops." It printed an exclusive interview with Gomez; it obtained an exclusive statement from Weyler on the death of Maceo; its correspondent Bowen was the only American journalist allowed to pass beyond Artemisa into the interior. The *Competitor*, a filibustering ship carrying arms and ammunition to the insurgents, was captured, and after a summary court-martial all on board were condemned to death; among those engaged in this filibustering attempt were two Americans, one of whom, Ona Melton, sent a special appeal to the *World* for aid, to which that paper responded so loudly that the other journals were compelled to take up Melton's cause, creating such a hullabaloo that the Spanish government deemed it wise to order a re-trial of the prisoners. Best of all for the *World*, the indiscretions of its correspondent, Sylvester Scovel, caused him to be temporarily jailed, enabling the paper to declare that he stood "in imminent danger of butchery by a decree of a drumhead court-martial." Scovel mass meetings were held, and the legislatures of some ten states passed resolutions demanding the journalist's immediate release. The other New York papers systematically played down the *World's* part in the affair, referring to Scovel merely as "an American correspondent," but their jealousy could not now dim the glory that was Pulitzer's.

The *Journal* by this time had a large staff in Cuba, including, besides Davis and Remington, Grover Flint, Frederick Lawrence, Charles Michelson, Bradley Johnson, George Bryson, Charles B. Pendleton, and Murat Halstead. When Richard Ruiz, a naturalized American arrested on a charge of train-robbery in Cuba, was found dead in his cell after two weeks of solitary confinement, George Bryson managed to get in to view the body and reported that the death had been due to head injuries. Scouting the official version that Ruiz had committed suicide by dashing himself against the floor of his cell, the *Journal* insisted that it was a plain case of murder and clamored loudly for war. "War is a dreadful thing," it admitted, "but there are things more dreadful even than war, and one of them is dishonor." It featured bellicose statements by Senators Cullom, Davis, Frye, and Gallinger, by Congressmen Boatner and Northway, all capped by an alleged interview with John Sherman, McKinley's incoming Secretary of State, which was published under the heading, "SHERMAN FOR WAR WITH SPAIN FOR MURDERING AMERICANS." Sherman's description of the "interview" was vigorous: "It is a lie from beginning to end. I am surprised that the *Journal* should make such a statement."

This was something of a setback, but the *Journal* quickly recovered its lost ground by printing a special article from Mrs. Ruiz, "My Life in Cuba," which described in vivid detail the horrors of the Spanish prison system.

Still, the desired war did not arrive. McKinley, whom the *Journal* had counted upon to overturn Cleveland's pacific policy, instead came out very distinctly for peace in his inaugural. As the year went on, in spite of the *Journal's* insistent harping upon McKinley's "betrayal of Cuba," the American public began to show signs of declining interest. Then in August 1897 occurred an incident such as the *Journal* was praying for. Evangelina Cisneros, described by the paper as "the most beautiful girl in the island of Cuba," daughter of a prominent Cuban insurgent, had been confined with her father in the mildly governed penal settlement on the Isle of Pines, but was now suddenly transferred to more rigorous incarceration in the Havana prison; according to her story, the reason for the transfer was that when a Spanish officer had brutally assaulted her her cries for help had brought her fellow-prisoners to the rescue and the officer had been severely beaten by them. Here at last was a chance to triumph over the *World*. What was the jailing of its masculine war correspondent who ought to have been able to take care of himself in comparison with the attempted violation of "the most beautiful girl in Cuba"!

Quite without authority, the *Journal* asserted that Señorita Cisneros had been sentenced to twenty years in an African penal settlement. It went on in its best style:

This tenderly nurtured girl was imprisoned at eighteen among the most depraved negresses of Havana, and now she is to be sent in mockery to spend twenty years in a servitude that will kill her in a year. . . . The unspeakable fate to which Weyler has doomed an innocent girl whose only crime is that she has defended her honor against a beast in uniform has sent a shudder of horror through the American people. . . . She was reared in seclusion and, almost a child in years, is as ignorant of the world as a cloistered nun. . . . This girl, delicate, refined, sensitive, unused to hardship, absolutely ignorant of vice, unconscious of the existence of such beings as crowd the cells of the Casa de Recojidas, is seized, thrust into the prison maintained for the vilest class of abandoned women of Havana, compelled to scrub floors and to sleep on bare boards with outcast negresses, and shattered in health until she is threatened with an early death.

In vain the *World* published the results of the investigations of Consul-General Lee, who learned from the girl's own confession that what had really happened on the Isle of Pines was that Señorita Cisneros, innocent "as a cloistered nun," had lured the commander of the island to her house, where men who had been secretly placed there attempted to assassinate him. Lee also testified that far from being confined among outcast Negro women or compelled to scrub floors, Señorita Cisneros had several rooms to herself and was being shown surprising consideration. All this information was quite useless. The woman-worshiping American public regarded the *World's* story as a libel on the virtue of the sex, and sternly rejected it.

On the *Journal's* appeal that cablegrams be sent on the girl's behalf to the Pope and the Queen Regent of Spain, among the thousands who responded were Julia Ward Howe, Clara Barton, the widows of Ulysses S. Grant and Jefferson Davis, the wives of Senator Mark Hanna and Secretary Sherman, a daughter of ex-President John Tyler, and a grand-niece of George Washington himself. When the Spanish government refrained from executing a sentence that there is no evidence it ever contemplated, the *Journal* received all the credit.

Then on October seventh came more thrilling news—the girl had escaped from prison—and on October tenth the most thrilling of all—she had been rescued by a *Journal* reporter and was on her way to New York on board an American ship. Karl Decker, the journalistic hero of this exploit, had simply rented a house next to the prison, from which vantage point he had been able to get to the girl's window and saw through the bars. On the arrival of Señorita Cisneros in New York, she was given a mammoth reception in Madison Square Garden and an elaborate dinner at Delmonico's, after which she was taken to Washington where she and Decker were presented to the President. The *Journal* received congratulatory telegrams from governors, senators, and the prominent women who had sent cablegrams—all of which, of course, were duly featured in its columns. A novelized version of the whole case was run for three months in the Sunday *Journal*.

Still, the war did not materialize. After all, now that Señorita Cisneros was safe, perhaps a war wasn't necessary.

Balking the *Journal's* outcries was the installation of the liberal Sagasta ministry in Madrid, the recall of Weyler, the appointment of the moderate General Blanco as his successor, and the announced willingness of Spain to allow a considerable measure of autonomy to Cuba. Once more, the excitement in America died down. In spite of all the efforts of William R. Hearst, there might have been no war but for an indiscretion of the Spanish minister, Dupuy de Lome, quickly followed by the probably accidental destruction of the *Maine* in Havana harbor.

The De Lome incident grew out of a letter written by the Spanish ambassador to José Canalejas, an unofficial Spanish agent in Cuba. In it, De Lome referred to McKinley's annual message to Congress in which the President had fairly boxed the compass in regard to Cuba: "The message has undeceived the insurgents, who expected something else, and has paralyzed the action of Congress, but I consider it bad. Besides the natural and inevitable coarseness with which he repeats all that the press and public opinion of Spain have said of Weyler, it shows once more what McKinley is: weak and catering to the rabble and, besides, a low politician who desires to leave a door open to himself and to stand well with the jingoes of his party." The

letter was obtained by an insurgent sympathizer who had secured employment in the office of Canalejas and was given to
the American press. The *Journal,* after asking and being refused exclusive rights of publication, did secure exclusive fac-
simile rights, which permitted an air of ownership in the story
which it featured in the most exaggerated manner. J. B. Wisan
in his authoritative work, *The Cuban Crisis as Reflected in the
New York Press* (1934), refers to "the *Journal's* vindictiveness
and evident pleasure in the incident," and makes the point that
"though the *Journal* had itself used far more offensive language
in its criticism of McKinley, it pretended extreme anger at De
Lome's insults, [charging] the Spanish Minister with 'the
greatest offense of which a diplomatic officer can be accused.' "
Unable to resist the inevitable rhyme of "De Lome" and
"home," it even broke into verse on the occasion.

Dupuy de Lome, Dupuy de Lome, what's this I hear of you!
Have you been throwing mud again, is what they're saying true?
Get out, I say get out before I start to fight.
Just pack your few possessions and take a boat for home.
I would not like my boot to use but—oh—get out, De Lome.

Hardly had the De Lome affair disappeared from the front
page when the *Maine* disaster occurred on February 15, 1898.
Although the cause of the explosion has never been determined
by impartial inquiry and presumably never will be—since the
United States Government refused to permit Spanish participation in the one-sided investigation and later, when the case was
reopened, after another one-sided investigation, had the wreck
towed out into deep water and sunk—nevertheless, the *Journal*
professed to know all about it from the first. "THE WAR-
SHIP *MAINE* WAS SPLIT IN TWO BY AN ENEMY'S
SECRET INFERNAL MACHINE" it announced on February seventeenth, with an accompanying diagram giving the
exact position of the mine which caused the destruction. Result:

its circulation on that day reached 1,025,624, at last overtopping that of the *World*. When the other papers, with the exception of the *World*, pleaded for suspended judgment, the *Journal* reiterated its sense of certainty in a scream headline: "THE *MAINE* WAS DESTROYED BY TREACHERY," and continued the same asseveration day after day.∤ Dismissing the plausible explanation of an internal explosion caused by faulty mechanism·and scouting the equally plausible one that the ship had been blown up by Cuban patriots eager to bring the United States into the war, it insisted that the destruction was the deliberate work of the Spanish officials—the one explanation that, unless one believed the Spanish government insane, was utterly incredible.

Unfortunately, a large section of the American public had by now been educated through the yellow press to accept incredibilities, and the majority of congressmen were in this class. Still McKinley hesitated, while the United States minister at Madrid, Stewart L. Woodford, sent word that the Spanish Government was willing to accede to all the American demands if only it could be given time to do so with traditional Spanish dignity. Forgetting its recent attitude in the De Lome incident, the *Journal* renewed its attacks upon McKinley with greater bitterness than ever. It featured a cartoon representing Uncle Sam sweeping from a ship's deck rubbish labeled "McKinley," "Wall Street," "Woodford twaddle," "Fake ultimatum," "Peace with dishonor," "Cowardly foreign policy," and "Peace-at-any-price." "McKinley and the Wall Street Cabinet," it shouted, "are ready to surrender every particle of national honor and dignity." It talked about "the *Journal's* war fleet of yachts, tugs, and correspondents." It came out bespangled with little American flags—a device to be later repeated in the World War. It announced that "Spain's powerful flotilla" was believed to be "stealing toward our shore."

In addition to playing upon the sentiment of honor and the

emotion of terror, the *Journal* featured an appeal to cupidity. "The future of Cuba is American," it announced prophetically. "Shrewd American speculators are traversing the Island . . . taking up options and making outright purchases at prices so low as to promise an enormous return in the future. . . . The exploitation of Cuba by American capital is a certainty."

As always, the *Journal* attempted to utilize the support of great names. It publicly invited ex-President Cleveland to serve on a committee gotten up by W. R. Hearst to provide a memorial to the victims of the *Maine* disaster, and it quoted an alleged statement of Theodore Roosevelt, Assistant Secretary of the Navy: "It is cheering to find a newspaper of the great influence and circulation of the *Journal* tell the facts as they exist and ignore the suggestions of various kinds that emanate from sources that cannot be described as patriotic or loyal to the flag of this country."

In both of these instances the paper was notably rebuffed. In refusing Hearst's invitation, Cleveland wrote, "I decline to allow my sorrow for those who died on the *Maine* to be perverted to an advertising scheme for the New York *Journal.*" Roosevelt roundly declared, "I never in public or private commended the New York *Journal* . . . I never have given a certificate of character to the *Journal.*" Roosevelt's denial made front-page headlines for Pulitzer, who tersely described the *Journal's* war news as "Written by fools for fools."

Nevertheless, Pulitzer continued to be almost as bellicose as Hearst, and by this time nearly all the New York papers had swung into line behind the young Californian who had found patriotism so profitable.

Of important editors, Edwin Lawrence Godkin on the *Evening Post* alone remained unaffected by the war hysteria. He deplored a situation in which "A blackguard boy with several millions of dollars at his disposal has more influence on the use a great nation may make of its credit, of its army and navy, of its name and traditions, than all the statesmen and philosophers and professors in the country. If this does not supply food for reflection about the future of the nation to thoughtful men, it must be because the practice of reflection has ceased."

Savagely, Godkin shot his poisoned arrows at both the *World* and the *Journal,* whose business was "not to promote public happiness or morality but to 'sell the papers.' The resources of type," he went on, "have been about exhausted. Nothing in the way of larger letters can be used, unless only a single headline is to be given on the first page. Red ink has been resorted to as an additional element of attraction or terror, and if we had a war, the whole paper might be printed in red, white and blue. In that case, real lunatics instead of imitation lunatics should be employed as editors and contributors. . . . A yellow-journal office is probably the nearest approach, in atmosphere, to hell existing in any Christian state. A better place in which to prepare a young man for eternal damnation than a yellow-journal office does not exist."

But Godkin was outmoded. Where he had one reader, Hearst and Pulitzer had scores. On April eleventh McKinley yielded to the pressure of newspapers and Congressmen, and the war at last was on.

With the approach of hostilities, there was much fear in America lest Admiral Camara's Mediterranean fleet should move by way of the Suez Canal to attack Dewey in the Pacific. Inspired as always by a mingling of schoolboy patriotism and the thought of sales, Hearst sent to James Creelman in Europe an extraordinary message which read as follows:

Dear Mr. Creelman:—
I wish you would at once make preparations so that in case the Spanish fleet actually starts for Manila we can buy some big English steamer at the eastern end of the Mediterranean and take her to some part of the Suez Canal where we can then sink her and obstruct the passage of the Spanish warships. This must be done if the American

monitors sent from San Francisco have not reached Dewey and he should be placed in a critical position by the approach of Camara's fleet. I understand that if a British vessel were taken into the canal and sunk under the circumstances outlined above, the British Government would not allow her to be blown up to clear a passage and it might take time enough to raise her to put Dewey in a safe position.

Yours very truly,

[Signed] W. R. HEARST

Fortunately, the occasion for this exhibition of superpatriotism did not arise. Such a violation of international law might easily have involved the United States in a war with Great Britain.

Much of the admitted incompetence of the government during the Spanish-American War is traced by Walter Millis in *The Martial Spirit* (1931) to journalistic interference with military measures:

The war extras followed one another through the streets in a torrential outpouring; and the war correspondents, flocking into every camp, every naval station, and into every possible or impossible theater of action, loaded down the wires with detailed accounts of every move made or contemplated. Any feeble opposition put up by the brow-beaten authorities on the score of secrecy was imperiously brushed aside. After all, if it was not the newspapers' war, whose war was it? When the Navy fitted out a vessel as a hospital ship, she was immediately stormed by whole battalions of reporters, who calculated that, as she would have to hurry from the scene of battle to land the wounded, she would be the first to reach the telegraph wires. Mr. Long [Secretary of the Navy] managed to keep them off; not, however, because they might reveal military secrets, but because he believed news to be "contraband of war" and thought that their presence might destroy the ship's neutrality. . . . Already, by April 26th, Mr. Pulitzer was selling 1,300,000 copies of the *World* a day; and as the editorial writers of the country settled to the serious business of conducting operations, a triumphant journalism was definitely in command. Even the sedate *Atlantic Monthly* stunned its readers by appearing, actually, with an American flag upon the cover and after that it seemed that patriotism could indeed go no farther.

In Cuba, however, it was different. There, where the fighting was to be done with bullets and bombs instead of words, the military assumed stern control, and the disgruntled journalists learned that they were no longer cocks of the walk. Pulitzer in particular had cause to be distressed. Stephen Crane, hired as a war correspondent because of his best-seller, *The Red Badge of Courage*, sent but one dispatch of importance, and that, though later confirmed by an official report, caused the owner of the *World* no end of trouble because it accused the Seventy-First New York Regiment of cowardice in a critical emergency. Hearst loudly denounced the report as a slander on the American army, and when Pulitzer tried to atone for the error of his correspondent—who was too young to realize that truth-telling was not a part of his function—by raising a fund for a memorial to the regiment, the money was coldly returned to him by the recipients. Next Pulitzer's impetuous correspondent, Sylvester Scovel, having a quarrel with General Shafter, struck the commanding officer in the face and was saved from court-martial only by the intervention of President McKinley. All in all, the war was a disappointment to Pulitzer. As Don Seitz says, "he never wanted another."

Matters went far otherwise with Hearst. At the beginning of the war, in return for giving the government his private yacht, the *Bucentaur*, he received an honorary commission as an ensign in the United States Navy. Delightedly, he purchased another ship, the *Sylvia*, and led a fleet of twenty tugs to Cuba. Good luck enabled him to participate—though in a somewhat minor capacity—in the Battle of Santiago. A boatload of Spanish sailors, escaping from the sinking *Cristobal Colon*, landed on the beach near where the *Sylvia* was anchored out of gunshot. Perceiving them huddled disconsolately on the shore,

Hearst ran his launch in, valiantly pulled off his trousers, and leaped into the knee-deep water, waving a big revolver and followed by his faithful reporters. The Spaniards were willing enough to surrender and were taken back to the *Sylvia* and compelled to kneel and kiss the American flag while Hearst's photographers took pictures of the exhilarating scene. That done, the *Sylvia* steamed down the line of battleships to the *Brooklyn,* where Hearst, who had resumed his trousers in the interim, officially presented his prisoners to Admiral Schley. The whole episode, of course, furnished excellent front-page copy for the *Journal.*

The last act of the journalistic comedy was in the nature of an anti-climax. After the capitulation of Santiago, the three Hearst correspondents who remained there, finding life a little dull, placarded the city with huge signs, "Remember the *Maine!*" They were probably merely trying to start something to enliven their reports, but since this revival of war hysteria might easily have led to riots and a possible massacre of Spanish prisoners, General Shafter summarily ordered the correspondents to leave the island. Hearst took up their cause with Russell Alger, Secretary of War, who sent to Shafter a series of excited cables: "The New York *Journal* people are in great trouble"; "the *Journal* has been doing good work"; "the New York *Journal* is in terrible distress." But for once Hearst did not have his own way. His correspondents were duly ejected. It seemed a sorry reward after the expenditure of so much patriotism on his part.

But this was only a minor incident. On the whole, the war had been a decided success for Hearst. It had brought him personal attention beyond his dreams, making his name known around the world, and it had increased the circulation of the *Journal* to over a million. Decidedly, whatever happened to Cuba and the Philippines, the war had been worth while. And, unlike Pulitzer, he would never cease to desire another, provided he could have it, as he had had this one, on his own terms.

Content with his success, he made approaches to Pulitzer to declare a truce between the *Journal* and the *World*. Pulitzer agreed, and all unfriendly utterances between the two papers abruptly ceased. Then, in the best of all possible moods, Hearst went off to Europe for recreation after labor.

CHAPTER VIII

Absentee Congressman

FEW Americans have ever visited Europe more often purely for pleasure than William Randolph Hearst, and few Americans have derived more pleasure from their trips. Constantly staying at the most luxurious hotels, financially able to gratify any whim of the moment, he gave free rein in Europe to his double passion for spending and for getting. Beautiful, costly, or unusual objects aroused in him an insatiable zeal for ownership. Pictures, statuettes, vases, and even mummies followed him back across the Atlantic to adorn his home at No. 123 Lexington Avenue, once owned by President Chester Arthur. The sellers of these objects often had to wait long for the payment of their bills; sometimes this was because Hearst did not happen to have the ready cash upon his person, but more often it was simply because they were tradesmen, and it had always been the tradesman's duty to await the nobleman's leisure in such matters.

Only in England was Hearst unhappy. There he was deliberately snubbed by the "best families" and in countless ways that the British know so well how to use he was made to feel that he was only a counterfeit aristocrat. The whole country seemed to him a kind of Harvard on a large scale and with more rigorous laws. On one occasion he is said to have been arrested for some minor escapade, and to have been much irritated by the London bobby's strange insensitiveness to offers that any New York policeman would have welcomed with alacrity. His earlier Anglomania gave way to a permanent Anglophobia, first publicly expressed at the time of Queen Victoria's death in 1901 when the *Journal* featured a number of disparaging stories about the queen's management of her domestic affairs, thereby naturally increasing the British animosity toward Hearst. For his part, he divorced himself completely from his affectation of British accent, manners, and clothes. A straw hat, checked suit, and rather loud neckties now formed his favorite attire. Henceforward he would be nothing but a true-born American.

Soon after the publisher's return to the United States, Bryan's second campaign for the presidency was launched. Hearst supported this as fervently as he had the former one. Again McKinley was assailed with a vituperative skill that Dupuy de Lomé would have envied; Davenport's dollar-mark cartoons of Hanna were resurrected and brought up to date; in return for a promise to start a party newspaper in Chicago, Hearst was made president of the National Association of Democratic Clubs, an organization that soon had in it as many as three million members.

The first edition of Hearst's Chicago *American* came out on the day of Bryan's nomination. The establishment of a new paper in Chicago was not an easy matter in those days, especially when the invader was as dangerous as Hearst was recognized to be. The rival papers hired thugs to run his newsboys off the streets. But such methods were not likely to terrorize an heir of the San Francisco vigilantes. Hearst hired more thugs than his enemies and ran their newsboys off the streets. When thug met thug, a fine battle would ensue. Teamsters and delivery men joined the holy war on behalf of their masters, until traffic became so disrupted that the police at last interfered to restore law and order. It was evident that Hearst had come to stay. How well he had mastered the methodology for such crises was shown years later when the Hearst papers in San Francisco employed identically the same means to keep Cornelius Vanderbilt out of their field.

Bryan's campaign was a fizzle. McKinley received 110,917

more votes, Bryan 151,917 less votes than in 1896. Hearst was greatly disappointed by his candidate's defeat, and this disappointment prompted an increasingly violent tone in his papers' denunciations of McKinley after the election. On February 4, 1901, soon after the assassination of Governor Goebel of Kentucky, Ambrose Bierce published a stanza in the *Journal* which both he and the publisher were later to regret:

> The bullet that pierced Goebel's breast
> Can not be found in all the West;
> Good reason, it is speeding here
> To stretch McKinley on his bier.

The poet always contended that his lines were written merely to indicate a dangerous spirit of unrest in the country, but they seem undoubtedly to have contained a threat. More menacing still was an editorial attack on McKinley in the *Evening Journal* of April 10, 1901, in which the words occurred: "If bad institutions and bad men can be got rid of only by killing, then the killing must be done." It is said that Hearst attempted too late to have the presses stopped in order to modify this editorial which had been printed without his personal knowledge, but he could hardly condemn severely what was after all only an extreme instance of the recklessness which he habitually encouraged in his papers' utterances.

Realizing, however, that this last editorial might prove a boomerang, he sent James Creelman to the White House with an olive branch. According to Creelman's account years later, "Mr. Hearst offered to exclude from his papers anything that the President might find personally offensive. Also he pledged the President hearty support in all things as to which Mr. Hearst did not differ with him politically. The President seemed deeply touched by this wholly voluntary offer and sent a message of sincere thanks." If so, the President may have regretted this message of thanks when later the attacks upon him were resumed with unabated vigor. The very week of the assassination a cartoon in the *Journal* depicted McKinley as a dancing Negro in a trust minstrel show led by Mark Hanna.

McKinley was shot on September 6, 1901, and died on September 14. The speed with which the public established a fancied connection between the Hearst press and the "anarchist" Czolgosz is shown by the resolutions adopted by the Grand Army of the Republic four days later:

Resolved—That every member of the Grand Army of the Republic exclude from his household 'The New York Journal,' a teacher of anarchism and a vile sheet, unfit for perusal by any one who is a respecter of morality and good government.

The boycott of the Hearst papers was taken up by many business organizations, libraries, and clubs; an anti-Hearst pledge was widely circulated not to patronize any news-stands, barbershops, or other places which subscribed to the "vile sheets"; in a number of towns, Hearst himself was hanged in effigy, often accompanied by Emma Goldman, handcuffed to him.

In December came a blast from the White House. President Roosevelt, in his first message to Congress, referred to his predecessor's assassin as "a professed anarchist, inflamed by the teachings of professed anarchists, and probably also by the reckless utterances of those who, on the stump and in the public Press, appeal to the dark and evil spirits of malice and greed, envy and sullen hatred. The wind is sowed by the men who preach such doctrines, and they cannot escape their share of responsibility for the whirlwind that is reaped." Everyone knew for whom these words were meant.

It was not, one would have supposed, a propitious moment for the victim of all this abuse to develop an aspiration for the United States presidency. Yet nothing less than that occurred in the strange convolutions of Hearst's mind. He had borne himself with unwonted dignity during the storm that burst upon him.

Bierce recorded with gratitude that Hearst never mentioned his offending poem to him, and added, "I fancy there must be a human side to a man like that, even if he is a mischievous demagogue." Perhaps it was not so much humanness as a complete aloofness from normal emotions, a contempt for the multitude so deep as to have bred utter indifference to its good or ill opinion. Whining, cringing, and apologetics were as foreign to Hearst's code as were some nobler activities. The only concession which he made to public wrath was to change the name of the *Morning Journal* to the *American*. His humanness was shown chiefly in the thought of how pleasant it would be to succeed the gentleman in the White House who had so scathingly attacked him.

The idea was not so mad as it may seem today. Hearst was still president of the National Association of Democratic Clubs, with their 3,000,000 members; his Washington correspondent, Max F. Ihmsen, was installed as secretary; the whole organization was on the road to becoming Hearst's personal property. Bryan was out of the picture, having no desire, as yet, to court a third defeat, and Hearst attempted to ensure his support by making a European trip possible for him through highly paid articles contributed to the *American* by the ex-candidate during a nine weeks' dash at top speed through Great Britain, Holland, Germany, France, Italy, Switzerland, and Russia in which he mastered every essential problem of those nations through the car windows.

With Bryan eliminated, what was there to prevent Hearst from taking his place? There was a notable dearth of able men in the Democratic Party. The Populists in the west were disorganized but they were still there, and the right kind of leadership could bring them back to join with the Democrats as in 1896. Even Hearst's recent reputation as a "red radical" might, if suitably toned down, be turned to advantage.

Such thoughts as these during his fortieth year led the publisher into a political career that was to prove for almost a decade fully as astounding as his journalistic one had been.

Hearst's own later idealistic explanation of his seeking public office ran as follows: "My early ambition was to do my part in newspapers, and I still propose to do a newspaper part. But when I saw mayors and governors and presidents fail, I felt that I'd like to see if I couldn't do better. I felt I'd like to go into office, any office almost, to see if I couldn't do the things I wanted to see done." Which, translated into more realistic language, meant that political office, any office almost, could be a stepping-stone to the presidency, but that some political office was a prerequisite. Hearst chose the easiest and most available, that of representative from the Eleventh Congressional District of the City of New York, an office entirely under the control of Charles F. Murphy, the reigning boss of Tammany Hall.

The publisher's decision to enter politics was opposed by most of his friends. There was still a journalistic tradition, more honored in the breach than the observance, that an editor should be independent of political parties, and should never sacrifice this independence by becoming a candidate for office. The experience of the one prominent journalist who had gone into politics, Horace Greeley, vainly seeking the presidency and dying of chagrin after his defeat, was not such as to encourage imitation. But Hearst knew that he should not die, and his determination remained unshaken.

First, he launched Brisbane as a trial balloon. He suggested to his editor that he run for Congress, and after the latter had agreed and it was evident that Tammany would accept him, Hearst announced that he had decided to do the running himself. Brisbane obediently retired, and Murphy was glad enough to take the owner of the *Journal* instead. Hearst was duly nominated, and nomination was tantamount to election. There was only one drawback: he had to deliver a speech accepting the nomination.

On October 6, 1902, pale and nervous, his large hands and feet very much in his way, William R. Hearst read his first political speech in a high-pitched trembling voice that hardly carried beyond the first row. In it, he presented his platform and his political philosophy:

I believe that of the eighty millions of people in this country, five or six millions (the most prosperous five or six millions) are ably represented in Congress, in the law courts, and in the newspapers. It would be immodesty on my part to imagine that I could add much to the comfort or prosperity of the few who are so thoroughly well looked after. My ambition is to forward the interests of the seventy millions or more of typical Americans who are not so well looked after. Their needs seem to offer a wider field for useful effort. At the same time let me say that I do not seek to divide the nation into classes or foster unreasoning dislike of one class by another. I can recognize and admire the genius and the generosity of the great captains of industry; of Mr. Pierpont Morgan, for instance, who gives a splendid hospital for poor women, educational buildings to Harvard University, and treasures of art to the Metropolitan Museum, but I feel that Mr. Morgan can take care of himself. I feel that any man who directs great capital will ordinarily be able to secure all that he deserves. My interest is in the average American citizen. The welfare of the country demands that he too shall secure a fair share in the advantages of prosperity. . . .

There was nothing very "anarchistic" in this, thought Murphy, who had been a little anxious lest his candidate veer too far to the left. It was quite in the style of President Roosevelt himself.

I do not mean to say that the genius of the great captains of industry is not of much benefit to the community in many ways; I do not mean to say that their charities are not highly commendable—

but I do say that a situation such as the present one brings into strong contrast the difference between the enormous power of the trust magnate and the helpless position of the average citizen, and sufficiently explains why I have always devoted my energies and abilities, whatever they may be, to the cause of the plain people and why I shall continue to do so. A real danger threatens the country today in the great power and arrogance of the trusts that defy the laws and laugh in the face of the President of the United States when he begs them to avert a public calamity. . . .

Still perfectly safe, thought Murphy.

Nothing is so important to the people as the regulation of this financial power which has suddenly overshadowed the power of the government itself, and the means of controlling these great industrial giants must be discovered and applied before the power of the trusts gets absolutely beyond control. Every sensible man knows that there is no objection to legitimate organization in business—organization that aims at greater economy or at greater efficiency and production. Such organization is inevitable and will be of benefit to the community wherever the community shall be permitted to participate in its advantages. But every fair-minded man knows that there is every objection to the injurious, illegitimate, illegal organizations known as the trusts, which absorb and suppress all competitors in order to establish a monopoly and exercise that monopoly—as in the case of the Beef Trust—to compel the payment of extortionate prices by the helpless public. . . .

Murphy's anxiety began to return; why need his candidate be so specific?

The question of how these criminal trusts may be effectually dealt with occupies the mind of every thoughtful man. To begin with, Congress must deal with the matter through law, and therefore Congress first of all must be made to represent the people and not the trusts. The public will never be protected against the trusts by a Senate in which the trusts occupy many seats and control a majority. A first step, therefore, will be "The Election of United States Senators by the People." Given the election of a truly representative

Congress, the next step will be such modification of the tariff as will permit outside competition with illegal combinations and will prevent the trusts from selling their products dearly at home while they sell them cheaply abroad. With the regulation of the tariff there must come wise application of the principles of "Government Ownership of Certain Public Utilities." It is not advocated that the government engage in all the branches of industry which the trusts have managed to monopolize. A natural beginning will be the government ownership of railroads and telegraphs. These are as legitimate objects of government ownership today as the post office was when that was first taken over by the government. . . .

Murphy wondered if he had a Populist on his hands; but it was all just talk, he reflected self-consolingly.

The anthracite coal mines, under ordinary conditions, would hardly have been thought of for government ownership, but the intolerable situation has made it advisable for the government to take possession of these coal beds and manage them for the people's benefit. Such action would not only solve the present problem, it would act as a salutary threat, influencing the other trusts and preventing them from defying decency in the Coal Trust fashion. Adequate laws must be passed to punish criminally trust owners and officers for criminal infractions of the law. The whole complicated system of civilized society, from policeman to President, was devised to prevent the powerful and unscrupulous individual from overriding the rights of his weaker brethren. The laws must now be applied and where necessary must be strengthened to protect the people against that powerful and unscrupulous criminal combination known as a trust. . . .

As soon as his painful ordeal was over, Hearst held out a cold, flabby hand to each of his supporters, and hurried home. His speech had been a perfectly safe one to deliver. Murphy would never, he knew, sacrifice the support of the New York *Journal* on account of a few words. Hearst's seat in Congress was as certain as if he had bought it in an antique shop. There was nothing in his speech that had not been said in Populist meetings a thousand times. His eye was not on his immediate audience but on the morrow's newspapers, the western voters, and the distant future.

A believer in omens would have noted two untoward events during Hearst's campaign. He brought on Mayor Eugene Schmitz of San Francisco to testify to his character in California. Schmitz performed his task creditably—but some years later he was himself discovered to be in the pay of the United Railways of San Francisco. And on election night at a fireworks display put on by the *Journal* in Madison Square the mortar used to set off the rockets exploded and seventeen people were killed or seriously injured.

But these omens would not be significant until several years had passed. Hearst was elected to Congress as easily as was expected.

While waiting for his term to begin, he indulged more continuously than usual one taste which he undoubtedly had in common with his lower-middle-class constituents—that fondness for vaudeville and musical comedy which he had first acquired in the classical atmosphere of Harvard. There was at this time on the vaudeville stage a popular clog dancer named George Willson, who had two young and pretty daughters, Anita and Millicent. Both girls were dancers in a musical comedy called *The Girl from Paris* playing in the Herald Square Theater. Hearst's devotion to the Willson sisters soon became the talk of the town; every night he and George Pancoast were to be seen in the front row; every night there were theater suppers and bouquets innumerable. At first, he was supposed to accord his favors to both sisters equally, but when the *Morning Telegram* put on a popularity contest, it became evident that he had a preference. The congressman-elect corralled so many votes for Millicent Willson that when the results were announced there seemed no question that she was New York's favorite actress.

According to the enthusiastic account of John K. Winkler,

"One observing Hearst's courtship of Millicent Willson would have set him down as a young dilettante whose whole time and attention were devoted to making more joyous the days of his lady fair. Hearst and Millicent Willson were like a couple of childrer in their love-making." On April 28, 1903, the children were happily married in Grace Episcopal Church by Bishop Potter, and on the same afternoon they left for Europe on their wedding trip.

During the succeeding years five children in all were born to them: George in 1904, William Randolph in 1908, John Randolph in 1909, and the twins, Elbert Willson and Randolph Apperson in 1915.

No congressman ever took his legislative duties more lightly than did Congressman Hearst. He rarely attended the meetings of the House, and when he did, he voted still more rarely. During the first and second sessions of the Fifty-Eighth Congress, which were continuous from November 9, 1903, to April 28, 1904, he responded to the roll-call but nine times. He did, indeed, introduce a number of resolutions of the most progressive character: an amendment to the Interstate Commerce Act, giving the Interstate Commerce Commission the power to fix railroad rates; an amendment to the Sherman Anti-Trust Act designed to strengthen it; an inquiry relative to alleged railroad combinations in the transportation of anthracite coal; a bill to appoint a committee for the investigation of trusts; one to establish a parcel post system; another to regulate towing at sea. All of these were enlightened measures, though far enough from that governmental ownership of the railroads and the coal industry which Hearst had promised in his speech of acceptance to promote. And, once having introduced his resolutions and seen them referred to the appropriate committees, where nearly all died a natural death, Hearst took no further interest in them save to give the impression through his newspapers that he was an exceedingly active congressman.

He had meant from the beginning to use his position in the House of Representatives merely as a springboard from which to leap to the presidency—an ambitious program, indeed, but not too ambitious for his aspirations. How the attempt was made in the spring of 1904, how it achieved an astonishing degree of success, and how it ultimately failed, will be narrated in a later chapter. Here it will be more convenient to complete the account of Hearst's career in the House of Representatives, to which body he was re-elected after his failure to obtain the Democratic nomination for President.

During the third session of the Fifty-Eighth Congress, which ran from December 5, 1904, to March 4, 1905, Hearst gathered together a small coterie of followers, including his colleague Baker of New York, Lamar of Florida, Shackleford of Missouri, Robinson of Indiana, and Garner of Texas. Two of these, Lamar and Shackleford, reintroduced his railroad rate bill of the previous session. This bill represented a mild effort to snatch the reform leadership away from President Theodore Roosevelt, who had repeatedly asked for legislation to strengthen the Interstate Commerce Commission but who did not wish to give it the authority to fix rates. Public opinion in this instance was more radical than the President, and those congressmen who had their ears to the ground were quick to respond. Hearst's bill was one of several which were similar to the Hepburn Act ultimately passed.

When his bill came up, Hearst was absent as usual, and John A. Sullivan, Democratic congressman from Massachusetts, after asking in vain for an elucidation of its terms, called attention to the fact that "although a year has passed the gentleman has not taken an opportunity to explain his own bill on the floor of this House, which I for one would have welcomed." His remarks were greeted with applause.

The incident led to the following news item the next day in the New York *American:*

The ignorance of many members of the House on the subject of this legislation is an interesting study. Mr. Lamar referred to it yesterday and Mr. Shober today, both in doubt as to whether this ignorance was due to congenital incapacity or indifference to the people's rights.

For example, a bald, red-nosed young man, whose name, it seems, is Sullivan, interrupted Mr. Lamar yesterday. He was identified, after investigation, as being from Massachusetts. Mr. Sullivan revealed his hitherto unsuspecting presence in the House of Representatives by asking some questions which showed that he knew nothing of the hearings before the Interstate Commerce Commission, the hearings before the House Interstate and Foreign Commerce Committee, and the Senate Interstate Commerce Committee, the many volumes of printed testimony taken at these hearings, or the character of the bills pending. . . .

But this time the New York *American* had caught a Tartar, or what was worse, a fighting Irishman. The gray files of the *Congressional Record* take on some color as they give Sullivan's reply to Hearst and Hearst's reply to Sullivan, with the Republican Speaker, "Foul-Mouthed Joe" Cannon, egging on both contestants in their unseemly quarrel and making no attempt to conceal his grinning delight in watching the Democrats at loggerheads.

Rising to a question of privilege on February thirteenth, Sullivan, after some introductory remarks, in which he quoted the offending article, proceeded as follows:

Mr. Speaker, this article does not touch my character, but it does affect me in my legislative capacity, and is a deliberate insult of one Member by another, so I propose to discuss it and the motives beneath it in such a manner as to afford the gentleman from New York a fair chance to reply, and I trust he will have the decency to avail himself of the privilege of this floor, after the fashion of a manly man, instead of hiding under the cover of further cowardly newspaper attacks.

Mr. ROBINSON of Indiana: Mr. Speaker, I make the point of

order that one Member cannot impugn the motives of another, and that he cannot, except in a parliamentary way, refer to a Member, and that this is not a question of personal privilege, which the gentleman originally said it would be.

The SPEAKER: The Chair infers from the remarks of the gentleman from Massachusetts that he is not impugning the motives of a Member in his representative capacity . . . the Chair gathers from his remarks that he is giving the motives of the gentleman from New York in his newspaper capacity. [Laughter.]

Mr. SULLIVAN of Massachusetts: Mr. Speaker, I may say in passing that I recognize my obligations to the gentleman from New York for his "discovery" of the hitherto unknown member. One should be duly thankful for political birth—even under the unhappy circumstances of being begotten in acrimonious colloquy and delivered in the columns of "the yellow journal." [Applause] . . . .

The writer raises the query whether my "ignorance" [of pending measures] was due to congenital incapacity or indifference to the people's rights. "Congenital incapacity" is a serious charge, yet obviously one which a person accused would not care to discuss. If the charge is true, he is not guilty but simply unfortunate, and it is surely a grievous misfortune not to be able to appreciate the value of the legislative services of the gentleman from New York. [Laughter.] But "congenital incapacity to understand" is a term that covers a wide range of mental and moral deficiencies. It covers the case of the moral degenerate who insolently casts his eyes upon the noblest of women whose virtue places them beyond the contamination of his lust. . . . And it includes the man who, totally bereft of the sense of proportion, raises his profaning eyes toward the splendid temple of the people's highest gift—the Presidency of the United States—blissfully unconscious of the woeful contrast between the qualifications requisite for that high office and his own contemptible mental and moral equipment.

Mr. ROBINSON of Indiana: Mr. Speaker, I renew my point of order.

The SPEAKER: The gentleman renews his point of order. The Chair will read the following from the *Digest* for the information of the House and for the information of the gentleman occupying the floor by unanimous consent. Page 155 of *Jefferson's Manual* says: "No person, in speaking, is to mention a Member then present by name, but to describe him by his seat in the House, or who spoke last, or on the other side of the question, etc.; nor to digress from the matter to fall upon the person by speaking, reviling, nipping, or unmannerly words against a particular Member." The parliamentary usage in this respect is perfectly plain, and the gentleman from Massachusetts will proceed in order.

Mr. ROBINSON of Indiana: May I ask the Chair to rule on the point of order I made? . . .

The SPEAKER: . . . The House will observe that the language used by the gentleman from Massachusetts would be unparliamentary if there were anything in the language to connect it with any Member upon the floor of the House. The Chair in passing upon the point of order cannot enter the domain of speculation to say whether it refers to any Member of the House. To illustrate, if it were set out as a matter of pleading in a declaration it would need an averment that would connect it with a Member of the House. So that upon the face of the language as uttered by the gentleman from Massachusetts the Chair cannot say that he is out of order. . . .

Mr. BAKER of New York: Mr. Speaker, I raise the point of order that the language did apply to a Member of the House, and it is shown in the almost unanimous applause of the Republican Members. [Applause and laughter.]

The SPEAKER: The Chair supposes it must rule upon that point of order. On the Speaker's left is the Republican side of the House, on his right the Democratic side. The members of both sides seem to be indiscriminately mixed. [Laughter and applause.]

Mr. SULLIVAN of Massachusetts: Mr. Speaker, if the gentlemen will possess themselves in patience for a little longer I shall conclude. . . .

The last charge is that of "revealing my unsuspecting presence in the House." I take it that the writer meant "unsuspected." If so, it is only just to remark that I have not been absent from this House more than three or four times in the three sessions of the Fifty-Eighth Congress. This is well known to the Members, and it is equally well known that some gentlemen are the most notorious absentees in this body—that they do not attend one day in ten, and have never been known to remain for an entire legislative day even upon those rare occasions when they condescend to grace us with their presence. Time and time again, when their votes on this floor were needed by that party which they profess to love, have we looked in vain for them. . . . And how about their services? Has any Member heard their manly, sonorous voices once upon this floor in the discussion of a subject, in the asking of a question, in the making of an amendment, in the offering of a motion? Not once! Silent, inarticulate, wrapt in impenetrable gloom, these legislative sphinxes sit enshrouded in the majesty of their fancied greatness. . . .

Their constituents evidently do not expect them to come here often, for by re-electing them they endorsed their record of absenteeism, apparently on the theory that they could do them less harm by their absence from the House than by their presence therein. [Applause and laughter.]

Many Members of this House must feel some curiosity to know why these gentlemen ever break their custom by coming into the House at all. Some of them come here solely because the position offers them an opportunity to exploit their candidacy for the Presidency of the United States. That such are candidates for the Presidency is a truth that has ceased to be startling, for after the country took a survey of them it discounted them as possibilities and breathed easier forthwith. [Laughter and applause.] There was a single precedent in their favor, for the Democratic Party had once nominated an editor; but they failed to remember that it had never nominated a mere check book. . . .

Perhaps the lesson of that failure has been read, and I trust that it has. But at all events a shrewd plan has been framed for the attainment of these great ambitions. A scheme of wholesale political assassination has been mapped out, evidently with the idea that only by destroying the respectable elements of the Democratic Party can their candidacy rise above the plane of farce comedy. And so the Democrats who refuse to follow the will-o'-the-wisp of Populism are threatened to be ground into the dust by this car of Juggernaut. . . .

The duty of Democracy is not to pave the way to socialism, but to prevent its achievement. Democratic faith is valuable or valueless to the country according as it opposes or fails to oppose the mighty force of its ancient faith against the rising sea of socialism, toward which every present policy of the Republican Party is fast driving us. . . .

Now, Mr. Speaker, I will conclude. If by my remarks I have checked the scheme of political assassination which has been marked out by a Nero of modern politics, or have even called public attention to its evil purpose, I believe I have performed a service to the House and to the country—to the House by insisting that each Member shall duly respect each other, at least outwardly, and to the country by exposing the malice that inspires these newspaper articles which operate to create in the minds of the people false impressions of their public servants. [Prolonged applause.]

Mr. HEARST of New York: Mr. Speaker——

The SPEAKER: For what purpose does the gentleman from New York rise?

Mr. HEARST of New York: Mr. Speaker, I ask unanimous consent for a personal explanation in reply to the gentleman from Massachusetts.

The SPEAKER: The gentleman from New York asks unanimous consent for a personal explanation in reply to the gentleman from Massachusetts. Is there objection? [After a pause.] The Chair hears none.

Mr. HEARST of New York: Mr. Speaker, it seems to me that the gentleman from Massachusetts has very largely exaggerated the article which appeared in my newspaper. He has altogether misstated the reasons for the publication of that article. Personally, I did not inspire or suggest the publication of that article, but I am entirely willing to assume all responsibility for everything that appears in my newspapers, no matter whether I inspire or suggest them or not. . . .

The gentleman from Massachusetts apparently criticises my action, or lack of action, on the floor of this House. I wish to say in reply to that that I am proceeding here in the way that I think most effective to my constituents. I have heard incompetents speak on the floor of this House for hours for the mere purpose of getting their remarks in the RECORD; and I have heard the best speakers deliver the most admirable addresses on the floor of this House without influencing legislation in the slightest particular. [Applause.] I do not know any way in which a man can be less effective for his constituents and less useful to them than by emitting chewed wind on the floor of this House. [Laughter.] There is a certain class of gentlemen who are peculiarly sensitive to newspaper criticism, and have every reason to be. I was criticised on the floor of this House once before by a gentleman from California, Mr. Johnson. That gentleman had been attacked in my newspaper for subserviency to the Southern Pacific Railway. He had gone back to his constituency for vindication, and the district which had elected him by 5,000 Republican majority repudiated him and went 5,000 Democratic. It was the first time that district had gone Democratic, and it has never gone Democratic since that time, so it was obviously in order to reject the gentleman from California, Mr. Johnson. Mr. Johnson had been indicted for forgery——

[At this point, Mr. Hearst of New York was interrupted by Mr. Payne of New York who made a point of order but then withdrew it. Before Mr. Hearst of New York could resume, Mr. Dalzell of Pennsylvania rose.]

Mr. DALZELL of Pennsylvania: Mr. Speaker, I desire to make a suggestion. If Mr. Johnson is to be criticised by the gentleman from New York, we ought to have what Johnson said. I am for fair play; let us have both sides.

Mr. HEARST of New York: Mr. Speaker, I thoroughly approve of that. . . .

The SPEAKER: The Chair does not rule on fair play. [Laughter.] The gentleman from New York is addressing the House by unanimous consent by way of personal explanation in reply to the gentleman from Massachusetts. The gentleman is entitled to the floor for one hour. The gentleman will proceed in order.

Mr. HEARST of New York: Mr. Speaker, Mr. Johnson was indicted in New York State for forgery and fled to the West, where he changed his name, but not his character or his habits. He was denounced not only by my paper, but by a Republican paper, the San Francisco *Chronicle*, for this indictment for forgery and for other faults or crimes that he had committed. It seemed to me just to the people of California, whom my paper represented, to tell the truth about Mr. Johnson, and I think the action of my constituents showed approval of the action of my newspaper.

I had no desire, really, to criticise the gentleman from Massachusetts, and if I had I should certainly not have done it in so puerile a way. When I was at Harvard College in 1885 a murder was committed in a low saloon in Cambridge. A man partly incapacitated from drink bought in that saloon on Sunday morning, when the saloon was open against the law, was assaulted by the two owners of that saloon and brutally kicked to death. The name of one of the owners of that saloon was John A. Sullivan, and these two men were arrested and indicted by the grand jury for manslaughter and tried and convicted. I would like to ask the gentleman from Massachusetts if he knows anything about that incident, and whether, if I desired to make a hostile criticism, I côuld not have referred to that crime?

Mr. BUTLER of Pennsylvania: Mr. Speaker, surely this is not a wash-shop. Is it within the power of a Member to object to a continuation of this? [Laughter.]

Mr. SULLIVAN of Massachusetts rose.

The SPEAKER: One moment. The House will be in order.

Mr. SULLIVAN of Massachusetts: Mr. Speaker, the gentleman from New York has asked me a question which I desire to answer, if he desires an answer. If he does, I shall answer it.

Mr. BUTLER of Pennsylvania: Mr. Speaker, I rise to a point of order. Is it within the power of any Member of this House to prevent a continuation of this discussion?

The SPEAKER: On the contrary . . . the gentleman from New York received unanimous consent, by way of personal explanation, to reply to the gentleman from Massachusetts, and is entitled to the floor for one hour, if he proceeds in order. . . . So far as the Chair is able to judge from the question of the gentleman from New York, the Chair cannot see that the gentleman is out of order. . . .

Mr. BUTLER of Pennsylvania: Mr. Speaker, if I understood the gentleman from New York rightly, he inferentially charged the gentleman from Massachusetts with either having murdered someone or conspired to murder.

The SPEAKER: He does not, from anything that the gentleman

HEARST AS "THE YELLOW PERIL"

A cartoon by Oliver Herford showing Hearst as an office-seeker, published in *Life*, August 17, 1922. Brisbane is supposed to have remarked to Herford: "At least, Oliver, you might have made me a bigger bug!"

has so far said. An averment would have to be made before the Chair could know that he is referring to any Member of the House. . . . The Chair assumes that the gentleman from New York was not referring to the gentleman from Massachusetts. . . .

Mr. BUTLER of Pennsylvania: Then somebody else committed the murder. Very well.

The SPEAKER: The Chair will state, in view of the remarks of the gentleman, that an accusation of homicide against a Member— even although the alleged offense occurred before he was elected to this House—would seem to the Chair to fall within the parliamentary prohibition of being calculated "to provoke disturbance and disorder and to bring the body itself into contempt and criticism." . . . The gentleman from New York, the Chair presumes and believes, is quite familiar with parliamentary rules and usages and will proceed in order.

Mr. HEARST of New York: Mr. Speaker, I really have nothing further to say except that I am proud to have incurred the hostility of that class of individual, and I shall make it my duty and my pride to continue to incur the hostility of that class of individual as long as I am in journalism or in politics. [Applause.]

What had happened in the Sullivan case was briefly this: Sullivan's father owned a small hotel, not a "low saloon," from which an intoxicated man was ejected by the father and son, then a boy of seventeen, with such force that the man had slipped on the pavement and broken his skull. Both the Sullivans were convicted of manslaughter, on very insufficient evidence; the boy was given a suspended sentence; the father served two years, but was then pardoned in the light of new evidence that fully exonerated him. Even more than in the Johnson instance, Hearst had mercilessly misused the facts of a man's early life. (The reader will have noticed how in the face of the evidence he repeated his earlier charge that Johnson went to California under an assumed name.) If Sullivan's speech resembled the baying of a bloodhound, Hearst's was like the venomous spring of a coiled rattlesnake. His medieval code of chivalry was not faring well in the stress of journalistic and political strife.

On the other hand, the catastrophe of the San Francisco earthquake and fire of 1906 touched his sympathies deeply and showed him in his most attractive light. Although he lost over a million dollars through the destruction of the *Examiner* building, he generously established several emergency hospitals, equipped two relief trains from the East, raised a fund of $200,-000 through his newspapers, and temporarily increased the wages of the San Francisco mechanics in his employ a dollar a day to enable them to meet the higher cost of living. He also introduced in Congress a joint resolution to appropriate $4,502,-500 for the re-erection of public buildings in San Francisco, Oakland, and San Jose.

For the rest, however, during the Fifty-Ninth Congress, Hearst's attention was almost entirely devoted to his mayoralty and gubernatorial fights, although he did introduce an obvious bill for the relief of San Francisco after the 1906 fire. He was present in his seat in the House a little more frequently (perhaps as a result of Sullivan's remarks), but the only important measure to receive his affirmative vote was the Hepburn Bill. On the other reformist issues that came up in one of the most exciting congresses ever held—on the Food and Drug Act, on a bill to enlarge the powers of the public health service, on a bill to restrict immigration, even on a bill to limit the hours of labor —Hearst was uniformly recorded as "not voting." The only important resolution which he introduced was a bill for the regulation of trusts that was somewhat milder than a similar one recommended by President Taft three years later.

What Frank Palmer wrote in *Collier's* on October 13, 1906, remained true to the end: "Hearst has accomplished nothing in Congress which he could not have done as an outsider working through a mouthpiece on the floor." But his congressional career, Sullivan's speech, and similar utterances elsewhere,

taught him one valuable lesson which he was never to forget—
the ease with which the most moderate reformist activities in
America can be dubbed "socialistic" and "dangerously radical."
This lesson, one may be sure, was duly set down in his retentive
memory for future reference.

CHAPTER IX

Millionaire Radical

HAD Hearst's career between 1903 and 1909 consisted solely of his congressional activities, he would have been little talked about outside of Washington. But, as already indicated, Congress was the least of his interests during those stormy years. And in actuality he was the most discussed man in America, with the single exception of Theodore Roosevelt. Those hard-working progressives in Congress, LaFollette and Beveridge, were unknown in comparison with Hearst, and even Bryan was almost forgotten in the noisy notoriety of his successor. For there can be no question that for half a decade Hearst really achieved his program of succeeding Bryan as the leader of the forces of popular discontent. In 1904 he rolled up 263 votes toward nomination for president in the Democratic national convention; in 1905 he came within 3,472 votes of being elected mayor of New York City; in 1906 he was defeated for the governorship of New York State by less than 60,000 votes; in the presidential campaign of 1908 he created an independent third party. Though these movements failed, all but the last came so near to success as to indicate a vast amount of popular support behind the candidate.

What was the cause of this support? What was the cause of Hearst? These were questions constantly asked in the newspapers and magazines of the period. Though many editors remained baffled by the problem, those who gave it the closest study came to practically identical conclusions which might be summarized by saying that the Hearst boom was a product of the times rather than a product of Hearst, or that it was a lucky combination of the two.

This generally accepted explanation was well expressed by the *Review of Reviews* in its issue of November, 1906:

"The significant thing is not so much Mr. Hearst himself as the Hearst movement. This movement stands for every phase of social and economic discontent. It has its tinge of fanaticism. In the minds of many adherents of it, the movement is idealistic and Utopian." Readers today will be at once reminded of contemporary analogues: the Epic campaign of Upton Sinclair, the Utopians, the Townsend Plan, the Share-the-Wealth movement of Huey Long, the political adventures of Father Coughlin. As the leaders of each of these later developments have known how to capitalize real grievances of the masses, so with the Hearst movement.

The *Review of Reviews,* though hostile to Hearst personally, continued:

It would be useless to minimize the plucky and aggressive fights that the Hearst newspapers have made against corporate monopolies and kindred evils of all sorts. There is wide difference of opinion as to the motives that have impelled this policy. But merely to disparage it as "yellow journalism" cannot alter the fact that it has brought to the Hearst movement a tremendous following of working men and plain citizens.

During the gubernatorial campaign of 1906 the *Outlook,* worried by the amount of Republican support which Hearst was receiving, sent out a member of its staff to try to learn the sources of his popular strength. The results of this investigation, published in the *Outlook* of October 20, 1906, are interesting:

In one of the larger cities a man sat in a cobbler shop with his stocking feet on a newspaper while the cobbler repaired his shoes. He was evidently a small tradesman. He was not a Party man, but he might be termed normally a Republican. He predicted, rather vindictively, that Hearst would "sweep the state." He put his support of Hearst on the ground of the increase in the number of swollen fortunes, the idleness of rich men's sons, and the difficulty of competing with big concerns. A retail merchant of good standing in a much smaller city, heretofore a Republican, though from a family of Democratic traditions, was roused against the oppressive power of big corporations; he resented the action of the Railroad Commission in delaying action on the franchise for a through trolley line which would improve transportation facilities between several cities; he felt—rather than knew—that the franchise was held up by a railway that disliked the prospect óf a competitor; he felt that the people were helpless because they had no way of holding the commission to account; he vaguely felt that somehow Mr. Hearst could, if he would, cure all industrial and political evils; he was inclined to doubt, not Mr. Hearst's ability, but his real intentions; when he was asked as to the value of Mr. Hearst's specific promises, he was not prepared to answer. A mild-faced, quiet-voiced workingman, a Republican all his life, confessed his adherence to Mr. Hearst and predicted that the vote for him would be a surprise. A deaf old man, excited by the Hearst meeting, walked along the street shouting so that he could be heard a block away: "That's the man! I've been a Republican all my life, and I've been voting for a lot of rottenness. Talk about a square deal! What we want is a new deal—all round!" [Was this the ignominious origin of Franklin Roosevelt's famous phrase?] A watery-eyed young fellow, who finally turned into a saloon, said that he had heard nothing but Hearst until the day before; "You wouldn't have known Hughes was running," was the way he expressed it.

In general, these men represented pretty fairly the groups which are supporting Mr. Hearst: the man who is embittered by class feelings and wants vengeance; the man suddenly roused against the unjust power of certain corporation managers, and about ready to accept any candidate who is vociferous in promising remedies; the unobtrusive socialistic workingman; the natural bigot who has fallen under the spell of Hearst; and the rather shiftless, thoughtless loafer who follows the herd to which he belongs. Unlike one another in many respects as these men are, they are alike in one respect, their reliance upon a single individual to deal with social and political ills. There was nothing of that sturdy self-reliance and instinct for self-government characteristic of those islanders off the coast of Maine whom Mr. Stowe tells about in another column; although none, except perhaps the first of these men, was apparently foreign of origin, their attitude toward public problems seemed to be that of the foreigner who looks to a kindly paternal government rather than that of an American who joins with his fellow-citizens in dealing with public problems at first hand.

Again contemporary analogues rush to one's mind. The yearning for "a kindly paternal government" and "reliance upon a single individual to deal with social and political ills" are more in evidence in 1936 than they were in 1906. Was Hearst the ancestor of Franklin Roosevelt? Or was he a Fascist born out of his due time?

Lincoln Steffens, writing on "Hearst, the Man of Mystery" in the *American Magazine* for November 1906 in an article which began, "All over the country all sorts and conditions of men are asking 'What about Hearst?'" reported, after a long personal interview with him, that Hearst was "cold, isolated, hard," "distinctly unmoral," "a boss who would like to give us democratic government, just as others of his class would 'give us' colleges and libraries and—good plutocratic government." And the writer added: "But we don't want Mr. Hearst to 'give us' democratic government. We don't want anybody to give us self-government. We want to get that for ourselves. . . . He seems to think that democracy is an end in itself, and that the end justifies the means—his journalism. So to give us a better government he would make us a worse people."

Years later, Lincoln Steffens retracted this judgment. In *The Autobiography of Lincoln Steffens* (1931) he criticized his own article severely, writing, "I did not understand then what a part dictatorship has to play in democracy. And I found, as his chief fault, that he was not moral; I was just getting over my own righteousness, but I had not yet arrived where Hearst was born, apparently, at the point of view whence one sees that it is economic, rather than moral forces that count. . . . He is so far ahead of his staffs that they can hardly see him; and so, of course they cannot make either this remarkable man or his perfectly rational ideas comprehensible to his readers, the people Hearst would like to see served." When Lincoln Steffens as late as 1931 could still see in Hearst a "servant" of the people, one can begin to understand how Hearst's followers could have regarded him as a Messiah in 1906.

The most significant sentence in Steffens's earlier and more intelligent description of Hearst was this: "He says that when he speaks of the people he thinks of Mr. Opfer's caricature of the 'Common People,' the thin little, worried man with the glasses. 'The commuter is about it,' he says." In other words, Hearst's appeal, like that of Long, Coughlin, and Townsend in the thirties, was to the lower middle class, that group which has furnished the mass support of Fascism in every country where Fascism has arisen.

The *World's Work* in October 1906 explained the character of the Hearst movement by the character of the Hearst newspapers:

These Hearst newspapers do not circulate among the most highly educated of the wealthy or the fashionable people of the cities wherein they are located. They sell for a cent, are printed in ink of various colors and with headlines of circus poster type. Their illustrations are fanciful and often sensational. The largest space is given to tragedies, to murders by women or on account of women, to elopements, to scandals and exaggerated descriptions of happenings in that class of society whose notoriety or wealth is best known. It is most natural that the men and women whose mental caliber is such that they prefer this kind of newspaper should believe that it is really William Randolph Hearst who writes and publishes all the things which his newspapers credit to him. The woman who reads on the editorials about "Baby" has a kindly feeling toward Mr. Hearst for his sympathetic and friendly advice. The man who buys his coal in half-ton lots regards Mr. Hearst as his champion. The saloon keeper who has had the price of his ice raised believes that if Mr. Hearst were in power the ice trust would be abolished. The tenement-house dweller who bemoans his gas bills regards Mr. Hearst as synonymous with fifty-cent gas. The motormen and streetcar conductors who read Mr. Brisbane's editorials hope for two dollars and a half and an eight-hour day as a result of Mr. Hearst's political success.

Nor were his followers wrong in expecting tangible results from his success, for tangible results had already been achieved. As the *Outlook*, one of his bitterest opponents, generously admitted in an editorial of October 6, 1906:

It is due to Mr. Hearst, more than to any other one man that the Central and Union Pacific Railroads paid the $120,000,000 they owed the government. Mr. Hearst secured a model Children's Hospital for San Francisco, and he built the Greek Theater of the University of California—one of the most successful classic reproductions in America. Eight years ago, and again this year, his energetic campaigns did a large part of the work of keeping the Ice Trust within bounds in New York. His industrious Law Department put some fetters on the Coal Trust. He did much of the work of defeating the Ramapo plot, by which New York would have been saddled with a charge of $200,000,000 for water. To the industry and pertinacity of his lawyers New Yorkers owe their ability to get gas for eighty cents a thousand feet, as the law directs, instead of a dollar. In maintaining a legal department, which plunges into the limelight with injunctions and mandamuses when corporations are caught trying to sneak under or around a law, he has rendered a service that has been worth millions of dollars to the public.

Just how many of these accomplishments—Hearst's greatest in the field of actual reform—stemmed from the mind of his leading attorney, Clarence Shearn, rather than from his own, there is no way of knowing. But since they represented a policy formed long before Hearst's connection with Shearn, it seems fair to ascribe their inception to the publisher rather than the lawyer, reserving to the latter the credit for their successful execution.

Besides his large following of small tradesmen, the labor unions, also, were at this time united in support of Hearst. Under the leadership of Samuel Gompers, the American Federation of Labor was entirely dominated by middle-class reformist ideals. Solomon Carvalho, Hearst's business manager, was most diligent in circulating the *American* in factory towns, and the paper loudly proclaimed its rôle as special defender of "the rights of Labor" as well as of "the rights of the People" in general. But here the results were less tangible. The attention of the Hearst press and of its legal department was given much more to the lowering of prices than to the raising of wages. For example, Hearst was a member of the Publishers' Association, and in that position did not exert himself in the least on behalf of hours, wages, or union recognition. As Frank Palmer wrote in 1906: "Far from leading a movement in the Association for higher wages or shorter hours, Hearst has raised no dissenting voice when the Publishers' Association has resisted the demands of the union. He has yielded to the trade union's demands only when business wisdom dictated retreat." True, his New York papers, together with the *World* and the *Herald,* paid a little higher than the current wage rate to printers, but only, as Palmer pointed out, in return for later hours at night. "Hearst's editions have not raised the rate of wages or lessened the hours of work of the employees of any concern in the United States. . . . The trades union men have bought his newspapers and voted for him. They have served him when they thought that he was serving them."

For the up-state vote, Hearst at this time brought out a new publication, thus described by Palmer: "It has part of the Goddard features and the 'comic sups'—pastoral Maud, the mule, never being left out, and urban Buster Brown never included—and advice on crop-raising as well as how to vote after the crops are harvested in November. To the initiated it seems too clearly a patchwork of Sunday 'stuff' done by the scissors, with agricultural special 'stuff' done by a stall-fed editor from Avenue A. . . ."

In spite of everything, however, there was a considerable disposition to give Hearst the benefit of the doubt on the score of sincerity. As the hostile *World's Work* put it in its issue of April 1906: "He takes himself seriously. He may once have held a creed that was made to order for journalistic success. But he now believes it . . . The Hearst of today· is, to a great degree, the product of Mr. Arthur Brisbane."

This notion of Brisbane as Hearst's better angel, originating in the unquestioned sincerity of Brisbane's socialistic father, whose traits and philosophy the son was supposed to have inherited, was destined to be gradually dispelled as successive years showed him always following his leader no matter to what strange goals the journey led. But in the beginning it was widely held and was often coupled with a belief that Brisbane supplied the real brains behind the Hearst movement. Thus in campaigning against Hearst, William Travers Jerome, district attorney in New York, won applause by demanding that his opponent "go to Brisbane and find out what his own platform meant." It was one of the merits of the Steffens article already mentioned that it adequately refuted this idea by simply quoting a letter and a telegram from Hearst to Brisbane. The letter read:

February 21, 1906.

Dear Mr. Brisbane:

Don't you think it would be a good Sunday editorial on corporation government, not to make it political, but sort of historical? Ask if a republic really exists today, if this country is governed by the people. . . .

We still maintain a republican form of government, but who has control of the primaries that nominate the candidate? The corporations have. Who control the conventions? The corporations. Who control the machinery of elections? Who count the votes to suit themselves? The corporations. Who own the bosses and the selected officials? Are the representatives at Albany and the representatives at Washington representatives of the people or of the corporations? Let any fair-minded man answer that question truthfully.

If the corporations do all this—and they surely do—can we maintain that this is any longer a government by the people? It is a government by a distinct class, and a government not for the greatest good of the greatest number, but for the special advantage of that class. Laws are passed for the benefit of the corporations, laws are interpreted for the benefit of the corporations, and such laws as are not to the advantage of the corporations are ignored. The people are neglected because they have ceased to be important as a factor in the government. . . .

Sincerely,

[Signed] W. R. HEARST.

The telegram was slightly longer than the letter. It ran:

Los Angeles, December 13.

Brisbane, N. Y.: Must be cautious in attacking courts, but nevertheless necessary to explain to the people the fact that they are governed by the judiciary. The corporations realize the importance of the judges, and have secured most of them. The people do not yet understand the situation. The legislatures make laws, but the judges interpret them, and they seldom fail to interpret them as the corporations desire. It is true, as Jerome said, that the judges go hat in hand to Mr. Murphy, but it is also true that Mr. Murphy goes hat in hand to Mr. Ryan [of the Standard Oil], and Mr. Ryan, who instructs Mr. Murphy and appoints the judges and governs the people, has his hat on all the time.

The fight must be made for honest judges, and it is only a phase of the fight against boss rule and corporation rule which is the great issue of today. We do not want the judges appointed either by legitimate executives or by corrupt bosses or by criminal corporations.

We want them elected by the people, responsible only to the people, and replaced at sufficiently short intervals to make them realize their responsibility. The people must appreciate the importance of the judiciary as well as the corporations realize it. They must own their judges, limit their power and make their impeachment easy. . . .

The one thing that hampers the progress of reform is Party prejudice. Party prejudice is used by clever schemers to divide the people and overcome them while divided. The people must unite for the interest of themselves and their fellow-citizens, and united they will be irresistible.

HEARST.

Brisbane was indeed more widely read than his chief, who was nothing of a student, and he presumably had more knowledge of Socialist philosophy, but Hearst was no whit inferior to his subordinate in realistic understanding of the political issues of the day. As early as June 6, 1899—several years before Roosevelt adopted the same platform—Hearst wrote over his own signature: "Combination and organization are necessary steps in industrial progress. We are advancing toward a complete organization in which the government will stand at the head and be the trust of trusts. It is ridiculous to attempt to stop this development. It is necessary merely to restrain it within proper lines and prevent the power of the trusts from being used to raise prices or lower wages or otherwise oppress the people." This was obviously a flexible program which lent itself to opportunism. Both Hearst and Brisbane were at heart opportunists and careerists. But with regard to the particular variety of opportunism to be selected at any particular moment, it was Hearst, not Brisbane, who made the decisions. Hearst was the Robinson Crusoe, Brisbane only his man Friday. Now as always, the owner of San Simeon, the Piedra Blanca, and Babicora, of the Homestake and the Ophir, of *Examiners* and *Americans*, would be his own master and, so far as fate permitted, the master of other men.

CHAPTER X

Perennial Candidate

HEARST early realized that in a nation-wide campaign for the presidency on a reformist platform his alliance with Tammany would tell against him. The fact that he ran ahead of his ticket in his first election to Congress encouraged him to believe that he no longer needed Murphy's assistance and he accordingly broke with the Tammany boss in 1903 by promoting a Fusion-Republican ticket in New York City. Then as the time for the presidential campaign of 1904 approached, he followed what was to be henceforth his permanent strategy by retiring into the background and allowing his candidacy to be promoted by others so that he could gracefully yield at the proper moment to public demand.

The "others" consisted of his newspaper staffs and his reporters who were shamelessly sent off from their journalistic jobs with instructions to devote themselves, at political rallies and in private conversation, to drumming up sentiment for Hearst, and to report to his campaign manager, Max Ihmsen, who was fully as important a factor in the Hearst boom as Brisbane, Shearn, or Carvalho. Under Ihmsen's tutelage, Hearst Clubs sprang up all over the country, and the national William Randolph Hearst League was organized, absorbing a considerable part of the older National Association of Democratic Clubs.

At the propitious moment Hearst returned from Europe and he and Ihmsen set forth in his private car to preach the gospel to the poor throughout the South and West. Discarded were now the check suit and straw hat of earlier, freer days; they were succeeded by a frock coat and slouched felt more in consonance with a message that must be radical yet respectable. At the same time, the seriousness of the speeches was enlivened by an accompaniment of brass bands, fireworks, and banners.

The conservative South proved unresponsive to these blandishments, but from the more volatile West the delegates thronged in. The states and territories beyond the Mississippi that had belonged to Bryan, and some that had not, gave Hearst in most instances their full support or a major part of it. These gains, however, were compensated by losses in the eastern states where the most that he could obtain were partial delegations from Maine, Rhode Island, and West Virginia. The issue seemed to turn upon Illinois. There the Chicago *American* under Andrew Lawrence wrought valiantly on behalf of its owner, but the old-line Democratic machine worked overtime to defeat him. Hearst secured delegates chosen by popular election; the Chicago bosses, Roger Sullivan and John P. Hopkins, secured through the state convention a set of handpicked delegates to contest their seats. The result hung upon the action of the Credentials Committee in the National Convention at St. Louis.

Hearst's headquarters at the Hotel Jefferson in St. Louis far outdid those of any of his rivals in spectacular display: ablaze with electric lights, streamers, and flags, with a generous use of all the latest Belasco stage devices. Tons of Hearst literature were passed out, and a continuous succession of speakers addressed the crowds in a large hall formed by throwing a number of suites together.

But the issue was not to be decided by electric lights, literature, or lecturers. In the convention, Bryan made a gallant fight for the seating of the Hearst delegates, but in vain. The battle for the nomination of the publisher was lost before the balloting began. Though Hearst increased his strength from 104 votes to a maximum of 263, there was no stampede in his favor such as had been hoped for, and the conservative Judge Alton B. Parker of New York was nominated. Hearst at once left for home, perhaps reflecting sadly on the $600,000 which his campaign had cost him. Several hours out of Chicago the Limited was flagged for Hearst to receive a telegram from Ihmsen and Lawrence begging him to return to the convention. Judge Parker had wired his henchman, "Blue-Eyed Billy" Sheehan (whose overthrow would later constitute the first political achievement of Franklin D. Roosevelt), to say that he was in favor of the maintenance of the gold standard—that issue having been skillfully avoided in the party platform—and that he could not accept the nomination on any other terms. This seemed to throw the election open once more, and Hearst hurried back to Chicago on the next train. But the convention, having once swallowed the Wall Street judge, declined to regurgitate him.

There seemed nothing for it but another term in Congress, which Murphy, anxious to avoid a further breach with the owner of the *American*, was willing enough to sanction. In Congress, Hearst brooded upon the meaning of his defeat. He saw that he had made the same mistake as Bryan in trusting to the West to the relative neglect of the East. The West alone could never elect a president. In the next election he must manage to carry New York State; if that could be accomplished, without at the same time losing his western votes, all would be well. The strategy of the situation seemed to call for the same bold tactics which had once carried Grover Cleveland to the White House: open defiance of Tammany and a pure reformist campaign—a dangerous program but one which if successful would put the presidential crown almost within his grasp.

There would be a mayoralty election in New York City in 1905, a gubernatorial election in 1906. If defeated in the first, he could try again in the second. But why should he be de-

ON THE HUSTINGS

Hearst campaigning for the governorship of New York.

feated? With all his New York employees hard at work in their own bailiwick, he ought to be able to defy Tammany successfully

The New York *American* and the *Evening Journal* now opened up a running fire on the Tammany mayor, George B. McClellan, finding something to criticize in everything he did. The William Randolph Hearst League of New York adopted the more impersonal title of the Municipal Ownership League which all of Hearst's employees who had not already joined now immediately entered out of a newborn enthusiasm for a full program of municipal ownership. And in due time, on October 4, 1905, a mass meeting was called by the Municipal Ownership League to save the city from the tyranny of Tammany. The meeting was addressed by Clarence J. Shearn, J. G. Phelps Stokes, John Ford, Max Ihmsen, and William Randolph Hearst. Carefully placed last on the list and with his way well prepared by the earlier speakers, Hearst, who had by this time sufficiently mastered the technique of campaign oratory, launched at once into a fiery denunciation of both the traditional parties:

Have we left any government by the people? You have your votes and the privilege of casting them, but for whom? For Mr. Murphy's puppet, or for Mr. Odell's puppet. If you want gas that will burn and not merely poison, you can vote for Mr. Murphy's puppet and you won't get it. And if you want a reduction in your extortionate bills, you can vote for Mr. Odell's puppet and not get it.

If you want decent treatment for your heroic firemen, your brave police, your conscientious clerks, your hard-working street cleaners, you can vote for Mr. Murphy's man and you won't get it; and if you want to retain the small portion of your public property still unstolen, you can vote for Mr. Odell's man or Mr. Murphy's man and you won't get that.

I do not believe the financial corporations are at fault. I do not believe that Mr. Murphy or Mr. Odell or Mr. Murphy's man or

Mr. Odell's man is at fault—I am afraid you are at fault. You are a sleeping majority, pledged by pygmies. Wake up! Nominate independent men. Men who will lead you to victory and restore this city to a government of the people, by the people, and for the people.

At the conclusion of his speech, Hearst men all over the place leaped to their feet to put his name in nomination. Some one moved that the nomination be made unanimous, and the motion was quickly carried. Hearst, pleading the unexpected character of the honor done him, begged for time in which to make up his mind as to acceptance.

The next day, like Cæsar on the Lupercal, he very gently put away the crown. But Ihmsen, Shearn, and the other leaders of the Municipal Ownership League were not to be denied. In response to their continued solicitation, he consented to reconsider his decision and within a few days dispatched the following letter to the Chairman of the League:

I have felt absolutely unable and unwilling to accept the nomination you have offered me, but I have at length decided to defer to your wishes and not to shirk a task that presents itself to me as a public duty.

The situation in this city is so grave and the condition of the public in the face of organized bossism is apparently so helpless that no man has a right to consider anything else, least of all his private affairs or personal inclination.

The one thing to be considered is the necessity of giving to the people an opportunity to vote for some man of whom it may at least be said that he would, if elected, represent those that voted for him and not any boss or corporation or selfish private interest.

If your convention believes that I am such a man I shall accept the nomination. . . .

In the cyclonic three weeks' campaign that followed, most of Hearst's energy was devoted to pointing out the personal iniquities of Boss Charles F. Murphy. He found himself obliged to go back to the time of Tweed to discover any parallel in political corruption. "Murphy," he said, "has made Croker admirable by contrast." "Under McClellan the Murphy graft in New York pales even the record of Van Wyck, the Ice Man." "Murphy is as evil a specimen of a criminal boss as we have had since the days of Tweed." "Murphy is as bold a buccaneer as ever sailed the political seas." "It is not the fact that Murphy is the boss of Tammany Hall that gives him his power and opportunity to plunder you. It is the fact that he owns the city government, and the little mayor at the head of the city government."

When Murphy retaliated by attacks on Hearst's private life, his editorial staff was sent out to testify to his model behavior. Speaking before the Presbyterian Ministers' Association of New York in October 1905 Brisbane answered the charge that Hearst was "a debauchee of a peculiarly depraved type" by offering the following evidence:

I know that this charge has been widely circulated. But I lived in the same house with Mr. Hearst for three years, and I know of nothing whatever to support it. He is a man who never drinks, who works hard every day until two or three o'clock in the morning. He is a big, strapping fellow, a man of domestic habits, and his little boy is a marvel of health and vigor.

Photographs of the young George Hearst adorned the pages of the *American* so frequently that one might almost have supposed he, rather than his father, was the candidate for mayor. Photographs of Mrs. Hearst in company with her son were added proof of her husband's fidelity. If more were needed, a portrait of His Holiness the Pope was reproduced, inscribed with a personal message of thanks to Hearst for financial aid to the Italian people during one of the periodic eruptions of Mount Vesuvius.

Sternly, the Hearst papers set their face against every indulgence of sexual depravity. A campaign begun by them in 1899 against the veiled assignation column in James Gordon Bennett's *Herald* was renewed with added vigor and carried on until that luckless publisher in 1907 was fined $31,000. Thus a double purpose was accomplished; a competitor was injured and the cause of morality was triumphantly upheld.

During this period, indeed, the Hearst papers became positively puritanical. When Anthony Comstock made himself ridiculous in the eyes of other New York editors by suppressing the magazine of the Art Students' League because it contained pictures of nude figures, Brisbane came out in defense of the prurient old man, lauding him as a guardian of the home. Not until Hearst was through with politics did his New York papers relax the severity of their asceticism.

This, of course, did not prevent their continuing even more than other papers to feature sex crimes, such as the Stanford White murder and the Terranova case. But here, too, they developed more thoroughly the technique of hinting at all the details which, they confided to their readers, a proper regard for decency prevented them from giving in full. So the imagination of the readers was stimulated—the end which Brisbane, if not Hearst, knew that Shelley had proclaimed to be the highest achievement of great art.

But we have been led somewhat beyond the three weeks' mayoralty campaign which finished with the results in as much doubt as at the beginning. John K. Winkler describes with admiration the behavior of the anti-Tammany candidate on Election Day:

Hearst spent most of Election Day in his headquarters. His watchers, manhandled and bleeding, staggered in with reports of thugs in control at the voting-booths. Ihmsen and the other managers were raging, but Hearst kept perfectly cool. "Attend to these men, and put others in their places," he directed. That evening, as incomplete returns showed a neck-and-neck race, he drummed on the wainscoting of the Lexington Avenue home. He sat in a small room, the green walls copied from the Château de Blois—Bourbon lilies and crowned porcupines daintily picked out in gold. A score of costly pictures stood on the floor, leaning against the walls. Here was a wonderfully painted and gilded Egyptian mummy-case standing on end under glass; there a complete suit of ancient German armor. On a pianola stood a gilded bronze statuette of Cæsar crossing the Rubicon and one of Napoleon as First Consul. In a corner gleamed Frémiet's golden St. George and the Dragon and under a window a beautiful porcelain Eve with Cain and Abel, as infants, playing at her knee.

There, in that "small" but adequately furnished room, amid the Bourbon lilies and the crowned porcupines, with memories of Cæsar and Napoleon on either hand, the champion of the people received the news that he had been defeated in one of the closest elections ever held in New York City.

Angrily, his papers claimed that he had been counted out, which seems not unlikely in view of the fact that the Tammany forces were better organized for both force and fraud than were the Hearst contingents. The latter succeeded in obtaining a recount of the votes, but it did not alter the final result which, according to the official figures, gave McClellan 228,397, Hearst 224,925, William M. Ivins, the negligible Republican candidate, 137,193.

Not unnaturally, the Hearst papers were no more convinced by the recount than by the original report. A cartoon in the *Evening Journal* depicting Murphy in prison stripes with a convict's close-cropped hair was accompanied by the following editorial:

Every honest voter in New York WANTS TO SEE YOU IN THIS COSTUME. You have committed crimes against the people that will send you for many years to State prison, if the crimes can be proved against you. Your dull mind cannot conceive of any REAL public opinion. But an awakening is ahead of you. YOU KNOW THAT YOU ARE GUILTY. The PEOPLE know it. You have swindled the poor as their employer; you have swindled the voting public as political manager of your miserable little gas tool. The people have found you out. If you persist in your effort to rob the city, your friends will soon find you in State prison.

Don't be such a fool as to repeat Tweed's question. He only stole MONEY. You have stolen VOTES. There could not be found in New York at this moment a jury to ACQUIT you. YOU. KNOW THAT.

Look out! If you ever sit in the prisoner's dock you will not come out, except in striped clothing. You were warned before election. Be warned now—or follow Tweed and the men BETTER THAN YOU that have worked for the State prison after working against it in public office.

The cartoon and editorial were plainly libelous, yet Murphy took no action. But a year later when various anti-Hearst papers reprinted them, he at once threatened to bring suit. For strange things had happened in the interval.

As the gubernatorial election of 1906 drew nearer, Hearst's rancor over his mayoralty defeat had cooled and he began to take stock of his position. As the up-state region was normally Republican and he had learned to his cost that New York City could not be carried without Tammany, it was necessary, however dangerous and unpleasant, to attempt to reknit his old alliance with this organization. At the same time, he could not fully trust Murphy, who might, conceivably, bear some resentment on account of the attacks upon him. Murphy must be frightened as well as conciliated. The needs of the situation called for a subtle threefold policy. First, to build up as far as possible the strength of his William Randolph Hearst Municipal Ownership League, whose name was once more changed, this time to Independence League, a title less embarrassingly specific and also of far nobler associations. Second, secretly to obtain as many delegates as possible to the regular Democratic convention. Third, on the basis of this double show of power, to strike the bargain with Murphy.

There was only one slight hitch in the carrying out of this

complicated program. The Independence League convention, called by Hearst's managers two weeks before the Democratic convention, insisted not only on nominating Hearst for governor but on putting a full ticket in the field for all the other offices. This was an obstacle, but Hearst realized that loyalty to the others on this ticket ought not to take precedence over the great good to accrue to the whole nation from his own election. He accordingly went on to make sure of, his delegates to the Democratic convention and was able at least to contest a sufficient number of seats to accomplish the deal with Murphy. The latter handed over to Hearst the chairman of the Membership Committee, State Senator Thomas F. Grady, an outstanding Tammany leader, who under Murphy's instructions threw out sixty anti-Hearst delegates including the entire group from Queens County elected by a majority of over 3000 votes. Grady later admitted that it was "the dirtiest day's work" in his whole life.

Hearst was thus nominated by the same methods which had brought about his defeat at St. Louis. No one can deny that he was an apt student in the school of crooked politics. Enough Independence League candidates—including John W. Goff, chief counsel in the Lexow investigation and Samuel Seabury, more recently chief investigator of Mayor Jimmy Walker—were accepted by the Democratic convention to give some semblance of a Fusion ticket representing both the regular Democrats and the League.

The voters of New York that fall were happy in having two "reformers" to choose between: the Independent Democrat, William R. Hearst, and the regular Republican, Charles E. Hughes, whose laurels won in his investigation of the insurance companies of New York were still fresh. Any other man but Hearst would have been embarrassed by the praise which his papers had heaped upon Hughes only a year before. On October 16, 1905, the *American* had commented favorably upon "the brilliant and uncompromising investigator who is following the path of financial perfidy and crime," and on December 30, 1905, when the investigation closed, it announced its contentment with the work of Hughes in the following paragraph:

No one in New York State will question the excellence of the work done by the counsel of the people, Mr. Charles E. Hughes. He has drawn from the management of the companies under litigation admissions which have damned them in the eyes of the public. He has done perhaps everything that could be done in the time at his disposal. If there should be no extension of time, Mr. Hughes can retire with perfect certainty that his work has had the approval and aroused the commendation of the people.

But Hearst's past commendation of Hughes meant as little to him as his past condemnation of Murphy. In October 1906 the *American* discovered that "as the net result of Mr. Hughes's investigation of the insurance companies, we have the substitution of ruthless Ryan for the more or less harmless Hyde." In the previous year the paper had particularly praised Hughes for "refusing to be the dupe of Ryan." But now it said, sarcastically, "We may hope, if Mr. Hughes is elected and investigates the State departments as he has investigated the insurance companies, that Mr. Ryan will soon have control of the banking institutions and the railway interests, as well as the insurance interests."

In regard to these allegations, the *Outlook* commented pertinently on October 20, 1906:

The fact that the transfer of stock from Mr. Hyde to Mr. Ryan took place, not as a consequence of the investigation, but weeks before the investigation was even decided upon; that Mr. Ryan put the stock into the hands of disinterested trustees; that, as a direct consequence of the investigation, one insurance president went practically into exile and another to death; that a new set of men have come into control of those companies in which abuses were discovered; and that, most important of all, a new body of drastic insurance laws was placed on the statute-book, Mr. Hearst knows as well as anybody. He made his statement apparently recklessly, assuming that most of those who heard or read it would not encounter the facts that prove it false.

The *Outlook* in the same issue cited another instance of similar tactics:

Recently a Hearst paper stated on its editorial page that Mr. Hughes, after receiving a retainer from the Attorney-General of that State to help him argue a motion in a gas suit, 'took the money and went to Europe. Not only has the Attorney-General denied this, but Mr. Hughes has explained that he prepared for the argument and argued the case, and has not asked or got a cent. And yet Mr. Hearst up to this week has refused to put Mr. Hughes right before the community on a matter that concerns his personal and professional reputation.

It was with reason that Ambrose Bierce, who left Hearst's service at about this time, confided to his notes a farewell remark in regard to his chief's mendacity: "I am not sorry that, discovering no preservative allowable under the Pure Food Law that would allow him to keep his word overnight, I withdrew."

As the *Outlook* remarked:

Disclosures have been made in the present campaign regarding the "Hearst movement" which would make even Mr. Hearst laugh if he had a sense of humor. [This was a little unjust; Hearst's humor, like everything else about him, was peculiar; bitter and ironical, closer to wit, perhaps, than to what is ordinarily called humor; but it certainly existed. It was not, however, the kind of humor that could ever be exercised at his own expense.] The central theme of his campaign has been opposition to "corporations," which is the word used to typify trusts. Mr. Hearst is said actually to be the head of fourteen corporations organized to avoid individual responsibility. [Mainly New York real estate companies discussed in a later chapter.] When the county committee of the Independence League rejected the Tammany-Hearst judicial ticket, they discovered that they were powerless to act, as the governing body was the Board of Directors of the Independence League, Incorporated. . . . Mr. Hearst has even said in one of his speeches that he was opposed to the use of money in politics. He thundered against the suppression of the will of the majority in party matters, but refused to allow the enrolled members of his League to select their own leaders. These are a few of the inconsistencies of Mr. Hearst's position, and yet it is doubtful if any-one could convince him that he is inconsistent.

The *Outlook* was certainly no friend to socialism, but it drew an interesting contrast between the personnel of socialism and that of the Hearst movement.

What makes the difference [it asked] in spirit, gentleness, and temper, between a Socialist and a follower of Mr. Hearst? Letters from both are pouring in on us constantly. The Socialist is patient, kind, open-minded, intelligent, and free from charges and abuse. The Hearstite, almost without exception, storms, threatens, and relies on stereotyped allegations of corruption. From the last Hearst batch are these:

"If you do not stop to publish those nasty things about Mr. Hearst my only wish would be to see you lose all your subscribers."

"Your continued insults to a man among men, William R. Hearst, a man that is a friend of labor, has so discusted me that I will not under any circumstances take your paper again."

"What on earth, has W. Hearst ever done to you that he must bear Weekly such unseething remarks that you make. And such silly, such Bious remarks that you make in your styled society paper, more fit for some bar-room trash, than the public."

Hearst's following undoubtedly included many men of honesty and ability, such as J. G. Phelps Stokes, John W. Goff, and Samuel Seabury, but his mass support came from the same group that read his newspapers, the least literate members of the lower middle class and working class. And in politics as in journalism he believed in giving his public what it wanted—which was not any fundamental social change, but a few specific reforms and a great deal of exciting personal vituperation.

His radicalism had grown less with each successive campaign. Federal ownership of major industries had become municipal ownership of public utilities and municipal ownership had become a few specific reforms and the reforms had become the single reform of eliminating Boss Murphy. But with all the will in the world, it was impossible to attack Hughes as Murphy had been attacked, so in the gubernatorial campaign reform was resurrected, the platform of the Independence League written by Hearst demanding an eight-hour day, a two-cent railroad fare, teachers' pensions, and the three-platoon police system, all tied together by Hearst in the grand old cause of "anti-monopoly" and "Americanism." In his acceptance speech Hearst said:

My program is not socialism, or radicalism, or extreme of any kind. It is simply Americanism. If this platform is not Americanism, then common honesty is no longer a measure of American morals. If this platform is not Americanism, then a free ballot and a fair count are no longer the basis of our American government. If this platform is not Americanism, then independence, equality, and opportunity have ceased to be American ideals; then Jefferson's teachings have been forgotten and Lincoln's labor was in vain.

The issue of "Americanism" was ill chosen, for there the Republicans were thoroughly at home. Theodore Roosevelt, realizing the importance of the New York election, sent Secretary of State Elihu Root into the state to revive the story of Hearst's connection with the assassination of McKinley. On November 1, 1906, Root announced himself as the President's official spokesman:

I say to you, with his authority, that he greatly desires the election of Mr. Hughes as governor of the State of New York; I say to you, with his authority, that he regards Mr. Hearst as wholly unfit to be governor, as an insincere, self-seeking demagogue who is trying to deceive the working men of New York by false statements and false promises; and I say to you, with his authority, that he considers that

Mr. Hearst's election would be an injury and a discredit alike to honest labor and to honest capital and a serious injury to the work in which he is engaged of enforcing just and equal laws against corporate wrong-doing.

President Roosevelt and Mr. Hearst stand as far as the poles asunder. Listen to what President Roosevelt himself has said of Mr. Hearst and his kind. [Root here read the passage in Roosevelt's first message to Congress quoted in Chapter VIII.] I say, by the President's authority, that in penning these words, with the horror of President McKinley's murder fresh before him, he had Mr. Hearst specifically in his mind.

And I say, by his authority, that what he thought of Mr. Hearst then he thinks of Mr. Hearst now.

Nor was it the Republican Party alone that Hearst had to fear. In a period when party loyalty was more esteemed than it is today, many staunch Democrats had not forgiven his flirting with the Republican-Fusion ticket in 1903 or his attacks on Tammany in 1905. And, on the other hand, many sincere members of the Independence League could not stomach the new alliance with Murphy. Hearst's policy of carrying water on both shoulders had gained him the nomination, but it bade fair to lose him the election.

Correctly judging that the regular Democrats outnumbered the Independence Leaguers, William Jennings Bryan attempted to come to his friend's assistance by extolling his party loyalty. Writing in his paper, the *Commoner,* he said:

Whatever we may believe of Mr. Hughes's personal disposition and probable action with respect to great public evils [even in the stress of battle Bryan could never adopt the billingsgate tone of the man he was supporting], there can be no reasonable doubt of Mr. Hearst. Through the efforts of his great newspapers he has proved his fidelity, and if any proof be lacking we find it in the fact that the representatives of these interests whose purpose it is to defy the law and plunder the people are among his most bitter opponents.

It is somewhat significant that among the first to charge that Mr.

Hearst is not a Democrat are those who either bolted from the Democratic ticket or grew cold and distant whenever the party prepared for a serious campaign against monopoly.

In 1896, when loyalty to the party was tested, William R. Hearst supported the ticket most heartily, and anyone who now challenges him must have better standing than the man who habitually bolts when the great corporations fail to control.

The Democrats of New York who have no axe to grind and who are interested solely in the public welfare should give their support to the Democratic state ticket headed by William R. Hearst.

Hearst's nemesis proved to be his home town, the city of New York. In 1905 Senator Pat McCarren, the Democratic boss of Brooklyn, had given him the votes of Kings and Queens counties against Murphy, but in 1906 McCarren had sent anti-Hearst delegates to the convention and had not at all appreciated Grady's action in unseating them. Accordingly, in the election he had his followers scratch their ballots, knifing the head of the ticket. All of the Democratic-Independence League candidates were elected with the exception of William Randolph Hearst.

Opportunism is the comedy of politics. Where the genuine radical is likely to be a tragic figure like the Gracchi, Rienzi, Robespierre, or Trotsky, staking all upon a single issue, the opportunist is essentially a comic character, a Gil Blas, Falstaff, or Peer Gynt of reality, for whom life is nothing more than a succession of rôles, so that when one project fails he merely turns to another with unshaken equanimity. Where the radical gives up his life, the opportunist simply discards a worn-out cloak and puts on a new one, becoming at length nothing but a succession of cloaks with nothing inside them; so the opportunist dies, too, but he takes longer about it.

Hearst had tried the Democrats and failed; he would try the Republicans again. In 1907 he promoted a Republican-Fusion deal to elect his political manager, Max Ihmsen, as sheriff of

New York. Once more he failed. Thenceforward he decided to have no traffic with either the Democratic or Republican bosses who had brought him nothing but ill-luck; he would devote himself single-mindedly to building up the Independence League on a national scale. So he threw the support of his papers behind Mayor Dunne of Chicago, who was seeking re-election; but Dunne was badly defeated by Busse, the Republican candidate.

The year ended in a blaze of libel suits. Busse brought suit against the Hearst papers for $150,000 because of what they had said about him. Hearst brought suit against the Chicago *Tribune* for what it had said about *him*. And then he brought suit for $500,000 against the New York *Times* for printing what President Roosevelt was said to have said about him. This last was the most interesting of the three cases. It arose from an article written by the *Times* Washington correspondent, Oscar King Davis, in which he reported a statement by Roosevelt to the effect that in California Hearst was now supporting Harriman of the Southern Pacific while attacking the railroad in his eastern papers where no damage would be done. As soon as the libel suit was instituted, Davis was sent to interview the President as to his sources for the story.

To my surprise [Davis wrote many years later in his book, *Some Inside Political History of Theodore Roosevelt and His Times* (1925)] I learned that the man who had given him the information was Franklin K. Lane, then a member of the Interstate Commerce Commission. Mr. Lane had been the Democratic candidate for the governorship of California only a few years before . . . and had kept extremely well informed as to political doings and developments in the State during all the time that he had been serving on the Interstate Commerce Commission in Washington.

The President made it plain that he was keen to have the *Times* beat the Hearst suit, if possible, and Mr. Lane readily agreed to give us all the help he could. . . .

"AFTER THE HARVEST"

Political cartoon from *Collier's* satirizing Hearst's unsuccessful
gubernatorial campaign.

The libel suit never came to trial. Whether it was started merely as a bluff, or whether Mr. Hearst, for some other reason, reached the conclusion that it would be better not to force the issue, I never knew.

In 1908 Bryan was nominated for the third time by the Democratic Party. This resurrection of the man whom Hearst had set out to succeed aroused all the latent envy in his nature. Although Bryan had twice attempted to come to his rescue in his time of need, Hearst insisted upon putting an Independence League ticket in the field—the effect of which would be to split the Democratic Party and render a Republican victory certain. This was his reply to Bryan's eulogy of his party loyalty three years before.

This time, with defeat inevitable, Hearst did not venture to run himself but put up Thomas L. Hisgen, an oil dealer of Springfield, Massachusetts, for President, with John Temple Graves, a feature writer in the Hearst newspapers, for Vice President. Independence League state tickets also were put up wherever possible. If these balloons should float, Hearst would have the nucleus of a national third party which might become strong enough to capture the election in 1912.

He campaigned energetically on behalf of his puppets, drawing fuel for his speeches from certain letters which had come into his possession written by John D. Archbold, Standard Oil vice president, to prominent members of the Republican Party —letters which will be discussed in detail in the following chapter. But he did not confine his attacks to the Republicans. Bryan, also, he asserted, had become an agent of the Standard Oil. "Mr. Roosevelt prosecuted the Standard Oil, and the Standard Oil went out of the Republican Party and into the Democratic Party. Mr. Bryan appointed Mr. C. N. Haskell, political paymaster of the Standard Oil, to be chairman of the Committee on Platform. Mr. Bryan made Mr. Haskell treasurer of his national campaign fund to collect from Standard

Oil substantial evidence of the great monopoly's appreciation."
Just as Hearst had formerly characterized Pulitzer in terms singularly applicable to himself, so now he ventured to describe
Bryan as "the world renowned loose skin man, who can re-
verse himself in his own integument so that you cannot tell
whether he is going or coming."

The verdict of the country upon the Independence League
was decisive. Taft, the Republican candidate, received 7,677,544
votes; Bryan, the Democratic candidate, 6,405,707; Debs, the
Socialist candidate, 420,464; Chapin, the Prohibition candidate,
251,660; and Hisgen, the Hearst candidate, 83,628. In his own
state of Georgia, John Temple Graves obtained 77 votes. Lang-
don, Hearst's candidate for governor of California, came in a
poor third. In Massachusetts and Illinois his representatives
made a miserable showing. Everywhere the country had repudiated Hearst and all his ways.

He himself could not yet believe it. Perhaps he had made a
mistake in selecting such weaklings to represent him. That they
had been selected because they were weaklings he had virtually
admitted. A Hearst writer who during the campaign had been
assigned the task of doing a series of denunciatory articles on
the boss rule of a certain western city had asked his chief, "Who
are the prominent men who have joined us in this work of
reform? I should like to talk to a few of them before I write
on the subject." To which the leader of what Hearst liked to
call "the Anti-Boss Party" had replied: "We have no prominent men associated with us. I don't want any prominent men.
If I have prominent men connected with me I will have to consult them—and I don't propose to consult anybody." But it was
evident that puppets were of no more use than prominent men.
It would be necessary for Hearst to gird up his loins and enter
the battle again in his own person.

So in 1909 he once more ran for mayor of New York, this
time against Judge William J. Gaynor, who had the support of

Tammany. All the old arguments against Murphy and anyone so low as to be a Murphy candidate were brought out and refurbished. But New York, too, was at last weary of this perpetual farce of the pot calling the kettle black. When the election returns came in, there was now no need of a recount. Hearst was beaten, not as before by four thousand but by twenty times four thousand.

Still his craving for political office, almost any political office, would not down. The next year with humbler aspirations he sought to run for lieutenant-governor on an Independence League ticket. But the Independence League was now politically as dead as he and could not be revived. The campaign was abandoned before election. This last humiliation convinced Hearst that he was through. He realized that he could not be elected to any office in the gift of the American people.

His eight years of political adventuring had cost him in the neighborhood of two million dollars, divided according to the researches of the New York *Post* approximately as follows:

Year	Campaign	Estimated Cost
1902–3	Tammany candidate for Congress	$ 75,000
1903	Promoter Republican-Fusion aldermanic deal	40,000
1904	Candidate for Democratic presidential nomination	600,000
1905	Independent candidate for mayor of N. Y.	200,000
1906	Democratic candidate for governor of N. Y.	500,000
1907	Promoter Republican-Fusion deal for Ihmsen	35,000
1908	Promoter Independent Party presidential campaign	300,000
1909	Candidate for mayor of N. Y., heading one type of Republican-Fusion ticket	?
	Total	$1,750,000

The years, too, had taken their toll in other more important ways. It was not so much, as many have thought, that the publisher gradually lost his political sincerity; he had never had more than a small modicum of that quality to lose. His Phebe Apperson inheritance of Utopian idealism had early vanished before the more powerful George Hearst strain, leaving only a kind of radiant haze behind it. But the radiance, too, was gone now. Those joyous days on the *Examiner* and *Journal* of happy sleuthing, corruption-hunting, and military ardor, when every fresh discovery of sin prompted some new departure in sensational journalism to the applause of mounting circulation— those days the publisher would see no more. That gay irresponsible zest which he had originally brought to the reformer's rôle, buoyed up by confidence that if the rôle were well played it would lead to steadily increasing power, could not survive an interminable series of defeats. Anyone less inveterately opportunistic than Hearst would have yielded long before. When at last he was forced to admit to himself that with all his wealth and unquestionable ability there was one thing, political office, that lay beyond his power to attain, it meant a profound shock to his prolonged infantile vision of a world made for his command. In time he would recover this vision, through other means, in part, but never wholly. The inferiority sense that had dogged him since his youth but that had been temporarily thrust into the background by his success with the *Examiner* and *Journal* permanently returned. He became more envious and suspicious. The old camaraderie with the members of his staffs disappeared. His natural aloofness from the normal human emotions of companionship and friendship intensified. In the beginning he had seemed a man of many potentialities; now his character had hardened in the grooves already formed; and a deadly chill enveloped it.

His last gesture on the political stage was not a graceful one. Not long after the election, there was an attempt to assassinate Mayor Gaynor. While his late opponent lay at the brink of death, Hearst, who had once more sought escape from his defeat in travel, received a message from several New York newspapers asking him to comment on certain unkind statements made by Gaynor during his illness. He sent the following reply:

I am exceedingly sorry that Mayor Gaynor was shot, and if Mayor Gaynor has said what you tell me, I can only add that I am exceedingly sorry that his injuries have affected his mind. . . . His experience did not abate his evil temper nor his lying tongue. The criticism of Mayor Gaynor's public acts by the Hearst papers has been temperate and truthful, dignified and deserved, unprejudiced and in the public interest. . . .

I personally will not take advantage of your columns to criticize Mayor Gaynor politically, first, because of his illness, and second because his mental as well as moral condition has eliminated him from political consideration.

Decidedly, among the virtues of William Randolph Hearst magnanimity was not included.

CHAPTER XI

Last of the Muckrakers

HEARST may be regarded as having been a muckraker from the beginning. In San Francisco he had started modestly by muckraking the emergency hospital, the life-saving service, and the traction companies; in New York he had muckraked the public utilities; his highest point of journalistic glory had been reached by muckraking the Spanish government in Cuba. After the war, he attempted to muckrake the Mormons, the New York *Herald*, Hanna and McKinley, Boss Murphy, Hughes, and Gaynor. In all this he had been in part a product of his era, that exciting period when America, newly conscious of its national greatness, had also become aware that in the course of attaining it the old ideals of liberty, equality, and political honesty had somehow been sacrificed. Like a giant who had fallen asleep in a cesspool, the nation awoke, rubbed its eyes, and beheld the sorry condition it was in. Its immediate reaction was to assume that somebody must have pushed it into the cesspool, and it set out to find the villain. When it discovered not one villain but hundreds, the first cry was the old cry, "Turn the rascals out!" To this cry, Hearst, as we have seen, was particularly ready to respond. His financial means and the opportunities for investigation afforded by his newspapers might have made him, had he cared to make use of them conscientiously, the greatest of the muckrakers. But where Lincoln Steffens, Ida Tarbell, Ray Stannard Baker, David Graham Phillips, and Upton Sinclair were tireless in documenting their evidence, Hearst found it much easier simply to trust to his own imagination or to that of Chamberlain, McEwen, or Arthur Brisbane. The result was that much of the muck which he raked up was muck which he himself deposited.

But his preference for the method of personal attack over that of the discussion of principles was not solely a matter of giving the public what it wanted. That there was also a subjective and pathological element involved is shown by the fact that he persisted in the method long after the public had become weary of it. True, when in 1907 the New York *World* committed the mistake of belatedly trying to muckrake Mary Baker Eddy, the Hearst papers came to the old lady's assistance, thereby, incidentally, establishing a permanent and highly useful entente with the Church of Christ Scientist. But this was rather an episode in the enduring, though latterly less open, feud with the *World* than an indication of any understanding on Hearst's part that the days of muckraking were over. On the contrary, in 1910 he was still vigorously at it, gleefully publishing a series of secret letters incriminating to both Murphy and Gaynor which he is said to have obtained by bribing a maid in the Murphy household. The spirit of envy, which lies so close to the inferiority sense and is so easily invoked for righteous causes, must surely have been at the root of Hearst's continued muckraking after the other journalists in the movement had left it for new fields.

His greatest achievement in the realm of exposure, the publication of the Archbold Standard Oil letters mentioned earlier, which ran from 1908 to 1912, came too late. Had they been published when Hearst first secured them in 1905, they would have shaken the nation; as it was, though they were instrumental in causing the political retirement of Foraker, the most scarlet of the various sinners exposed, the story of political corruption was by that time too familiar to cause the shock it would have brought a few years before. And the series of publications ended, as will be seen, in something worse than a lame and impotent conclusion.

The letters were obtained in the following manner. In the household of John D. Archbold, vice president of the Standard Oil Company and respectable deacon of the Methodist Episcopal Church, there had been for twenty years a trusted Negro butler named James Wilkins. Wilkins had a reprobate stepson named Willie Winkfield. And Willie Winkfield was fond of shooting craps at the Little Savoy, a Negro dive on West Thirty-Fifth Street. In consequence, Willie often needed cash. He was employed by his stepfather's kindly patron in the Standard Oil offices at 26 Broadway, but his small wage did not enable him to satisfy his gambling propensities on the generous scale which his expansive nature required. Accordingly, Willie conceived the happy thought of burglarizing Archbold's letterbox and selling the contents to the press. He communicated this subtle idea to Charlie Stump, a white employee, who in turn communicated it to the New York *American*, which eagerly welcomed the suggestion. Every afternoon, Winkfield and Stump would wait until the other employees had left and then conduct their raids; the letters would be photographed during the night and returned early the next morning so that their temporary absence would never be suspected. Hearst obtained the correspondence late in 1904 or early in 1905, but for three years no hint of the affair transpired.

It was not until September 17, 1908, during the presidential campaign, that the bomb was exploded. Then in the course of a speech at Columbus, Ohio, Hearst made public the most damaging of the letters, preluded by the following remarks:

I am not here to amuse you and entertain you with oratory, but I am here to present to you as patriotic American citizens some facts that should startle and alarm you and arouse you to a fitting sense of the genuine danger that threatens our republic.

I am not here either with empty assertions but with legal evidence and documentary proof. I ask you to rally to your country's needs, to rescue your country from the greatest danger that can threaten a republic—the danger that is within the gates—the corrupting power of unscrupulous and criminal wealth.

I am now going to read copies of letters written by Mr. John Archbold, chief agent of the Standard Oil, an intimate personal representative of Mr. Rockefeller and Mr. Rogers. These letters have been given me by a gentleman who has intimate association with this giant of corruption, the Standard Oil, but whose name I may not divulge lest he be subjected to the persecution of this monopoly.

(1)

26 Broadway, New York.
March 26, 1900.

Dear Senator:

In accordance with our understanding I now beg to enclose you certificate of deposit to your favor for $15,000. Kindly acknowledge receipt and oblige,

Yours very truly,

JNO. D. ARCHBOLD

(2)

April 17, 1900.

My Dear Senator:

I enclose you certificate of deposit to your favor for $15,000. We are greatly at a loss in the matter, but I send this, and will be glad to have a very frank talk with you when opportunity offers, and if you so desire.

I need scarcely again express our great gratification over the favorable outcome of affairs.

Very truly yours,

JNO. D. ARCHBOLD

Both letters were addressed to "Hon. J. B. Foraker," Republican Senator from Ohio. Upon their publication, Foraker at once gave out a public statement that the certificates of deposit had been given in return for legal services that had nothing to do with politics and that he had never performed or been expected to perform any act on behalf of the Standard Oil in his capacity as senator. Hearst thereupon released two more letters.

(1)

26 Broadway, New York.
February 16, 1900.

My Dear Senator:

Here is still another very objectionable bill. It is so outrageous as to be ridiculous, but it needs to be looked after, and I hope there will be no difficulty in killing it.

Am anxious to hear from you as to the situation as a whole.

Very truly yours,

JNO. D. ARCHBOLD

Addressed to Hon. J. B. Foraker,
1500 Sixteenth St.,
Washington, D. C.

(2)

26 Broadway, New York.
March 9, 1900.

My Dear Senator:

I have your favor of last night with enclosure, which letter, with letter from Mr. Elliott commenting on same, I beg you to send herewith. Perhaps it would be better to make a demonstration against the whole bill, but certainly the ninth clause to which Mr. Elliott refers should be stricken out, and the same is true of House Bill No. 500, also introduced by Mr. Price, in relation to foreign corporations, in which the same objectionable clause occurs.

Am glad to hear that you think that the situation is fairly well in hand.

Very truly yours,

JNO. D. ARCHBOLD

Addressed to Hon. J. B. Foraker,
Senate Chamber,
Washington, D. C.

These were the most damaging of the letters in Hearst's possession, but during his Columbus speech he read others also, implicating a Republican congressman, Joseph C. Sibley, and showing a close connection between Archbold and Senator Mark Hanna.

The letter from Sibley to Archbold told of a visit paid by the Congressman to President Roosevelt and ended as follows:

For the first time in my life I told the President some plain if unpalatable truths as to the situation politically, and that no man should win or deserve to win who depended upon the rabble rather than upon the conservative men of affairs. I don't know as he really liked all I said, but he thanked me with apparent heartiness. Anything you may desire here in my power please advise.

Sincerely yours,

JOSEPH C. SIBLEY

After reading this effusion, Hearst commented: "You gentlemen, I, Mr. Hisgen—all of us are the rabble. Seekers after office cannot depend upon us: they need the conservative citizens, these magnates of the great criminal trusts!"

The letter from Archbold to Mark Hanna ran as follows:

26 Broadway, New York.
March 20, 1903.

My Dear Senator:

To our amazement, it is reported that Smith W. Bennett is making a canvass for the Attorney-Generalship in Ohio. Mr. Bennett is a brother-in-law of F. S. Monnett, recent Attorney-General, and was associated with Monnett in the suit against us in that state. If there is any possible danger, which I cannot believe, of Mr. Bennett's candidacy assuming serious proportions, I would like to tell you something of our experience and impressions of the man in connection with that case. I am sure, however, that you will agree that Ohio is not so poorly off as to take that sort of timber for its Attorney-General. I will be very glad to hear from you on the subject.

Sincerely yours,

JNO. D. ARCHBOLD

Two weeks later, on September 20, 1908, while speaking in Memphis, Tennessee, Hearst attempted to implicate Joe Bailey, Democratic senator from Texas, in the Archbold transactions. After reading a letter from Sibley to Archbold in which "the miserable little Standard Oil spy in the House," as Hearst denominated him, informed Archbold that "Senator B., a Democrat" would be a "tower of strength and safety" and suggested that a conference be held with him, Hearst went on:

Mr. Sibley does not say who Senator B. is. We'll have to do a little Sherlock Holmes work. Let us see. The vowels of the alphabet are a, e, i, o, and u. It can't be Senator Bully as there is no Senator Bully. It can't be Bolly for the same reason. It can't be Senator Billy unless Mr. Sibley is calling some Senator by his first name. It can't be Senator Belly. Can it be Senator Ba—? Why, to be sure, there is a Senator Bailey and we have heard his name mentioned before in connection with Standard Oil. Another thing that makes me suspect the Senator referred to may be Senator Bailey is this letter from Mr. Archbold asking Senator B. to come down to New York and step up to the captain's office quickly.

And he quoted: " 'We are anxious to have a talk here at as early a date as possible with Senator Bailey of Texas.' "

It was a telling speech, though there was nothing in the correspondence actually to prove that Senator Bailey succumbed to Archbold's blandishments. Other letters published later did, however, show that Senators Matt Quay and Boies Penrose of Pennsylvania both received large amounts from Archbold and that Mark Hanna asked "Dear John" for a "liberal subscription" to the Republican campaign fund.

When the revelations went on week after week, President Roosevelt issued the following public statement in regard to them:

Mr. Hearst has published much interesting and important correspondence of the Standard Oil people, especially that of Mr. Archbold with various public men. I have in times past criticised Mr.

Hearst, but in this matter he has rendered a public service of high importance and I hope he will publish all the letters dealing with the matter which he has in his possession. If Mr. Hearst or anybody else has any letter from me dealing with Standard Oil affairs I shall be delighted to have it published.

After the election, Roosevelt invited Hearst to call at the White House, and the two had a forty-five minutes' conversation, in the course of which the President is said to have asked whether the publisher had found any "gossip" connecting him with Archbold, to which Hearst is said to have replied, "Nothing that I intend to publish at this time." As a matter of fact, he had nothing at all beyond evidence that in the early days before the Standard Oil fight arose Roosevelt had occasionally invited Archbold to visit him at Oyster Bay, plus the fact that Mark Hanna, with or without Roosevelt's knowledge, had requested the contribution to the campaign fund.

The interesting question remains: why had Hearst waited for three years before giving the Archbold correspondence to the public? The "danger threatening the republic—the danger within the gates" had surely been as great in 1905 as it was in 1908. Yet Hearst had not been so "startled and alarmed" but that he had allowed the republic to be undermined for three more years before calling attention to its perilous situation.

The explanation is not far to seek. In 1905 Hearst had set out to unseat Theodore Roosevelt as President of the United States. The men implicated in the Archbold correspondence—Foraker, Hanna, Quay, Penrose—were all bitter enemies of Roosevelt. The publication of the letters at that time would have redounded to Roosevelt's advantage more than to Hearst's. But the situation was different in 1908. Roosevelt was then out of the picture, and Hearst as head of the Independent Party was campaigning against both the Republicans and Democrats. It was a more suitable moment for the revelations and for attempting to involve in them the prominent Democrat, Senator Joseph Bailey of Texas.

The publication of the correspondence had no perceptible effect on the election of 1908, but during the dull years that followed Hearst continued to bring out intermittently further batches of Archbold letters until in 1912 the whole series was republished in *Hearst's Magazine* accompanied by elaborate scholia from the pen of Hearst himself. On one occasion the Hearst gloss, cabled from London where the publisher happened to be, ran as high as 7000 words, which were said to constitute the longest message ever sent over the cable up to that time.

Then came the anti-climax—an article entitled "Mr. Hearst's Forgeries" by Arthur Gleason in *Collier's Weekly*, October 5, 1912. In it, the writer proved that in five of the letters the same Archbold signature had appeared, enlarged or made smaller by an engraving process. He also published the following official statement by W. L. Smith, president of the L. C. Smith & Brothers Typewriter Company:

These letters, namely, letters alleged to have been written by Mr. John D. Archbold to Hon. M. S. Quay, *February 13, 1900;* letter alleged to have been written by General Grosvenor to Mr. Archbold, *September 27, 1904;* letter alleged to have been written by Mr. Archbold to Senator Quay, *July 18, 1898;* letter alleged to have been written by Mr. Archbold to Senator Hanna on *January 19, 1900;* letter alleged to have been written by Mr. Archbold to Senator Penrose, *October 13, 1904,* are all of them unmistakably written on the L. C. Smith & Bros. typewriter containing elite type, or known to us as No. 6 type. No. L. C. Smith and Bros. typewriting machine equipped with elite or No. 6 type was placed upon the market or manufactured earlier than *June 15, 1905.*

Arthur Gleason commented pertinently:

Mr. Hearst has many genuine facsimiles in his possession. Photographs were made in his *American* office of genuine original documents. Why is he using forgeries? In particular, why has he used forged documents in the Penrose exposure? Stump told me that he carried original Penrose material to the *American* office, just as he carried Hanna material. . . . How foolish of Mr. Hearst to pull a real leak on the invisible relationship of Standard Oil with the government, and then create a series of forgeries in order to exploit that secret accurate information!

The best explanation that we have seen of this recurrent phenomenon in Hearst's career is given in a hitherto unpublished letter by one of America's well-known writers who was intimately associated with Hearst for several years, and who still occasionally does special articles for the Hearst press. For obvious reasons his name cannot be given.

In respect to his veracity, I came to the conclusion long ago that he does not know the difference between a truth and a lie. I mean he really doesn't. He is utterly lacking in the judicial temperament. Anything that corroborates his own views must necessarily be true. Any arrant and palpably obvious faker can come along and sell him a grotesque collection of forgeries and lies about Mexico, Japan, Russia, or Communists. Later, when the lies are exposed and ridiculed after their publication, Hearst still has no regrets. Even if they are lies, he says, they ought to be true, and they have in them the spirit of truth, if not its reality. Of course it is impossible to convince a man of this type by a display of facts, or to deal with him at all on a factual basis. Through these chinks in his demeanor you see the spirit of a fractious, whining child who plays that the dream is true, even if it isn't.

There is in him, and rather strongly developed, the puerile, unethical amorality of a child. When he wants a thing he wants it right then and there, and he will get it if he can regardless of expense . . . long involved reverberations, or what not. And when he gets enough of anybody or anything they are dropped just as a monkey in a zoo drops the shell of a nut; an idle, inattentive, careless dropping. Apparently he never gives the matter another thought.

I feel pretty certain that I know the inner source of Hearst's personality. It is a vast inferiority complex; one of the world's top-notchers in its psychological relation to actuality. He was raised as a spoiled child, and taught that he was young lord and master, millionaire by natural right, and superior to the common run of mankind. Then he was sent to Harvard and out in the world. He learned, to his surprise, that people in general did not take him at his own valuation. They did not pay much attention to him, in fact. His adolescent conviction of superiority became, by inversion, a pitiable state of inferiority which could be overcome only by a complete defiance of all standards. That's Hearst.

In the sphere of controversy the over-stimulated and defiant inferiority complex goes the limit. Objective truth does not exist. To admit that somebody is right and that he is wrong in a major matter would be so disastrous to Hearst's ego that it is out of the question. Therefore, no slithering ray of doubt must be allowed to penetrate; if it got inside it might cause incalculable wreckage, like a firecracker in a powder mill. The personality is closed, impenetrable, and if it is caught in a lie, the proof is simply disregarded.

It was certainly a man insulated against "slithering rays of doubt" who one day in June 1912 penned the following:

INSTRUCTIONS TO THE HEARST PRESS

Make a paper for the nicest kind of people—for the great middle class.

Don't print a lot of dull stuff that they are supposed to like and don't.

Omit things that will offend nice people. Avoid coarseness and slang and a low tone. The most sensational news can be told if it is written properly.

Talk as a gentleman should. Be reliable in all things as well as entertaining and amiable.

Do not exaggerate.

Make the paper helpful and kindly. Don't scold and forever complain and attack in your news columns. Leave that to the editorial page.

Be fair and impartial. . . . Make a paper for all the people and give unbiased news of all creeds and parties. Try to do this in such a conspicuous manner that it will be noticed and commented upon.

If you cannot show conclusively your own paper's superiority you may be sure the public will never discover it.

A succession of superior papers will surely tell. When you beat your rivals one day, try hard to beat them the next—for success depends upon a complete victory.

CHAPTER XII

Pacifist Patriot

IN THE presidential campaign of 1912 the logic of Hearst's
political philosophy should clearly have made him a supporter
of Theodore Roosevelt rather than of Woodrow Wilson. In the
leading article of the November 1911 issue of the *World Today*
a paper (later to be called *Hearst's International*) purchased by
him in that year, he reiterated his position on the trust problem
with that clarity of expression which was always his in those rare
moments when he was not under the immediate sway of personal
ambition. The article was entitled "Combination a Phase of
Progress: its Evils must be Eliminated; its Advantages must be
Retained." Hearst's argument was summed up in the following
words:

The trust is a labor-saving device that can lower the cost of production. The trust is also a great power which can raise the price of
its commodities, rob its weaker rivals, corrupt legislatures and oppress
the public. These evil deeds of the trusts should be made criminal
and adequately punished. The trusts should be regulated and restricted, but they should not be destroyed and, what is more, they
cannot be.

Elsewhere in the article he wrote: "Mr. Taft may call this
state socialism or whatever he pleases, but calling a thing ? name
does not discredit it if the thing itself is right and furnishes a
solution and the only solution to an acute problem."

All this was essentially identical with the program of the Progressive Party and was essentially opposed to Woodrow Wilson's
endeavor to revive free competition. Furthermore, Wilson's

endorsement of the "open shop" was in fundamental conflict with Hearst's pretended labor policy. But we must remember that Hearst was the perfect pragmatist, in the popular meaning of that term; normally, words and ideas were to him merely instruments of action, weapons in the struggle for existence; truth was that which "worked"—for his own advantage. He had insisted too often on the hustings that he was a Jeffersonian Democrat, too often had denounced the trusts in wholly unmeasured words to make it safe for him to move into the other camp. Furthermore, the other camp did not want him. He was still as much persona non grata in Washington as ever. Mrs. Phebe Hearst on her visits East was frequently invited to the White House by both Roosevelt and Taft, but this hospitality did not extend to her son. Save for his forty-five minutes' conversation with Roosevelt about the Archbold letters, Hearst himself was excluded from the sacred precincts and the Hearst reporters at the press conferences with the President were usually received with the greatest coldness and sometimes not received at all. So for all these personal reasons, in the campaign of 1912 Hearst supported the man whose political philosophy he despised, and opposed the man whose political philosophy was almost the same as his own.

There was too little liking, however, between Hearst and Wilson for the publisher to have any standing with the new administration. Wilson had not forgotten that when he was governor of New Jersey he had been called by Hearst "a sham progressive" or that the publisher had gone to Baltimore to work for Champ Clark's nomination in the recent convention; and Hearst had not forgotten that Wilson and Gaynor had joined forces to denounce him back in 1910. The new President had been barely a month in office when Hearst wrote a letter to the editor of the Washington *Post*, published on April 14, 1913, in which he criticized Wilson for delivering his message to Congress in person, for too much reading of the London *Times*, and for favoring a low tariff. His own Anglophobia gave him a quick eye for any signs of Anglomania in others. The letter read:

The Federalist method of a speech by the President was a mere adaptation of the British usage of a speech to Parliament from the throne. The aristocratic Adams approved it and practised it. [As did also the aristocratic Washington, whom Hearst thought it best not to mention.] But Thomas Jefferson, who founded the Democratic Party and introduced into American political life the simplicity which has since characterized it, adopted the modest democratic method of writing a message to Congress, expressing his views and offering suggestion for legislation. . . .

Mr. Wilson gained his degree of doctor of philosophy by an essay which contended flagrantly in the face of fact that the English parliamentary form of government was superior to the American congressional system. To be sure this essay of Mr. Wilson's was written some time ago and might be considered an early and outgrown expression of a Federalistic affection for England, were it not that Mr. Wilson has only comparatively recently delivered an address in which he declares that he gets his information on world events from the columns of the London *Weekly Times.*

Certainly the London *Times* is, or at least once was, an excellent paper, but there is no publication on the face of the earth so completely and absolutely saturated with the English prejudice toward all other countries, and toward America in particular, as the London *Times.* . . .

Mr. Wilson's opposition to the protective principle is not inherently or essentially Democratic. Mr. Wilson is FUNDAMENTALLY opposed to the principle of protection, and his idea of radical, ruthless tariff reduction is but an expression of the English free-trade theories of Cobden and Mill. Mr. Wilson is an English free-trader.

Since Wilson had campaigned for election largely on this very tariff issue, anyone but Hearst would have been embarrassed to reconcile his own support of the candidate with this later rebuke for doing just what the candidate had pledged himself to do.

His economic precepts and practices continued to be as inconsistent as were his political theories and political actions. During this his middle period he still posed as a friend of union labor, yet when a printers' strike swept Chicago he worked with the other publishers to beat the strike by employing gun thugs. As of old his papers attacked the gas rings, yet one fine morning his readers in Chicago were surprised to note that the attacks had ceased; later they observed that the gas companies were advertising heavily in the Hearst papers.

Hearst's general program continued to involve that curious combination of avowed liberalism in domestic matters and avowed imperialism in foreign affairs that had marked it from the beginning. On the Pacific Coast his papers kept up a running fire against Japan, which had now taken the place of China as the head and front of the "yellow peril" always threatening the prosperity of California—hated Japan, which had captured for itself that Chinese trade on which America, or some Americans, had counted. Toward Mexico, after the overthrow of Diaz (the benevolently minded friend of the Hearst properties) the Hearst press adopted an attitude of consistent hostility. And with regard to Great Britain, the Hearst papers were ever on the alert to detect new evidences of that power's heinous imperialistic plots.

During Wilson's fight for the repeal of the Panama tolls which had been passed in defiance of the government's solemn promise, Hearst was the bitterest of all the President's critics. His cartoonist, Winsor McCay, almost rivaled the earlier notoriety of Davenport by his series showing Wilson as a graceless schoolmaster misrepresenting to his pupils the great patriotic events of American history. The New York *World* pointed out that "Mr. Hearst apparently has learned nothing from the assassination of William McKinley" and insisted, with some exaggeration, that his attacks upon Wilson were "more malicious, mendacious and incendiary" than those upon McKinley prior to the assassination.

Still, compared with his campaigning period, these were relatively quiet years for Hearst. Yellow journalism had temporarily
worn itself out—as anything based upon mere sensation must in
time—and Hearst was forced to accommodate himself as best he
could to the new mood of the public. His papers, though yel-
lower than others, became much less yellow than of old. His last
venture on a large scale in the old-time appeal to commingled
purity and lust was a campaign put on by the San Francisco
Examiner in 1912 to clean up the Barbary Coast, the city's
celebrated and picturesque red-light district. And here Fremont
Older, editor of the *Bulletin*, took the headlines away from his
rival by a daring act. The church of the Reverend Paul Smith,
a Methodist preacher chosen by the *Examiner* to head its
crusade, was located near the Barbary Coast, and into it one
Sunday evening marched hundreds of prostitutes, marshaled
thither by *Bulletin* reporters. There ensued what was probably
the only mass meeting of prostitutes known to history. Overwhelmed with questions, obviously framed in the *Bulletin* office,
which he could not answer, the Reverend Smith was put to
shame in his own temple.

Hearst had a few minor troubles during these quiet years. A
British firm brought suit against him for $18,155 still due on
$46,205 worth of antique furniture bought between 1908 and
1913. He countered by bringing suit against the company for
$3000, claiming that he had been overcharged that amount for
an Elizabethan chimney piece which had turned out not to be an
antique at all.

On December 13, 1913, the New York *Times* carried a news
item headed "WILLIAM R. HEARST CAN'T SLEEP." It reported a
suit brought by the publisher to enjoin the New York Central
from switching freight cars at night on the West Side above
Seventy-second Street. Hearst testified that though he had put
double windows in his apartment at Eighty-sixth Street and

Riverside Drive, his slumbers were continually broken by the noise of shunting cars. He won his suit, but only to have the decision reversed by a higher court.

Meanwhile, far away on the Pacific Coast he was disciplined by the Associated Press for republishing his San Francisco *Examiner* in Oakland under the title *The Oakland Examiner* as if it were a local paper, and was compelled to discontinue the practice.

Almost equally annoying was an incident that lost Hearst the services of one of his ace reporters, Roscoe Conklin Mitchell.

Mitchell had the best reputation for accuracy of all the men on the Hearst press. Before he joined that organization, he had been the only reporter whom Roosevelt had allowed to interview him at Oyster Bay on his return from Africa. When the New York *American* secured Mitchell, it had been regarded as a great victory for that paper. Soon afterward he had demonstrated his value by obtaining personal permission from Secretary of the Navy Josephus Daniels to accompany the United States warships to Vera Cruz after an edict had been issued barring all Hearst reporters from that expedition. Sent to cover the Niagara Conference between Mexico and the United States, he wrote an accurate report, optimistic in tone, covering the initial proceedings. Buying a Hearst paper the next day, he was surprised to see that not a word of his dispatch was published, but instead a wholly fictitious report hinting that President Wilson was yielding in the most humiliating way to the Mexican demands. Indignantly, Mitchell threatened to resign, but received the following consoling telegram from Bradford Merrill, the Hearst manager in New York: "Be philosophical. . . . No reflection on you. Good soldiers are patient even if superior officers make mistakes. Be resigned without resigning." But the "mistakes" continued; a fantastic message from Carranza was published ten days in advance of the real one. Mitchell resigned. Again

Bradford Merrill telegraphed: "Why resign without cause? We should greatly regret it. Please be good soldier and good boy." But Mitchell remained impervious to this touching appeal.

When the World War broke out in 1914 it found Hearst in a very different mood from that in which he had been at the time of the Spanish-American War. In the first place, he was now fifty-one years old and less inclined for personal adventure. In the second place, and more important, the World War was not his war; he had not originated it, and he could do nothing to guide its development. The war was on too vast a scale to be monopolized by one or two sensational newspapers like the little skirmish in Cuba; with the strict censorship everywhere enforced there was no opportunity for scoops; when sensations were coming thick and fast from every side the market was already flooded; worst of all, the Hearst reporters, discredited in Washington, were at a disadvantage with those of other papers in obtaining official news. In every way, the war was, from Hearst's point of view, an utterly disgusting war. So he became, momentarily, an ardent pacifist.

Early in August 1914 he attempted to organize a mighty peace campaign among the newspapers, to be led with appropriate éclat by his Chicago *Examiner*. His Chicago editor, Andy Lawrence, wrote to the Socialist New York *Call*, seeking to enlist its participation in this campaign. The reply of Chester M. Wright, managing editor of the *Call*, was an epistolary masterpiece:

Dear Sir:

Your invitation to the New York *Call* to join with the Chicago *Examiner* in what you term "a great international peace movement" is highly interesting.

It is not long since the Hearst newspapers were lashing themselves into a frenzy of "patriotism" in an effort to embroil the United States and Mexico in war.

Every person who follows newspapers closely remembers the pro-war attitude of the Hearst newspapers in connection with the California Anti-Alien Land Law.

The Hearst newspapers have left no line of type unset that might drive the United States into war with Mexico and Japan. . . . And now you ask the New York *Call* to assist you in leaguing the Kings abroad and the representatives of Big Business at home in an international peace movement.

Permit me to suggest that you showed far more acumen in the case of the well remembered Chicago newspaper strike than you are showing now.

In that great strike you stood out as one of the most intense antagonists of the working people. As publisher of the Chicago *Examiner* you did your share in breaking up homes and filling the hospitals— you and your colleagues on the Chicago *American* and on the allied Big Business newspapers of Chicago.

. . . It cannot be that you have forgotten the assaults and the murders of those eventful months. There was a war in which you stood for war.

And now you talk of peace. Mr. Lawrence, your plea for peace is too ridiculous. It is too obviously what is known as a "Hearst play" for circulation. It is one of those situations in which you can prattle to your heart's content to the working class, knowing while you do it that you run no risk of injuring any of those interests that Hearst papers never injure.

You will have to omit the New York *Call* from the list of papers you are trying to enlist in this cause. The New York *Call* and the great Socialist movement for which it stands have fought too long for peace not to be able to continue the fight without the aid of unclean hands. . . .

No words, however, could bring any blush of shame to the cheeks of William Randolph Hearst. Almost as if to document Chester Wright's charges, on September 28, 1915, the New York *American* renewed the attack on Japan under the headline, "JAPAN'S PLANS TO INVADE AND CONQUER THE UNITED STATES REVEALED BY ITS OWN BERNHARDI."

There followed what purported to be "a literal translation"

of the first part of a Japanese work entitled *The War Between Japan and America*. The book was published, according to the *American's* account, by "The National Defense Association of Japan, whose membership includes the highest naval officers, army officers, cabinet and government officers of that country, and whose president is Count Okuma, the Premier of Japan." The article went on to state, "It is the most popular book in Japan, and it is now in its sixth edition; more than a million copies have already been sold."

The Japanese Consul-General, who had never heard of this marvelous book, cabled home for information and received the following reply from the Foreign Office: "*The Dream Story of the War Between Japan and the United States* is a trashy work written by a certain newspaper reporter at the time the California land question was hotly discussed. It appeals only to a few jingoists and has received no recognition by the intelligent public. During July 1913 the publisher of the book fabricated the name 'National Military Association' and gave it as the responsible author of the book. Such an organization, of course, has no existence in Japan." Incidentally, since Japanese editions normally ran to only about five hundred, the sale had been around three thousand copies, instead of "more than a million."

The *American* had not been content with trying to palm off an old book on its public under the guise of a new one, or with giving it an incorrect title, or even with ascribing it to mythical authors. Examination showed that the translation itself was badly garbled. For example, the original gave a brief description of California, opening with these sentences:

The beginning of the anti-Japanese question in California, U.S.A., is not of today. Therefore it is necessary to speak of the land and affairs of California. On the south it is bounded by Mexico and on the north it touches Oregon.

This passage was rendered by the Hearst translator as follows:

The Problem of California is so much in the mind of the Japanese at present and also in view of the fact that we intend to colonize it shortly, that we give its description. On the north, California is side by side with another small state—Oregon—and it is bounded on the south by the territory of our great and powerful ally—Mexico, who will help us against the United States when the time comes.

In the original there was no mention of the Panama Canal, so the translator added this sentence out of his own or his employer's mind: "The Americans boast of their Panama Canal, but it is only too ridiculously simple for us to dynamite it effectively—at the cost of an old ship full of powder."

The Hearst papers also reprinted what they called "A highly popular picture in Japan, which purports to be a prophetic view of the Japanese invading army landing at San Francisco." An untranslated date in the corner of the picture revealed that it was made in 1895. It really depicted a landing of Japanese troops in China during the Chinese War.

When President Wilson sent the punitive expedition under General Pershing into northern Mexico to break up Villa's band of outlaws which had made forays across the frontier, the Hearst papers loudly cried that this was not enough:

We have sent a meager army into Mexico to avenge a mighty wrong. . . .

Why should our army confine itself to a restricted zone where it will be neither a menace to Mexicans nor a protection to Americans! Our army should go forward into Mexico first to rescue Americans and, secondly, to redeem Mexicans!

Our flag should wave over Mexico as the symbol of the rehabilitation of that unhappy country and its redemption to humanity and civilization.

Meanwhile, the accuracy of Hearst's general war news was about on a par with that of his translation of *The War Between Japan and America*." To be sure, the Hearst newspapers announced that his International News Service maintained "the greatest newsgathering organization the world has ever seen . . . with representatives in every first-class city in Europe, on every battlefield . . . with more than 80 correspondents, many of them of world-wide fame." Among these famous correspondents were Herbert Temple, European Manager of the International News Service, John C. Foster and Lawrence Elston on the London staff, Franklin Merrick in Paris, Frederick Werner in Berlin, and Brixton D. Allaire in Rome.

The editors of *Harper's Weekly*, being strangely unfamiliar with any of these great names, decided to investigate. A cablegram to Robert P. Skinner, United States Consul-General in London, asking about Temple, Foster, and Elston, brought the reply, "Persons quite unknown to me." Paris was similarly unacquainted with any Franklin Merrick. No Frederick Werner could be discovered in Berlin. The acting president of the Foreign Press Association in Rome reported: "No press correspondent named Brixton D. Allaire belongs to our Foreign Press Association and nobody in Rome, as far as I could ascertain, knows Mr. Allaire." The Hearst press was merely republishing news items from European papers and affixing the name of the appropriate mythical correspondent. If not the greatest newsgathering organization the world had ever seen, Hearst's was certainly the most remarkable, with a non-existent European manager and non-existent correspondents in London, Paris, Berlin, and Rome.

Hearst's treatment of the war news published in his papers was motivated, first, by his personal hatred of Great Britain, and second, by the fact that the bulk of his readers were Irish-Americans and German-Americans. But in the beginning he was very cautious. Thus, on September 9, 1914, the New York *American* published a picture of British troops with descriptive matter under it reading, "This is the type of English soldier who is doing such tremendous work on the battle front in France," although the same picture appeared the same day in

EDITORIAL · SPECIAL ARTICLES
AUTOMOBILES

New York Tribune

EDITORIAL · SPECIAL ARTICLES
AUTOMOBILES

PART III EIGHT PAGES

SUNDAY, MAY 12, 1918

PART III EIGHT PAGES

HEARST'S WORK FOR A FIGHTLESS WAR

By Kenneth Macgowan

Next Week—Sowing Distrust of the Allies

REAPING THE FRUITS OF ANGLOPHOBIA

For weeks in the spring of 1918 the N. Y. *Tribune* ran articles like this in its Sunday editorial section. The Hearst cartoon series "History Reversed" was reproduced, showing President Wilson handing to the British everything we had fought for in the Revolutionary War and the War of 1812. At the same time the daily *Tribune* gave extensive space to news of the mounting anti-Hearst boycott.

Hearst's *Das Morgen Journal* with the description changed to read: "British troops that run so fast that it is not possible for the Germans to capture them."

Gradually, however, he grew bolder. He sent to Germany a living, flesh-and-blood correspondent, William Bayard Hale, who, with or without Hearst's knowledge, had been in the employ of the German embassy, and Hale's excessively pro-German dispatches, sent over the German government's radio station at Sayville, L. I., were heavily featured in the Hearst press. The Hearst papers also devoted increasing space to attacks on the British censorship, to emphasis on British interference with American commerce, and to defense of the Irish insurrectionary movement.

At last Hearst went so far as to give open support to Jeremiah A. O'Leary's American Truth Society, an organization composed almost exclusively of Irish-Americans and German-Americans. O'Leary, taking advantage of a strong anti-Wilson vote in New York and New Jersey, had sent a telegram to the President, accusing him of working in the British interest, citing the recent election returns, and ending with the question, "Well, sir, will you respond to popular disapproval of your policies by action?" To this discourteous demand, Wilson had returned a still more discourteous answer: "Your telegram received. I would feel deeply mortified to have you or anybody like you vote for me. Since you have access to many disloyal Americans and I have not, I will ask you to convey this message to them." The next day, September 29, 1916, the New York *American* commented on this exchange of telegrams as follows:

If these telegrams mean anything, they mean that O'Leary, an American citizen, is opposed to President Wilson's policies of submission to British aggression upon our commerce and British blacklisting of American firms and British seizure of American ships, as well as Mr. Wilson's policy of encouraging huge war loans and huge supplies of munitions to prolong the European conflict—and that

Mr. Wilson regards any American who expresses opposition to these policies of his as a disloyal person, whose vote and support he would be ashamed to have.

It is not known what connection, if any, there was between this incident and the action of the British government on October 11, 1916, in denying the further use of the mails and cables to Hearst's International News Service, but in any case the British government was reasonably sure that the American government would not look upon its action with disfavor. On October 29 the French government followed the lead of the British, and soon afterward the Canadian government debarred all Hearst papers from the Dominion. The effect of all this foreign fury was at first merely to increase the anti-Allies fury of the Hearst press and in particular to sharpen its attacks upon the Allied censorship.

But the tide of American sentiment was now unmistakably turning against Germany, and on February 26, 1917, Hearst, who was wintering at Palm Beach, received a telegram from Caleb R. Van Hamm, managing editor of the New York *American*, suggesting that it was time for him to indulge in a little censorship on his own account:

> Earnestly urge immediate action to check or stop Hale despatches. They come by wireless and are surely picked up. Despite your well-known attitude of neutrality, these despatches are so worded as to permit the inference that Berlin is dictating our policy. I find we are drifting into a situation akin to the false McKinley one, only accentuated manyfold. I urge we check Hale and all agencies that tend to throw discredit upon our declared attitude of sturdy Americanism.

Hearst had previously attempted to meet this danger in a characteristic manner by printing the New York *American* with a red, white, and blue title, and by running the stanzas of the "Star-Spangled Banner" at the top of the editorial page. He now decided to increase these patriotic efforts. On the day of the Van Hamm wire, S. S. Carvalho received a telegram from Hearst which indicates the latter's bewilderment at the course events were taking:

Why not run the red, white and blue title that we had for last edition through all editions for a few days during these troublous times? I think it will meet popular sentiment. Also please run little American flags to right and left of date lines on inside pages, like Chicago *Herald*. Our editorials should be patriotic without slightest criticism of administration. I guess Germany is going to sink every ship that tries to run the submarine blockade and this means three things—first, that we will get into the war; second, that England will be starved into submission in less than six months; third, that Germany will then have time to devote to us, and this country will soon be in a condition similar to warring European countries. We must prepare in every way. Can we say these things editorially?

By the next week, however, he had recovered his courage, sending Carvalho on March third another even more revealing telegram:

If situation quiets down please remove color flags from first page and little flags from inside pages, reserving these for special occasions of a warlike or patriotic kind. I think they have been good for this week, giving us a very American character and probably helping sell papers, but to continue effective they should be reserved for occasions.

On March fourth the publisher sent a further helpful suggestion to the New York *American*:

McCay could make strong eight-column cartoon, occupying in depth two-thirds editorial page, showing smaller figures Uncle Sam and Germany shaking their fists at each other on left side page and on right side big head and shoulders of Japan, with knife in hand, leaning over into picture and evidently watching chance to strike Uncle Sam in back. Title of picture to be "Watchful Waiting." "Look out, Uncle Sam, your neighbor, Japan, is eagerly waiting an opportunity to strike you in the back."

After war was actually declared, Hearst surrendered, but his surrender was by no means unconditional. He adopted the interesting policy of feeding the flames and at the same time trying to extinguish them, pouring oil from one hand and water from the other. Thus his papers featured Red Cross and Liberty Loan drives and enthusiastically joined in the effort to recruit as many troops as possible, but they also continued to prophesy defeat for the Allies and they urged that the United States get out of the war as quickly as it could. In July, 1917, they ran headlines such as this: "STRIPPING OUR COUNTRY OF MEN, MONEY, AND FOOD IS A DANGEROUS POLICY," and editorials like the following: "If the Allies should succumb to the submarine warfare inside of three months—as they certainly may—they are beyond any effective help of ours, and we are simply wasting sorely needed men and supplies by sending them abroad. . . ." But the popular response to this effort was so unfavorable that a counterstroke was attempted—of such brilliance that full justice can be done to it only by quoting the New York *American's* account.

On August 29, 1917, a news story from Paris, headed "HEARST GIFT PRESENTED TO JOFFRE," continued in this wise:

Appropriate military ceremonies marked the presentation of a handsome gift from William Randolph Hearst and the Hearst publications to Marshal Joffre today. The gift was a handsome bound volume of clippings from American publications of news matter and other references to Marshal Joffre and the visit of the French mission to the United States. It is valued at several thousand dollars. . . .

The ceremony was held in the Place Ecole de Guerre. It was of a purely military character. General Pershing and staff arrived early, accompanied by John H. Duval, foreign representative for *Harper's Bazar*, a Hearst publication, who represented the donors.

When the Pershing party arrived, they found Marshal Joffre waiting. There were warm greetings, after which General Pershing explained the object of the visit. He told Marshal Joffre there was

HEARST IN WAR-TIME

One of a series of New York *Tribune* cartoons, attacking Hearst as
unpatriotic, which ran in the fall of 1918.

no figure nearer the American heart than Joffre, who at the historic Battle of the Marne stemmed the tide of the German invasion, thus saving France and the civilization of the whole world.

General Pershing then introduced Mr. Duval, who said William Randolph Hearst and his associates were glad it was in their power to give some token of the great love and esteem in which America and Americans hold the French people and Marshal Joffre. He said the clippings would serve to show the universal delight of the American people in the visit of Marshal Joffre to the United States, which had cemented the alliance of the American people with the democracy of the old world. He called attention to the obligations of the United States to France, which had twice sided with the great American Republic in the hour of need.

Marshal Joffre responded, saying he would value the souvenir, which would always call to his mind the pleasant hours spent in America. He feelingly recalled the wonderful receptions tendered the French Commission in every city it visited. Then, turning to Mr. Duval, he asked him to convey his thanks to Mr. Hearst.

"I do not read English," he said, "but my wife does, and she will translate the contents of this beautiful book to me."

If the volume contained a complete file of clippings from the Hearst newspapers during the period, the Marshal and Madame Joffre must have experienced somewhat mixed emotions during the reading!

Hearst's tortuous and ambiguous policies during the World War bore evidence at every turn of their ignoble origin. Although in many instances he supported what today is recognized to have been the wise and liberal attitude—as in his opposition to the war loans, munition shipments, espionage bills, the unseating of the New York Socialist assemblymen, etc.—his course was always guided much more by personal than by public considerations. As so often before, he supported the right cause from the wrong motives, and in the long run the evil motives vitiated his endeavors and rendered his assistance harmful rather than helpful to the cause he represented. Back of his hostility to American entrance into the war there apparently lay nothing more recondite than the persistent animosity against Great Britain originally engendered by the snubs he had received from British high society and the persistent desire for circulation which led him to emphasize the appeals to his special German-American and Irish-American constituency. If there were any nobler motives at work in the recesses of Hearst's mind, they were hopelessly confused with these habitual ones.

In spite of his caution, Hearst soon found himself for the second time an object of national obloquy. During the spring of 1918 the New York *Tribune*, which, to be sure, was hardly an unbiased witness, ran a series entitled "Coiled in the Flag, HEARS-S-S-T," in which it declared:

Since the United States entered the war the Hearst papers have printed: 74 attacks on our allies, 17 instances of defense or praise of Germany, 63 pieces of anti-war propaganda, 1 deletion of a Presidential proclamation—total 155—or an average of nearly three a week, while America has been engaged in the life and death struggle with civilization's enemy.

Large sections of the American public had not waited for the *Tribune* to make these discoveries. During the latter part of 1917 and the spring of 1918 anti-Hearst demonstrations took place all over the country. Hearst was denounced as pro-German, he was accused of trying to defeat the Allies, he was charged with being a traitor to his country, he was hanged and burned in effigy. Among other places, these sadistic celebrations were held at Elmira, Jamestown, Port Jervis, and Plattsburg in New York; at Elizabeth, Englewood, Jersey City, Cranford, Rumson, Sterling, and Rutherford in New Jersey; at Macon in Georgia; at Santa Fe and Albuquerque in New Mexico; at Redlands, Santa Monica, Pasadena, and Long Beach in California. Hearst's papers were banned in many cities and were publicly burned in others. He was barred from the Boston Club;

AS A SEDITIOUS ALIEN
Another of the *Tribune's* series, showing Hearst wearing a German
infantryman's cap and carrying propaganda bombs.

he was referred to in many western papers as "Herr Wurst"; a delegation of angry women in New Mexico demanded that he be interned.

The outcry became so great that the Judiciary Committee of the Senate, appointed to investigate pro-German propaganda, was obliged to devote considerable attention to the Hearst press. But it would have been decidedly awkward for this committee to condemn as pro-German the recipient of the public thanks of Marshal Joffre. Hearst himself was not called before it, and no action was taken against his publications.

It is reasonable to believe, however, that from all the turmoil Hearst drew a lesson supplementing that which he had learned in 1901. He saw how easy it was to bring the charge of "disloyalty" even against men who were acting with the most patriotic intentions. This lesson, too, was stored away in his memory for future reference.

CHAPTER XIII

Patron of Hollywood

TO BE an object of national detestation at the age of fifty-five is not a pleasant experience, particularly when one has earned it not through any defense of principles or personal integrity but through mere maladroitness in compromise. Hearst's extreme unpopularity at the close of the war might well have had disastrous mental consequences for the publisher but for his good fortune in finding a new interest just at this time to divert his thoughts from public questions. His intimate friendship with Miss Marion Davies and the absorption in the movies that followed were undoubtedly most beneficial in restoring that fiction of superiority which was absolutely essential to his being. His successful flouting of public opinion by the openness of his relations with the beautiful actress enabled him to feel that he was an exception to the ordinary rules made for lesser men—a special privilege which he jealously guarded by continuing to maintain the strict moral standard of his papers on the general question of sex irregularity and by continuing to attack any inclinations toward "free love" wherever that hideous monster showed its head.

He had been dabbling—more than dabbling—in moving pictures for some time. In March 1913 Edgar B. Hatrick, director of the photograph department of the Hearst press, suggested to "the Chief"—as Hearst likes to be called both by his subordinates and friends—that it would be a good idea to take moving pictures of the presidential inauguration of Woodrow Wilson. The pictures were taken and were exhibited with huge success to a Broadway audience on the evening of March 5, 1913.

From this came the notion of a regular news-reel to compete with the *Pathé Weekly*, and in February 1914 the *Hearst-Selig Weekly* entered the field. It was found more profitable to make a joint arrangement with the Pathé News Reel Company, in which it was stipulated that Hearst's name should appear on the title of each weekly news film. The working agreement was cancelled by Pathé in October 1918 because of Hearst's attitude on the war. His own news reel was continued separately and after various changes of name became the *Hearst Metrotone News*.

Hearst also experimented after 1913 in the making of regular moving pictures, producing several serials in connection with Pathé. He established an elaborate studio and sank a great deal of money in the enterprise with small result. One reason for his failure was that under the influence of the Belasco school of stage technique he insisted that all the "props" be real—perhaps an over-compensation for the fakery of his newspapers; another reason may have been that he also insisted upon personally directing his plays. As usual, he was not discouraged by financial losses which he could well afford; he felt that he needed only a suitable star to make the venture a success. In 1918 he found her, or thought he found her, in Marion Davies.

Miss Douras, Brooklyn born, and the daughter of a minor local politician, changed her name to Marion Davies when she got a job as a dancer with the *Chu Chin Chow* company in 1916. There seems to be a slight discrepancy as to the date of her birth, which is given both as 1897 and 1900. January 3, 1900, is the date now in general use. She was educated at the Convent of the Sacred Heart at Hastings, N. Y., but left it for the stage at the earliest opportunity. From *Chu Chin Chow* to the Ziegfeld *Follies* was the next step in her rise to fame. It was while she was performing for the great Ziegfeld that Hearst first made her acquaintance. Her brother-in-law, George W. Lederer, is credited with having brought about the first meeting of the two, hoping that Hearst might give her a chance in the movies. Hearst not only gave her a chance but made her the chief and soon the sole star of his producing company. Not only is she the only star of Hearst's Cosmopolitan Corporation, she is also its president with a salary of $104,000 a year.

Miss Davies appeared in two films during 1918: *Runaway Romany* and *Cecilia of the Pink Roses*. Simultaneously, the motion-picture editors of the Hearst papers in New York, Chicago, San Francisco, and Los Angeles "discovered" her. She was hailed as the "find" of the year. She was photographed and interviewed almost endlessly. *Burden of Proof*, *Belle of New York*, *Getting Mary Married*, and *The Dark Star* were the vehicles for Miss Davies's talents in 1919, *The Cinema Murder* and *April Folly* in 1920, *Buried Treasure* and *The Restless Sex* in 1921. In every instance the Hearst press gushed forth enormous praise, but other papers were not overly enthusiastic, nor was the audience response any too gratifying. Miss Davies's most successful years were 1922 and 1923: during the former she starred in *Beauty's Worth*, *The Bride's Play*, *Enchantment*, *The Young Diana*, and *When Knighthood Was in Flower;* during the latter in *Adam and Eve* and *Little Old New York*, the one unquestionably big hit of her career.

By this time Hearst had moved his studio to Hollywood and established close contacts with the moving picture colony. Miss Louella O. Parsons (wife of Dr. Harry Martin) now appeared as movie-writer-in-chief for the Hearst press. Her daily column of chatter was run in most of the Hearst papers and read by millions of people, although her *faux pas* equaled those of Mayor Hylan. On one occasion she told her readers that a Mr. John Dos Passos, "who is, I believe, a New York author," would soon be in Hollywood. When the RKO studios announced that they were about to film *Green Mansions*, Miss Parsons informed her public that the author, W. H. Hudson (dead these many years) was being brought out to help in preparing the screen version. Hollywood insists that she expects William Shakespeare to drop in at her office any day, but possibly this is an exaggeration. Nevertheless, by virtue of her position in the Hearst machine, she was soon able to become a veritable autocrat over the movie colony. When she previewed a film it had to be run off for her alone so that her concentration of mind might not be interfered with by any interlopers. From time to time she turned out "scenarios" which of course were accepted regardless of merit until every major company came to have a "Parsons shelf" of unproduceable scenarios whose purchase was checked off under such headings as "good will" or "advertising." As mistress of ceremonies on the "Hollywood Hotel" hour sponsored by the Campbell Soup Company, she forced even important stars to heed her beck and call as guest performers. No one in the movie colony dared to give a large party without sending special invitations to Dr. and Mrs. Harry Martin. The screen actors learned that it paid to have Dr. Martin as their physician even though his fees were extraordinarily high. Thanks to the Hearst tie-up Dr. Martin also became chairman of the State Boxing Commission, noted for its slovenliness and inefficiency.

The Martin-Parsons dictatorship was naturally pleasant to Hearst, since at any time he could break it with his little finger, and so was himself an autocrat of autocrats. Life in Hollywood, too, was pleasant, and the publisher delighted to entertain his sycophantic admirers.

At one such party, arrangements were made to have a special edition of the Los Angeles *Examiner* printed and distributed to the guests. The whole front page was done over for the occasion, with all kinds of unique stories about the various celebrities at the party. And the heading, "A Paper for People Who Think," which appears directly under the title, was changed to read, "A Paper for People Who Drink." Unfortunately, the press room failed to reset the original head in time, and several thousand issues of the next morning's *Examiner* were printed and distributed before the error was discovered.

A much more serious contretemps which has never been explained to the satisfaction of every one occurred in the fall of 1924.

Thomas H. Ince, noted motion picture director, died under somewhat mysterious circumstances, on November 19, 1924. The first news stories appeared in the Los Angeles *Times,* the New York *Times,* and other papers on the twentieth, and were very vague. They described his death as having been "due to heart disease, superinduced by an attack of indigestion." According to these reports, he had been on "a yachting party." He had gone to San Diego on Sunday evening of the previous week with Dr. Daniel Carson Goodman, head of the Cosmopolitan productions, was taken ill on board "the yacht," was removed to shore, was attended by a doctor and two nurses, was rushed home and died a few hours thereafter. The next day's papers announced that the yacht was the *Oneida* (Hearst's private yacht) owned by the International Films Corporation (Hearst's corporation). "The party aboard the yacht, it was said, was given by William Randolph Hearst. Among other guests were Marion Davies and Seena Owen, film actresses, Elinor Glyn, noted British authoress, and Dr. Daniel Carson Goodman." Still others in the fatal party were Charlie Chaplin and Theodor Kosloff. The story of Ince's illness was now more detailed: it told how he suffered an attack of acute indigestion on Monday morning and after attempts to give him relief on the yacht were unsuccessful, was taken off at San Diego and put on a train for Los Angeles, but because of the seriousness of his condition was removed from the train at Del Mar to the Stratford Hotel, whence he was again removed on Tuesday night to his home in Benedict Canyon, where death occurred some hours later. The death certificate was signed by Dr. Ida Cowan Glasgow.

Ince's body was shown to friends and relatives for one hour, from nine to ten A.M., on November 21, at the Hollywood cemetery chapel. The services were strictly private, there being no pall-bearers. Strothers and Dayton were the funeral directors in charge, and John Garrigues, a theosophist of South Pasadena, delivered the funeral address. Immediately following the funeral, the body of Ince was cremated. Among those at the last rites, beside members of the family, were Douglas Fairbanks, Mary Pickford, Marion Davies, Charlie Chaplin, and Harold Lloyd. Hearst was not present at the funeral, it being his usual custom to avoid such gatherings, nor was it mentioned in the papers that he sent any floral offerings, despite the fact that he had been intimate with Ince and that the two were supposed to be engaged in a common enterprise that would tie their film fortunes together.

Rumors and counter-rumors spread thick and fast through the movie colony and the cities of Los Angeles and San Diego. But no word of this got into the public press until December 11, when the Los Angeles *Times* carried a front-page story stating that "District Attorney Chester C. Kempley [San Diego], who has been conducting an inquiry into certain phases of the death of Thomas H. Ince, motion picture magnate, announced today that he has completed his investigations and that he has uncovered nothing to justify him in proceeding further with the matter." Said the District Attorney: "I began this investigation because of the many rumors brought to my office regarding the case and have continued it until today in order to definitely dispose of them. I am satisfied that the death of Mr. Ince was caused by heart failure as a result of acute indigestion. There will be no further investigation, at least so far as San Diego is concerned. If there is any investigation of the stories of liquor drinking on board the yacht where Mr. Ince was a guest, it will have to be in Los Angeles, where, presumably, the liquor was secured." (This was, of course, during the days of prohibition.)

Along with this, there appeared a statement over the signature of Dr. Daniel Carson Goodman, who listed himself as general manager of the International Film Service Company, Inc., to the effect that he had gone with Ince to the yacht, that there had been no drinking on board, and that, as a qualified physician, he was able to declare that Ince had died of acute indigestion.

The above does not coincide with the story run in the New York *Times* of December 11 and 12, declaring that the doctor and nurses testified that Ince had been under the influence of liquor and that he admitted having drunk a great deal of bad liquor on the yacht. ("Bad liquor" does not sound like Hearst; but in 1924, under the beneficent tyranny of the prohibitionists, it was sometimes difficult even for millionaires to obtain liquor that was not poisonous.)

The scandal was not entirely hushed by the testimony of the District Attorney and Dr. Goodman.

In the fall of 1926, the Chicago *Tribune* carried a story quoting District Attorney Robert E. Crowe of that city to the effect that he thought the Hearst papers should stop shouting "Who Killed McSwiggin?" (That unfortunate Irishman, killed a few weeks before in Cicero, Illinois, while in the company of several known gangsters, had been an assistant in the district attorney's office, and the Hearst papers were featuring the affair every day.) Crowe declared that the police were doing the best they could to find the murderers of McSwiggin, and that unless the Hearst press let up on its campaign he would have to raise the question, "Who Killed Thomas H. Ince?" Immediately after Crowe's challenge the Hearst papers dropped the case of the McSwiggin murder.

This is all the published "evidence." Anyone visiting Hollywood can hear half a dozen conflicting stories, all allegedly based on the secret statements of one or another of the guests on the yacht and may, if he has nothing better to do, spend the rest of his life in sifting them. So far as the general public is concerned, the Ince case is likely to remain a mystery. It aroused so much curiosity and comment that it seemed necessary to include it in a complete story of Hearst's life, but the authors have no desire to draw any unfavorable inferences. The only safe conclusion is that the Ince affair, whatever its true nature, must have been profoundly unpleasant to Hearst.

It had no effect, however, upon his moving picture enterprises other than to substitute for the projected alliance with Ince an actual alliance with Metro-Goldwyn-Mayer. A modest bungalow studio, said to have cost $75,000, was erected for Miss Davies at Culver City—her house in Santa Monica is somewhat larger than the historic Vanderbilt residence on Fifth Avenue, New York—and she worked there happily for ten years. Then, to anticipate chronologically, the Cosmopolitan Productions were suddenly shifted to the Warner Brothers–First National lot in Burbank. The cause of the break, according to Hollywood gossip, was that Miss Davies had wanted to appear in *The Barretts of Wimpole Street* and had been talked out of it by the M.-G.-M. officials on the ground that the play would not be a screen success, after which the lead was given to Norma Shearer, wife of Irving Thalberg, M.-G.-M. producer, and the play was almost as much of a success on the screen as it had been on the stage.

But one might go on endlessly with the small-town Hollywood gossip about Hearst and Miss Davies. The wonder is that the publisher himself was able to stand the atmosphere of the place for so many years. To be the Czar of Hollywood—and he was not quite that—would have been a tame ending for his loftier ambitions. But these were not dead; they re-emerged repeatedly during the twenties, to come forth most powerfully of all in the early thirties. It is high time for us to turn back to Hearst's unending, apparently unendable, political career.

CHAPTER XIV

Outdemagogued Demagogue

ALTHOUGH Hearst had not been nominated for public office since 1910, through his papers he had continued to exercise a very considerable political influence in New York City and Chicago. Andrew M. Lawrence, who was in charge of the Chicago section of Hearst's newspaper domain, is described by Winkler as "a posturing, pompous man, somewhat resembling Mussolini facially and in physique"; nevertheless, like Mussolini, he had ability of a hard-driving kind, and he established an alliance with Mayor Carter Harrison such that the Hearst-Harrison machine functioned efficiently for a number of years. But in New York, where the temperamental Hearst himself was at the helm, the political policies of his organization veered with every breeze, just as they had done from the beginning.

In 1913 he supported the Fusion candidate, John Purroy Mitchel, on a reform platform against Tammany, but then as usual he broke with his own candidate after the latter had been successfully elected. In 1914 there was a movement to secure his nomination as the Democratic candidate for United States senator, but nothing came of it. On August 25, 1914, the New York *Times* carried a news item headed: "HEARST SENATORIAL BOOM COLLAPSES"; the item read:

On the eve of the Democratic conference, opinion here [at Saratoga] is that William Randolph Hearst has been eliminated as a possible nominee for United States Senator in the primaries. The Hearst boom received its death blow at a meeting of a sub-committee on platform this evening when it was decided that the very first plank in the State platform should be one indorsing the policies of the Wilson Administration.

The next day Hearst came out with a statement that he had no desire to be a candidate unless the public interest demanded it, but that he himself also intended to give the President his full support. "I am not in accord with many of the national administration's policies," he said, "but I believe that in time of stress it is a citizen's duty to sustain the government of the nation." Even this patriotic statement did not convince the majority of the Democratic conference that the public interest imperatively demanded his election.

Nor did his support of the President preclude his bending every effort to defeat Roger C. Sullivan, the Wilson candidate for Senator in Illinois, or his later giving enthusiastic aid to "Big Bill" Thompson of Chicago in the latter's violent anti-British campaign.

By 1917 Hearst's influence among the Irish and German groups in New York City had become so great that he received a heavy preferential vote in the Democratic primaries for mayor. But he no longer had the heart for the kind of fight that was necessary to win a popular election. The senatorship was one thing; it could be given him in a gentlemanly manner relatively behind the scenes by the party leaders; but the mayoralty was a different proposition, as he had twice found to his cost. So when the Tammany leaders approached him, he contented himself with naming the candidate, one John F. Hylan, an obscure sub-sub-boss who would be certain to take the orders of the man who put him in. The position of king-maker had many advantages over that of king, as Hearst had come to see.

During the Hylan–Mitchel campaign, Hearst expressed himself as follows about the man whom he had supported in 1913. "I have no personal hostility to Mayor Mitchel. He is an amiable young man, but without character or principles. He has a silly ambition for social recognition and a weak willingness to place himself entirely in the hands of selfish and sinister interests and allow himself and his great public office to be used for the private advantage of these selfish interests and against the public welfare." There was beginning to be a note of sameness in Hearst's political attacks.

As the campaign progressed, a third mayoralty candidate developed surprising political strength. This was the Socialist leader, Morris Hillquit. Arthur Brisbane, perhaps haunted Hamlet-like by the ghost of his dead father, conceived a way of paying honor to principle and at the same time aiding Tammany. He sent the following telegram to his employer, who was at the moment in Los Angeles:

> There is actual possibility of Hillquit's election. . . . Conditions ought to disturb corporations working for Mitchel. They will sweat and pay taxes on their personal property if Hillquit is elected. Shall I write editorial warning corporations that their effort to get everything from Mitchel may cost them dear through Hillquit's victory? If they understood situation and danger they would drop Mitchel and vote for Hylan. Editorial would describe Hillquit's ability and sincerity. Remarkably able lawyer. Rosenwald . . . says . . . one of ablest men in country. Can write editorial in such way as to transfer many votes from Mitchel. . . . Please reply.

Hearst's answer, wired not to Brisbane but to Carvalho, was short, sharp, and decisive:

> Brisbane wants to write editorial praising Hillquit. Brisbane thinks Hillquit may be elected. Of course Hillquit will not be elected although government's policy will make Socialists very strong. Editorial of kind Brisbane suggests would be construed as disloyalty to Hylan and upset all our plans. Please prevent it.

Hylan was elected, and then a remarkable thing happened: Hearst did not break with him. On the contrary, during his first term of office, the mayor visited the publisher; in Florida, the two lounged around the beach together and ended by becoming friends for life. Hylan was a slow-witted product of the Catskill Mountains who had come to New York as a daylaborer, then had risen to be a motorman on the Brooklyn elevated, and eventually, after painfully mastering enough law to be admitted to the Bar, had found what seemed like a permanent place as a minor henchman of the Tammany machine until Hearst chose to pick him up and make him great. During his eight years of office, the incredible *faux pas* of the mayor and his wife afforded endless merriment to the wags of the metropolis. He was solemnly pompous and ineffably dull. But he was just the man that Hearst, still smarting from the criticism heaped upon him during the war, now needed to have at hand to restore his sense of superiority. Too stupid even to be dishonest or to detect dishonesty in his friends, Hylan reverentially learned Brisbane's editorials by heart to repeat in his speeches and in all things obediently followed Hearst's directions.

But the other Tammany politician whom Hearst had helped to a prominent metropolitan office was a horse of a very different color. Al Smith was no lumbering mountaineer, but a sharp-eyed son of the East Side who had grown up in the atmosphere of "Big Tom" Foley's saloon at Center and Franklin Streets. He, too, was personally honest, but in his case honesty was complicated by intelligence; he was no man's fool. Sent to the Assembly by Foley in 1903, he held his place in the legislature for twelve consecutive terms, during which he mastered not only every trick of local politics but every detail of state government and finance. Murphy brought him back from Albany to New York in 1915 to run for sheriff, and Al Smith's breezy manner, East Side pronunciation, and slangy repartee had as much to do with his election as had the support which he received from Tammany. In the campaign of 1917, to quote J. K. Winkler, "Al Smith raged through the platforms like a gale, laughing, joking, arguing, with elemental force; and it was generally agreed that Smith's wit, satire, and sound common sense contributed largely to the overwhelming victory of the Hearst-Tammany candidates."

Nominated for governor in 1918, Smith realized that he still needed Hearst's support, and sought an audience which the publisher was graciously pleased to accord. But Hearst was already uneasily conscious that his own eggs were imperiled by the cowbird he had helped to hatch. He exacted a promise to endorse the policy of public ownership which the publisher had now for years held over the heads of his candidates like a kind of Damocles' sword; he knew well that public ownership was something the candidate could not achieve but that the failure to achieve it would always afford a convenient ground for attacking him later if that proved desirable. And Smith for his part believed that once in the governor's chair he could dispense with this millionaire patron whose languid yet arrogant manner offended every instinct of his East Side soul. So the temporary entente was formed, with reservations on each side, and Smith was elected by the narrow majority of 15,000 votes over his Republican opponent, Charles S. Whitman.

The storm broke the next year, and it was Hearst who forced the issue. With Bryan completely discredited by his war-time pacifism, and with Wilson's star declining, his old longing for the presidency reawakened in the publisher's breast. Too late, he realized that Al Smith as governor of New York stood squarely across his path. It was necessary to do away with him, and quickly. A heaven-sent opportunity seemed to be afforded during the summer of 1919 by a milk famine in New York City caused by a sudden increase of prices decreed by a combination of the large milk-distributing companies. Hearst demanded that the governor do something about it. The governor replied that he had no constitutional power to fix prices. The war was on.

The Hearst papers declared that Smith was a tool of the

Milk Trust barons; cartoons showed them greeting him with a wink and the remark, "You Know Me, Al"; finally a whole series was devoted to representing pitiful groups of tenement-house children pleading with the stony-hearted governor for a drop of milk before they died.

Smith didn't mind the accusation of being linked with the Milk Trust; that was the sort of charge with which Tammany politicians were familiar; but he objected ,to being represented as an assassin of babies; he, the kind-hearted Al Smith, who, as everybody knew, positively loved babies. He challenged Hearst to debate with him in Carnegie Hall, each party to be privileged to ask the other any questions concerning either his public or his private life.

Even aside from this provision Hearst dared not accept the challenge. Though far from ineffective as a public speaker, he knew that he was not to be compared with Al Smith as a rabble-rouser. His own efforts in that line had been most successful when recorded, with Brisbane's assistance, on the printed page, not orally. He knew, too, that his long masquerade as a friend of the people would be over if he ventured to expose his cold, aristocratic manner to contrast with the warm heartiness of this genuine man of the people who spoke their language naturally and was skilled, as Hearst had never been, in finding the way to their more generous emotions. Hearst's pet trick of distracting attention from issues to personalities had now been turned against him. In declining the challenge, he tried to cover his retreat by asserting that Smith must answer for his conduct in the milk scandal "to the people," not to him.

But Smith was not satisfied with thus winning by default. He went alone to Carnegie Hall on the appointed night of October 29, 1919, and unburdened his soul on the subject of William Randolph Hearst. In his accustomed manner, he struck directly at that weakness of his opponent which was most undeniable: in this case, Hearst's long record of vituperation.

In the last analysis [he said] there is nothing very remarkable about the assault upon me. Follow back the history of this man's newspapers since he came to this part of the country and you will have to read out of his newspapers this remarkable fact: That in this great democracy, in this land of the free and in this home of the brave, there has never been a man elected to office yet that has not been tainted in some way. Is that right or is it wrong? That is not a severe statement to make because it is the truth.

If the Hearst newspapers were the textbook for the children of our schools, they would have to spell out of its every line that no man can be trusted in this country after he is put into public office; that no man thinks enough about it; no man has enough of regard for it; no man has enough of real Christian charity to do the thing right; no man that ever held great public office had enough of respect and regard for his mother and his wife and his children and his friends to be right in office. About that there can be no question, because no man in this state, from Grover Cleveland right down to today, has ever escaped this fellow. We all know that. The children on the street know it.

All those in the audience who liked to dream of how they themselves would behave if in public office, all those who were conscious of their own regard for mothers, wives, children, or friends—in other words virtually all those in the audience—responded to Smith's speech. The governor was victorious, the publisher was defeated, and the starving children in the tenements were quite forgotten. Smith's speech was printed and reprinted all the way across the continent, and he began to be definitely named as a presidential possibility.

Seeing that his attempt to demolish Smith had miscarried so badly, Hearst decided to cease attacking him. There were other roads to the presidency besides the governorship of New York. One of them was a senatorship. It would be pleasant after all these years to tread in the safe footsteps of George Hearst once more. There would be a senatorship in New York vacant in 1922. If he could secure Boss Murphy's support, that senatorship would be his. With Hylan's assistance, the oft-cemented, oft-broken alliance with Murphy was again established.

And then in the Syracuse convention of 1922 Hearst's new ship of state was barely launched when it foundered on a rock. The rock was Al Smith, who still, after three years, was unappeased for Hearst's aspersion of his good name in the baby episode. When Murphy announced his choices, "Smith for governor, Hearst for senator," Smith incontinently refused to run on the same ticket with the publisher. For three days Smith was besieged in his hotel, to which he was confined with a lame foot, by deputation after deputation from Murphy, but he remained immovable. Convinced of the necessity to sacrifice either Smith or Hearst, Murphy did not hesitate. He telegraphed to Hylan: "I can't budge Al. The delegates want him and they don't want Hearst. Sorry. I did my best." Back came a telegram from the publisher: "Please be sure not to allow my name to go before the convention. I certainly would not go on any ticket which, being reactionary, would stultify my record and declarations of principle. . . ."

Hearst was now nearly sixty, and he seemed to have fewer political friends than he had had twenty years before. He was almost ready to give up. Wearily, after Smith's nomination, the publisher supported the ticket. He could at least show the candidate and the world that he had been most unjustly accused in Carnegie Hall. "Our campaign for genuine Democratic principles and policies," he announced, "must be conducted without personal prejudice. We may entertain regrets that progressive ideals did not have what we consider fullest expression, but we should harbor no resentment."

In spite of his genuine Democratic principles and policies Hearst supported Harding as an exponent of progressive ideals against Wilson's Cox. He hated the League of Nations because to his mind it represented a union of the two most detestable things on earth, Woodrow Wilson and Great Britain. And he kept on his payroll William B. Shearer, the big-navy lobbyist who did such valiant work in wrecking disarmament conferences.

After Harding's election, Hearst was once more frequently invited to the White House. He and Harding had several tastes in common and thoroughly understood each other. Harding might have visited San Simeon on his western trip, as did Coolidge later, but for the fact that he died before he got there.

But as yet Hearst was not quite ready to put all his fortunes in the Republican boat which he could not hope to captain. He preferred to lean upon good old John Hylan. And he still had his memories of what now seemed in retrospect those golden days when he himself had been the head of the great Independent Party. With Hylan's assistance and that of "Big Bill" Thompson, mayor of Chicago, whom Hearst had supported for years, there being between them the common bond of Anglophobia, might not a third party be launched successfully? So Hylan was sent out to Chicago to confer with Thompson and to make a speech redolent of Hearst and Brisbane. The central idea advanced was that of forming a "cities bloc," headed by New York and Chicago, to operate if possible within both the Democratic and Republican parties, or, if they proved incorrigible, then to take the lead in organizing a third party to fight the "corporations and international bankers."

The program had one disadvantage; if New York City were to play the rôle of reformer on a national scale, it would be necessary for it first to clean up the muck-heaps in its own back yard. Valiantly, for the last time, Hearst attempted to eliminate Boss Murphy. In the elections of 1923 the Hearst papers savagely attacked Tammany's judiciary ticket, with the result, alas, that Tammany won one of the most decisive victories in its whole history. Joyously, Murphy announced that Hearst was "politically dead," and that henceforward "the lying filthy newspapers under the Hearst management" would be excluded from his home, it no longer being necessary to read them even for the purpose of refuting them.

Murphy died in 1924, precluding the possibility of any further alliances or wars with him. But "Big Tom" Foley, Al Smith's friend, still lived, and at about this time a pleasant opportunity occurred to show up Foley, who had never been a friend of Hearst, in his true colors.

The situation developed in the following way. Edward Markle Fuller and William Frank McGee, owners of E. M. Fuller & Company's bucket shop, failed on the Consolidated Exchange for more than four million dollars. It was shown that they had grossly misused their clients' money, and they were tried three times for grand larceny but on each occasion obtained a hung jury. Nosing around to discover the source of their obvious political protection, a Hearst reporter named Nat J. Ferber unearthed a check from Fuller & McGee to Foley for ten thousand dollars.

Also involved in these transactions was Fuller & McGee's attorney, William J. Fallon, a New York lawyer notorious for his success in saving shady business concerns from the legal consequences of their crimes. Victor Watson of the New York *American* got in touch with "Ernie" Eidlitz, a Fallon employee discharged for forgery, who asserted that his chief had bribed a juror named Charles W. Rendigs. Fuller and McGee, on their fourth trial, broke down and confessed. Charles W. Rendigs also confessed. The three received appropriate sentences, and an indictment for bribery was brought in against Fallon. Then the latter jumped his bail and disappeared.

The course of events had unfortunately shifted the limelight from Foley to Fallon, and the Hearst papers had to follow where the limelight led. They featured a full description of the fugitive and raised a great hue and cry over his escape from justice. Eventually, the police, by following Fallon's mistress, an actress named Gertrude Vanderbilt, discovered the refugee right in New York City. The Hearst papers happily announced in headlines, "SLIPPERY BILL FALLON CAPTURED." But in the upshot, the publisher had less reason to be satisfied.

On his trial, the lawyer claimed that he was the victim of a Hearst conspiracy. Speaking of himself affectedly in the third person as he always did, he said, "The *American* deliberately started out to destroy Fallon, and if I were like Watson I would prove it to you in one session." Eidlitz, he insisted, had been terrorized by the *American* but had later revealed to him the whole base plot.

Eidlitz said to me that he told Watson he was fearful he would be arrested, and that he knew I had the birth certificates of the children of a moving-picture actress, and that I knew Mr. Hearst had sent a woman, who pretended to be a countess, to get evidence against his wife. He said he had told Watson that I intended to use that information to blackmail Mr. Hearst. Eidlitz said he told Mr. Watson that I had the number of the car and the name of the man who went to Mexico with the same party, the same moving-picture actress. He said a few days later Hearst communicated with Watson, and said to Watson: "Fallon must be destroyed." . . . I have here in court the actual birth certificates of the illegitimate children of a certain motion-picture actress.

Fallon did not produce the certificates; neither his word nor that of Eidlitz nor indeed that of anyone connected with the slimy case was worthy of particular credence; and in any event, whether his statements were true or false, what had the private life of Hearst to do with Fallon's bribery of Rendigs? But the pure-minded jury reacted as pure-minded juries are wont to do and returned a verdict of acquittal. Thus the curious legal situation was created that Rendigs served his sentence for having been bribed by Fallon while Fallon went free because he had not bribed Rendigs. It was essentially similar to the legal fiasco of the Fall-Sinclair Teapot Dome trials. But at any rate, puritanic gossip-mongers could lick their greasy chops anew at the expense of Hearst.

The revival of the Ku-Klux Klan during 1923–5 presented a difficult problem to Hearst because of its entanglement of personal and political considerations. On the one hand, his strong Catholic constituency—he had received the official blessing of every Pope down to Pius XI—made open support of the Klan out of the question; on the other hand, large numbers of his German-American readers were enrolled in the organization, and its attacks were leveled especially at Hearst's greatest enemy, Al Smith. In this dilemma, the publisher and his creature Hylan attempted to straddle the issue by indulging in a little mild censure of the Klan and letting it go at that. During Smith's attempt to capture the Democratic nomination for the presidency in 1924, they simply kept their hands off.

The next year Governor Smith decided that the time had come to punish Hearst and Hylan. He promoted the cause of a new candidate for the mayoralty of New York City, dapper Jimmy Walker, clothed like a fashion plate, expert in wisecracks, pleasantly expansive in the use of other people's money. The dashing Jimmy represented what the average New York petty-bourgeois would like to be; dull, frugal John Hylan represented what this petty-bourgeois had been in the past and wanted to forget. Hurried s o s calls on behalf of the sinking Hylan were sent óut to San Simeon.

Hearst came to his favorite's assistance with a personal letter to the New York *American* on August 29, 1925, in which he praised Hylan for his two genuine accomplishments, establishment of a municipal subway and maintenance of the five-cent fare—though in Mayor Thompson's Chicago Hearst had not objected to the eight-cent fare—and then went on to call Smith a liar for saying that Hylan was a Ku-Kluxer. Smith's answer was published on September 3, 1925:

William Randolph Hearst, the owner of the New York *American*, in a letter to you, published August 29th, raised certain questions to which I desire to reply.

Nothing that comes from him is worthy of consideration, but I cannot let the opportunity pass to say something about his insolence in attempting, from his California home of San Simeon, to dictate the politics of the city of New York, and I cannot get over his effrontery in assuming to speak for the Democrats of this country.

Mr. Hearst, in his letter to you, said that I told a lie. It will not be very difficult for the people of New York to make a choice between myself and Mr. Hearst when it comes to a question of veracity.

Mr. Hearst's entire statement is a lie and I will prove it. He says that I attacked the Mayor as a Ku-Kluxer. That is a wicked, premeditated lie. What I did say is the truth and it was as follows:

"While the Democrats of the city of New York, with the Democrats of the eastern part of the country, stood day in and day out during the long hard siege in Madison Square Garden against the forces of religious and racial bigotry, not so much for me as for what I represented in the fight, where was Mayor Hylan? In secret conference with the representative of the Klan."

Send word to Mr. Hearst in California that that is the truth. It has already been admitted by Mayor Hylan. . . .

Mr. Hearst . . . is the last man in the world who should attempt to be the judge of what is undemocratic, un-American, or unpatriotic, unless he is prepared to point to himself as a shining example. . . . He never had any interest in any party or in any convention except to help himself. . . .

Hearst's reply indicated how far he had already drifted from his moorings in New York politics and the extent to which he had already lost touch with his former constituency there:

The distinguished Governor of the great State of New York has taken three days laboriously to prepare a vulgar tirade that any resident of billingsgate or any occupant of the alcoholic ward in Bellevue could have written in fifteen minutes in quite the same style but with more evidence of education and intelligence. The Wall Street friends of Governor Smith have enabled him to remove his domicile and his refined person from the neighborhood of the Bowery, but he still reverts in manner of thought to the familiar localities of Five Points and Hell's Kitchen, if this may be said without undue offense to these historic localities.

To sneer at the East Side was not the way to win votes for Hylan. After this blunder of his enemy, Smith could ramp on joyously. In a speech in the Bronx, he declared:

Hearst is out of the picture. He hasn't any business to make even a suggestion to the Democratic Party, because he has not got a vote. He was not enrolled. So out with him! The owner of the enchanted palace with a thousand hills and a thousand cows grazing. While he and the mayor were out brushing the flies off the grazing cows on the thousand hills, they were both engaged in shipping the bull on to New York.

Walker was triumphantly nominated over Hylan. This meant the final elimination of Hearst as a factor in New York politics. But it also meant much more than that. Al Smith was rapidly coming to be accepted as the national leader of the Democratic Party, and when he read Hearst out of that party and his action was overwhelmingly vindicated at the polls, this signified a national as well as local rejection. Hearst consoled himself by buying, sight unseen, St. Donat's castle in Wales—he had told his agent that he wanted an "English castle," but Wales was just as good.

The year 1925 marked the end of the publisher's long pose as a political liberal. He now at last discovered his true affiliation with the group that by all the laws of logic—if logic had been ever applicable to him—he ought to have been associated with from the beginning, namely, the Republican reactionaries.

In 1926 he supported for the governorship of New York against Al Smith none other than Ogden Mills, trustee of the New York Trust Company, director of the Atchison, Topeka & Santa Fe Railroad, director of the Mergenthaler Linotype Company, director of the Shredded Wheat Company, director of the Crex Carpet Company, director of the Continental Paper & Bag Mills Company. Gleefully, Al Smith announced that Hearst had given Mills "the kiss of death," and so it proved. The aid of the Hearst papers proved much more of a liability than an asset to the Republican candidate, who was hopelessly defeated.

The next year Hearst came out openly in support of Andrew Mellon for the presidency of the United States. A long article written by him appeared in the New York *World*, December 9, 1927, under the heading, "HEARST REGARDS MELLON AS IDEAL FOR PRESIDENT." In it, he discussed the four Republican candidates, Mellon, Hughes, Hoover, and Dawes, and elaborated his reasons for preferring the president of the Mellon Bank and owner of the American Aluminum Company to the other candidates:

Judged by the standard of notable service to his party and his country, Mr. Mellon is the outstanding figure.

Reviewing the records of two Administrations—that of President Harding and that of President Coolidge—the conspicuous achievement of each administration was made by the Treasury Department under Mr. Mellon. . . .

There was perhaps no time in the history of this republic when the financial condition of the country was as serious and as complicated as it was immediately after the great war.

To bring the country through its financial difficulties and establish it so thoroughly and so quickly on a sound financial basis, with no disturbance to business, but, on the contrary, with even a benefit to business, undoubtedly distinguishes Mr. Mellon as a great Secretary of the Treasury and a great executive, to be compared only with Alexander Hamilton.

As a matter of fact, while Alexander Hamilton had the keen and clear mind to solve the confused financial situation of this country at the beginning of its existence and to lay down principles which have been followed ever since, it is obvious from Hamilton's personal career that he in no way possessed the executive ability of Mr. Mellon.

Hearst did not explain why it was that although these transcendent merits of Hamilton's superior had been evident for six years, he himself had never recognized them until after he was thrown out of the Democratic Party by Al Smith. But he did go on to answer the objections to Mellon in a self-revelatory manner:

What objections are raised to Mr. Mellon as a candidate for the Presidency?

There are only two—first, that he is not young; and the answer to that is that he is young enough to conduct with overwhelming success the most difficult position in the whole public administration.

The second objection raised is that he is a wealthy man; and the answer to that is that this fact has not influenced him in his conduct of the Treasury Department, the one place where his wealth and his connections might be of danger to the community, if they were of danger at all.

Had Hearst really never heard how Mellon, from the day he took office, had labored to reduce lower and lower that income tax which his new admirer had always pretended to support? Or had this, too, now become a part of the secretary's "overwhelming success"? But the eulogy was not yet finished. Piling Pelion on Ossa, Hearst continued:

Moreover, it ought to be remarked in this connection that Washington seems to have made a satisfactory President . . . and Washington was the wealthiest man in the United States in his time.

Wealth honestly acquired, and as a measure of clear business vision and sound business judgment and high executive qualities, is in no way inconsistent or incompatible with patriotic and effective public service, as Washington proved in his day and as Andrew W. Mellon has proved today.

Besides Washington and Mellon, did not Hearst also have in mind a third wealthy patriot of sound business judgment and high executive qualities, who like them was getting a little old (sixty-four to be exact) but was still young enough to fill creditably any position that might be offered him in the public administration? But Mellon might not be nominated. It would be well to hand a few flowers to the other candidates also. Of Herbert Hoover, the publisher found this to say:

He is . . . a man of moderate and thoroughly sound progressive views. His great program for the development and control of the waterways and waterpowers of the nation is a plan conceived wholly in the public interest—a plan broad enough and beneficial enough to be worthy of Secretary Hoover's great reputation as one of the leading engineers of the world.

Secretary Hoover, like Secretary Mellon, served with the utmost credit in both the Harding administration and the Coolidge administration, and these two fine public servants have done much to redeem the Harding administration and to distinguish the Coolidge administration.

The president of the Central Trust Company of Chicago was a little more difficult to handle, but Hearst did his best.

Charles G. Dawes [he wrote] is very much the type of man of President Coolidge. . . .

Some of the popular qualities of Theodore Roosevelt, who likewise stepped from the Vice Presidency into the Presidency, also belong to Vice President Dawes. He is vigorous in his advocacies, but conservative in his opinions, and he has a breezy, democratic manner and mode of expression which are extremely engaging with the public.

Only from Hughes could Hearst expect nothing, and Hughes was accordingly dismissed with scant courtesy as having been, together with Senator Borah, "mainly responsible for the agreement with England which resulted in our destroying the great battleships which would have given America the supremacy of the seas; while England destroyed nothing but the plans and the blueprints of battleships yet to be built . . . apparently in Justice Hughes's mind an equal sacrifice."

Aside from Hearst's persistent Anglophobia, every issue that he had ever stood for was tacitly repudiated in this remarkable letter. And yet, the publisher remembered, Smith was going to be nominated as the Democratic candidate and he might, just possibly, win the election. The new Hamiltonian recalled that he was also a Jeffersonian, and four days after the effusion was printed he published a second signed statement in the New York *World*, which read:

Smith's record as Governor has been notable and his record, plus his popularity, has transformed the State of New York from a state which was almost surely Republican into a state which can now be considered safely Democratic . . . If Governor Smith is nominated, he should have the united and whole-hearted support of his party. . . .

Shamelessness, it would surely seem, could go no further.

Yet Hearst, if no other, could still surpass himself in this direction, as will be seen in the ensuing chapter.

CHAPTER XV

Purveyor of Forgeries

THE most sensational episode in Hearst's long career as journalist came in 1927 with his publication of a number of documents, prepared for by an announcement of "amazing revelations" soon to come and introduced in the first issue devoted to them by a scare headline: "MEXICO PLOT AGAINST U. S.!" The documents were published in a far-flung endeavor to produce war with Mexico, promote United States intervention in Nicaragua, develop popular animosity toward Japan and Russia, and, incidentally, ruin the reputation of four senators along with that of the most liberal American magazine of those years, the *Nation*. The undertaking was conducted on a magnificent scale worthy of the genius of its proponent.

The "documents" were run day after day in all the Hearst papers from November 14, 1927, to December 10, 1927, under such headings as:

"MEXICO SOUGHT JAPAN'S ASSISTANCE DRAFT OF PROPOSED TREATY SHOWS."

"CALLES FINANCED CHINESE RADICALS."

"OFFICIAL DOCUMENTS PROVE MEXICO AIDED REVOLT IN NICARAGUA."

"MEXICO SENT $1,000,000 TO PUSH ANTI-U. S. REVOLUTION."

"CALLES DONATED $100,000 TO SOVIET."

"CALLES TRIED TO BRIBE AMERICAN PRESS."

"CALLES ORDERED U. S. CLERGYMEN PAID $210,000."

"$2,400,500 MEXICO FUND USED IN NEW YORK."
"MEXICO PLOT AIMED AT SENATE: CASH ORDERED PAID 4 SENATORS."

Readers were assured: "These documents are not copies. They are the originals in every case and they bear the recognized and attested signatures of the President and the leading representatives of the Mexican government." And then in bold-face type: "There is no question of the authenticity of these documents as records of the government in Mexico."

According to Hearst's own account given later before the special Senate committee, the acquisition of the precious documents was first suggested by a mysterious friend, "an American citizen resident in Mexico," whose name was revealed in confidence to the members of the committee but was never made public. This friend, learning that documents were for sale implicating the Mexican government in anti-United States activities, out of pure patriotism wrote to Edward H. Clark, "a perfectly well-known business man in New York," to the effect that the documents ought to be secured and published for the safety of the United States. Mr. Clark, also perfectly well known as executor of the Phebe Hearst estate and chief financial adviser of William Randolph Hearst, immediately consulted the latter, and the mysterious friend in Mexico was authorized to proceed with the undertaking. It was decided "to employ the most capable and trustworthy investigator" in all Mexico, who was discovered by John Page, a Hearst correspondent, to be one Miguel R. Avila, a Texan half-breed formerly in the United States Secret Service in some minor capacity. Avila, still according to Hearst's story, succeeded in getting a number of initial documents by bribing various government clerks; later these clerks became frightened and fled to San Antonio, bringing with them further documents; finally, Avila was planted in the office of the Mexican Consul-

General in New York and produced still more documents. Avila certainly was "capable"; he seemed able to discover any document desired almost at a moment's notice!

No attention was paid in Congress to the "amazing revelations" until on December 9, 1927, the charge against the senators was published. This consisted of an alleged authorization signed by the Controller-General of Mexico for the payment of $1,115,000 to four United States senators whose names were carefully deleted in the newspaper reproduction of the documents.

The same day, in the Senate, David Reed of Pennsylvania rose to a question of the highest possible privilege. After quoting from Hearst's Washington *Herald*, Mr. Reed said: "Mr. President, as long as that story appears in print untested, uninvestigated, undenied, the honor of every member of this body is at stake." He therefore offered a resolution "that a special investigating committee of five Senators shall be forthwith appointed by the President of the Senate."

The resolution was agreed to unanimously, and Vice-President Curtis appointed a committee consisting of Reed of Pennsylvania, Robinson of Arkansas (the present Democratic leader in the Senate), Johnson of California, Bruce of Maryland, and Jones of Washington.

On December 13 the powers of the Committee were broadened to cover an investigation of the authenticity of any of the documents published in the Hearst papers between November 14 and December 10.

Meanwhile, the situation was enlivened by the publication in the *Nation* of a forged document purporting to show an authorization by the Mexican government of a payment of $25,000 to the *Nation* and its editor, Oswald Garrison Villard, in return for favorable propaganda. This document, with names deleted, had been previously published in the New York *American* after proof of its falsity had been submitted and assurance had been given by the *American* that it would not appear.

A few days later, a $500,000 libel suit was filed by Dr. Ernest Gruening of the *Nation's* staff against the *American,* Hearst, Arthur Brisbane, and others for statements accusing him of "communist" activities on Mexico's behalf.

In an open meeting of the Senate committee on December 16 the testimony of the leading principals was taken: the four senators, who turned out to be Borah, Heflin, Norris (ill but testifying by deposition), and LaFollette—the documents alleging that Borah had received $500,000, Norris and Heflin each $300,000, and LaFollette, for some reason, only a miserable $15,000; Dudley Field Malone, charged with having been the go-between who carried them the money; Arturo Elias, the Mexican Consul-General; all of whom categorically denied the accusations; and, on the other side, Hearst himself, Victor Watson, editor of Hearst's New York *Mirror;* E. D. Coblentz, editor of the New York *American;* John Page, writer of the stories; and the capable Avila.

Hearst's own testimony was the most interesting. A part of it ran as follows:

Q. Did you investigate whether money had been actually paid to United States senators?

A. No, sir, we didn't.

Q. Did you go to the senators mentioned and ask them?

A. No; we could not without revealing the contents.

Q. Have you any evidence that any senator received any such money as mentioned here?

A. No. In fact, I do not believe they did receive any money.

Q. Have you ever heard of any evidence to sustain such a charge?

A. No; I do not believe the charge.

Hearst's attitude on the stand showed a ne plus ultra of effrontery in this cool disclaimer of belief in a charge that had been spread across the continent by his papers. So far as could be made out from his testimony he seemed now to believe that the money had been paid by the Mexican Government to somebody but had never been received by anybody in particular.

Hearst's motive in deleting the names was reluctantly admitted by him.

Q. Did you consider the liabilities for the libel you might be subjected to?

A. Yes, I guess so.

Q. You had that liability in mind when you did not use the names?

A. Probably.

Had any effort been made to determine the authenticity of the documents? Oh yes; they had been shown to Ambassador Sheffield in Mexico, who glanced at them and said they looked all right to him; furthermore, they had been shown to the counsel of the embassy, Mr. Schoenfeld, who said that the signature of Calles ought to be verified. Was this ever done? Oh yes; not by Hearst himself, but by somebody or other in the organization. Were there any further investigations? Well, an attempt was made to show the documents to President Coolidge and Secretary Kellogg, but they declined to examine them. Anyway, further investigations were made by Hearst's editors, E. D. Coblentz and Victor Watson; he himself did not recall the details. How much money had been paid for the documents? $20,150. Who had received it? Well, it was given to Avila, who distributed it to the Mexican Government employees. What effort had been made to check the honesty of Avila? Well, Victor Watson could tell all about that.

Taking the stand, Victor Watson explained that the documents which were obtained by Avila when planted in the Consul-General's office fully corroborated his earlier documents.

In fact, as Victor Watson proudly proclaimed, he himself, "as a trained newspaper man," first conceived the brilliant idea of this verification. Unfortunately, Senator Reed seemed skeptical of its brilliance.

Q. When you planted Avila in the Consulate General did it occur to you that Avila was there for the purpose of corroborating himself?

A. It did not impress me that way at all.

Q. Well, was it not asking a man to get documents to prove the authenticity of documents he himself had procured?

A. Yes, but I see nothing wrong in that, provided he could get the documents.

On December 19, Senator Norris, on his sick bed, wrote an open letter to Hearst which was spread on the *Congressional Record*. It read in part:

To William Randolph Hearst:

A fair analysis of the recent articles published in the Hearst papers showing an alleged attempt by Mexican officials to bribe United States Senators and editors of various publications, and an analysis of your testimony before the Senate committee, leads to the inevitable conclusion that you are not only unfair and dishonest but that you are entirely without honor.

It is not necessary to consider any other evidence in order to reach the fair conclusion that in them you are making an attempt not only to besmirch the character of some of our own officials and journalists but that you are trying to excite an animosity and a hatred on the part of our people against the Mexican Government, which, if your articles and alleged official documents were true, would inevitably lead to war between the two countries.

Your attempt to shield yourself from blame by not publishing the names of the four senators and the editors alleged to be implicated, when properly analyzed, only shows the maliciousness of your attack and adds to the dishonor of your motive. You publish the alleged official documents with the names omitted and, at the same time, state that you stand ready and willing to deliver the original documents to any Senate committee that may be appointed to make an investigation.

You know that the publication of these charges, with the names omitted, must inevitably lead to the appointment of an investigating committee, and that, therefore, the names which you have concealed are bound to be published and that, in fact, the very withholding of the names adds to the curiosity and to the interest of an investigation.

You knew, therefore, to begin with, that the action you had taken would bring about the publication of the names and you cannot, in ordinary honesty, shield yourself or excuse yourself for the failure to give publicity to the names in the beginning. . . .

The real reason why you pursued this course was to save yourself from a libel suit, and the fact that you took this course shows that you, yourself, did not have confidence in the genuineness of the documents which you were publishing, because, if they were genuine, you ran no risk in their publication. Your admission that in taking this course you had in mind the saving of yourself from damages in a libel suit is an admission that you believed, yourself, that these alleged official documents were forgeries. . . .

The ordinary observer will not cease to take notice that the four senators mentioned were all prominent in the Senate in their opposition to interference by our government in the affairs of Mexico. It is rather remarkable that it is only this class of senators whose reputations are attacked. . . .

It is likewise peculiar that Calles, the President of Mexico, would spend his hard cash to bribe senators who were already advocating non-interference—a policy that he himself was anxious to carry out. . . .

What is your motive, Mr. Hearst? You have testified before the committee that you have very valuable properties in Mexico. It is almost common knowledge that you were in favor of the overthrow of the present government. You evidently believed that if a revolution could be started it would mean financial benefit for your investments in Mexico. . . .

In other words, for the sake of your financial investments, you were not only willing to ruin the reputation of honest and innocent men but you were willing to plunge our country into war with a friendly neighbor, and thus increase the army of widows and orphans and wounded and crippled soldiers.

The record which you have made in this matter is sufficient to place your publications in disrepute in the minds of all honest men, and it demonstrates that the Hearst system of newspapers, spreading like a venonomous web to all parts of our country, constitutes the sewer system of American journalism.

George W. Norris

Hearst's answer appeared on December 20, four days after the meeting of the Senate committee where his forces had made so poor a showing. He still asserted that "The plain facts of this whole Mexican matter are that these Mexican documents are apparently quite authentic, and that no proof whatever has been produced of their lack of authenticity." The circumstances of their acquisition were then stated, after which Hearst went on:

I held these documents for five months, carefully considering what was the best course to pursue and what was the most considerate course to pursue.

And it was only when the authenticity of the documents became almost overwhelmingly established, that publication began.

It is true as Mr. Norris said and as I told the committee, that I have property valued at approximately four million dollars in Mexico, which I had possessed in peace and security through the friendship and favor of the Mexican Government.

Certainly nobody but a perfect jackass—and Senator Norris is not that—at least not a perfect one—could imagine that my property holdings were benefited by losing the friendship and favor of the Mexican Government.

As a matter of fact, in publishing these documents there was strong probability—in fact, the near certainty—that these properties would be confiscated at the earliest possible moment by the Mexican Government. . . .

However, I can stand the loss of these properties through the publication of the Mexican documents better than I could have stood the loss of my self-respect through the cowardly suppression of these documents out of consideration for my own interest rather than the interests of my fellow American citizens.

Finally, as for the alleged evil motives in endeavoring to reflect upon the insurgents in the Senate through the publication of these documents, that seems to me to be the most asinine statement that can be picked out of Senator Norris' scrap-heap of misrepresentation and billingsgate.

My papers have always been in the main supporters of the insurgent group of Senators.

Senator Borah I have had occasion to support and commend probably more than any man in the Senate.

I do not know that I have ever supported Senator Norris, but then I cannot recall that he's ever done anything worth supporting. . . .

As a matter of fact, I am an insurgent myself. . . .

Since Senator Norris was the acknowledged leader of the insurgents, just how Hearst could have supported the insurgent group without ever supporting Senator Norris was a problem which he did not explain. Nor did he trouble to explain that a war between the United States and Mexico, which would probably result in American annexation of Chihuahua, where his chief properties are located, would have been even more beneficial to his own interests than to those of his "fellow American citizens." Neither did he mention the increase in circulation caused by publication of his sensational charges.

The experts employed by the Senate Committee examined the documents during Christmas week and found them all to be transparent forgeries. They were filled with incredible errors in grammar and spelling; the signatures patently did not correspond to originals; the alleged telegraphic messages had never been sent; the alleged typewritten copies had manifestly all been written on a single typewriter.

Why had John Page, the translator of the documents, never discovered any of these facts? Anticipating this question, John Page deemed it an appropriate time to disappear.

Faced with the approaching debacle, Hearst kindly offered to assist the Senate with his own handwriting experts who then for the first time examined the documents and fully corroborated the Senate's experts. Forewarned of their report, Hearst endeavored to cover himself in one of the lamest excuses ever offered by any man in public life:

If the handwriting experts should all agree that the documents we have produced bear evidence of having been fabricated, I will not dispute that decision further than to maintain persistently, and I believe patriotically, that the logic of events gives every evidence that the essential facts contained in the documents were not fabricated, and that the facts—the political facts, the international facts—are the things which are of vital importance to the American people and to the loyal representatives of the interests of the American people.

The documents might be false, but the alleged facts known only through the documents must be true! Hearst's "logic of events" was evidently something quite different from Aristotelian logic.

On the same day, the Hearst experts gravely announced that the documents were a fraud, made out of whole cloth from top to bottom. And a week later, on January 11, 1928, the Senate Committee brought the investigation to a close with its report that there was not a scintilla of evidence to show that any American had received or been offered money by the Mexican government for purposes of propaganda. Spread on the *Congressional Record* this last day was an editorial from the Los Angeles *Times* of January 6, summarizing the case:

The annals of yellow journalism [it said] will be searched in vain for anything remotely approaching this performance by Hearst. . . . It is a black record, the blackest in American journalism, the most gross abuse of the right of a free press in this or any other country's history. To call his proven fakes inflammatory is to understate their tenor. They accused a neighbor country of repeated acts of war;

accused Japan of plotting against the peace of the United States; they accused the United States Senators of treason; they accused dozens of high and reputed officials and prominent citizens of the blackest of crimes against patriotism; all without investigation, equivalent, or mitigation.

The evidence presented by the Senate Committee was so overwhelming that the Hearst press beat a hasty retreat, conveniently covering it up by a series of screaming headlines on the Parker-Hickman kidnap-murder case, which happened opportunely at this time.

Calles, Mexico, and the "Red" scare were left behind. Readers were worked up to a new frenzy in the manhunt for young Hickman. And another great moral issue had been found by the Hearst editors.

A major result of Hearst's "amazing revelations" was that the friendly relations between Mexico and the United States were so jeopardized by them as to make necessary the sending of Lindbergh to Mexico to counteract the effect.

A minor but significant result was that Hearst, after much effort, located the hideout of John Page and re-employed him at a handsome salary.

CHAPTER XVI

Patriot Redivivus

HEARST probably felt that he had been very unjustly used by Senator Norris when the latter accused him of trying to foment war with Mexico. How could anyone believe that he desired war with any nation? Had he not that very year, in listing the blessings of modern civilization, said, "The most important achievement of all would seem to me the abolition of the utterly uncivilized and wholly savage institution of war"?

This had been uttered at Oglethorpe University, Georgia, where his son John Randolph was in attendance. John Randolph, who was later dismissed from Harvard for low grades, wasn't much of a student and got no further than the sophomore year even at Oglethorpe, but the "university" was duly grateful for having a millionaire's child in its catalogue, and so bestowed the degree of Doctor of Laws upon the millionaire himself. Not to be outdone in gratitude, Hearst, after a suitable interval, bestowed upon the college a four-hundred-and-forty-acre wooded tract. In this matter of honorary degrees, a college can always trust a millionaire, if he is a gentleman, sooner or later to do the right thing. Hearst's gratitude was doubtless quite sincere; henceforward, even though he had been unable to obtain an A.B. from Harvard, he could boast that he held an LL.D. from Oglethorpe University, Georgia.

It was at the time of his investiture in the purple hood that he made the optimistic remark quoted above in regard to the abolition of war. But he also, in his speech on that occasion, made another even more surprising observation. "The time is ripe," he said, "to advocate the co-operation of the English-speaking people of the world to maintain peace." And he went on to elaborate a plan for a kind of minor League of Nations composed of the United States, Great Britain, Ireland, Canada, Australia, New Zealand, and South America.

Great was the amazement of the readers of the Hearst newspapers when they learned of this speech. Mayor Thompson of Chicago, who was busy as ever denouncing all things British, fairly shuddered, wondering if he had harbored a snake in his bosom all these years. Had Hearst suddenly grown senile and reverted to his adolescent Anglomania or had his purchase of St. Donat's castle led him to imagine that he had really become a British peer?

The explanation was much simpler. Hearst had floated a fifteen-million-dollar bond issue on behalf of his various enterprises, and this was being handled by a British subsidiary, the Anglo-London-Paris Company. After all, the publisher did not believe in cherishing old grudges beyond the point of reason.

Still, the elimination of Great Britain as an object of attack left a certain vacancy in his life. For thirty years the iniquities of the Empire had furnished fuel for his tongue and pen; had his theatrical interest not been confined to musical comedies and the cinema, he might well have sighed despondently:

> Farewell the neighing steed and the shrill trump,
> The spirit-stirring drum, the ear-piercing fife!
> Farewell! Othello's occupation's gone!

Sub-consciously, he set out to find a substitute for the vanished enemy, and by good luck he found that it was not necessary to transfer the feud farther than across the Channel.

Hearst had always been very fond of France, its tolerant moral atmosphere being much more to his taste than the prudishness of England. Furthermore, the French had been much quicker than the British to forgive his attitude in the World

FEELING WORRIED?

Hearst appearing before a Senate inquiry to explain why his newspapers published forged accusations of bribery against four U. S. senators.

APPRAISING PRESIDENTIAL TIMBER

Hearst with his candidate, Governor Alfred M. Landon of Kansas (center). Publisher Paul Block is at the right.

War. Had he not striven to atone for it by that magnificent gift of clippings to Marshal Joffre? So when Hearst and his friend Miss Davies visited Paris in the summer of 1928 they were received with the courtesy and hospitality for which the French are famous. And there seemed no reason to suppose that the publisher consciously had aught in view beyond a very pleasant vacation, such as he had often had before, until chance threw in his way the opportunity to obtain some secret governmental documents. And this time there was no doubt that the documents were genuine, being nothing less than the draft of a proposed treaty between France and Great Britain, with accompanying memoranda, in which France offered certain concessions to the British navy in return for similar concessions to the French "defensive" forces. Their publication would refute those doubting Thomases who said that the Hearst papers never managed even to steal anything except forgeries—and it was obviously also Hearst's sacred duty to apprise the world of the secret machinations of French diplomacy.

There is some doubt as to just how the documents were secured. Hearst's own statement was that they were not obtained in any underhanded way but by "good, direct, 'Go-and-get-it' American methods"—which sounds almost as if he had burglarized the Foreign Office. Presumably, however, the documents were not procured in quite such a direct way as that. According to the official version of the French government, Hearst's confidential private secretary, Harold J. T. Horan, obtained them through the connivance or negligence of two minor officials, M. de la Plante and M. de Noblet, but both of these men were later exonerated by a French court. There is also a much more sensational and elaborate account which appeared in the royalist paper, *L'Action Française* on August 14, 15, and 16, 1930. Though its source makes the latter highly suspect, it has never been answered either by the French government or by Hearst.

The first, and so far as Hearst is concerned most important, of these three issues of the royalist paper began by giving the background of the proposed naval pact, which aimed to establish a closer entente with Great Britain to the military detriment of both Germany and the United States: Great Britain agreeing to uphold the French right to defensive submarines and "trained reserve forces," and the French promising to support Great Britain's contention that there must be no limitation on light cruisers. It was a typical instance of the jockeying for military advantage which characterized the policies of all nations, including the United States, during the period of so-called "disarmament" measures. As such, much to the approval of *L'Action Française*, it ran counter to Briand's attempt to bring about a rapprochement with Germany, and, according to the paper's interpretation, Briand secretly desired the publication of the pact in order to discredit it.

At this point, Hearst enters the picture. "Mr. Hearst's visit to France at that time [said *L'Action Française*] was a political venture that had been arranged a few months before by Madame de Jouvenel [a protégée of Briand] and Alain de Lèche [an agent of the Prefecture of Police] in America during a lecture tour. As soon as he arrived in France, Hearst, a notorious enemy of France, received a scandalous welcome by the Bienvenue Française [under Madame de Jouvenel] . . . Lèche established direct and personal relations between Hearst and Briand."

Then comes the climax:

As to Mr. Hearst, what he wanted to get was the *very text* of the naval compromise that had been kept secret both in Paris and London. After much bargaining and numerous steps, on September 19 at 7 P.M. Hearst went to Quai d'Orsay where he had a long talk with Briand. Meanwhile, exactly at the same time, his mistress Marion Davies happened to be at the Foreign Office, too. The next day, September 20, Hearst was in possession of the pact and also of an authentic mimeographic copy of the circular letter [brief instructions to be sent to ambassador].

Certainly this story of the night visit, with its implication that either Briand personally gave the pact to Hearst or that Miss Davies filched it from some desk while they were talking, reads remarkably like a moving-picture scenario.

The newspaper account went on to tell how Hearst left his treasure trove with Horan for transmission to New York and then took the first boat for England. On September 22, 1928, still according to *L'Action Française*, Horan sent the following cablegram to Universal Service, New York:

Stansbury on his way with authentic letter of Berthelot [the circular letter] to all French ambassadors and containing the real text of document in question. Am sending only four hundred now. Please inform if you want the whole approximately 4,000 or summary.

A second alleged message was published, unsigned but obviously from Hearst and sent from London to Horan on September 22 after the French authorities had complained to the latter about his giving out the information. This read:

I do not understand why French authorities dissatisfied with you. I got the naval agreement in the manner you know and have given it to you to be communicated in full to our papers. Besides the publication of the pact is a great advantage under circumstances as it was feared in America it might be far more serious than it is. If the French authorities want to expel me as completely undesirable I shall be quite pleased but I intended to expel myself from the country anyway.

If this telegram is authentic—its authenticity and that of the previous one are denied by Horan—it would clearly prove three things: first, that Hearst, not Horan, obtained the documents in the first place; second, that Hearst had known of the existence of the naval pact before leaving America ("it was feared in America," etc.); third, that he had gone to France seeking trouble and intending "to expel himself from the country." Unfortunately, *L'Action Française* being what it was, there is nothing clear about the case.

The French government took no further action at this time against Hearst, but contented itself with arresting Horan, putting him through twelve hours' questioning, and threatening him with imprisonment or deportation—both of which he avoided by departing speedily on his own initiative.

In the summer of 1930, Hearst, at San Simeon, suddenly decided that he would like to take another trip to Europe. Probably no one who professed such utter preference for his own country to all others ever chose to spend so much time away from it. San Simeon at the moment was full of guests, so Hearst, with the lavish hospitality so characteristic of him on his own estate, simply invited all who would to accompany him to Europe at his expense.

The party went first to London and then to Paris, where the publisher spent four days at the Hotel Crillon, quite unmolested, after which he departed for Bad Nauheim to spend a month taking the cure there. On his way back to Paris, he gave out an interview to the *Frankfurter Zeitung* in which he asserted that the Versailles Treaty had subjected the Teutonic peoples to the domination of Belgium, France, Italy, Yugoslavia, Czechoslovakia, Poland, and Lithuania. If he was once more trying to expel himself from the country, this time he succeeded. On the morning of his arrival at the Crillon he was notified that he would have to leave France within four days. Not staying to contest the point, Hearst left immediately and on the train wrote his reply to the French Republic, which was published soon after his arrival in England in the London *Evening Standard* of September 3, 1930:

I have no complaint to make. The French officials were extremely polite. They said I was an enemy of France, and a danger in their midst. They made me feel quite important. They said I could stay in France a while longer, if I desired, and they would take a chance on nothing disastrous happening to the Republic.

But I told them I did not want to take the responsibility of endangering the great French nation, that America had saved it once during the war, and I would save it again by leaving it. Furthermore, I was like the man who was told that he was going blind, and who said he did not mind, as he had seen everything anyhow. Similarly, I had seen everything in France, including some very interesting governmental performances. Then I asked M. Tardieu's emissary to express to M. Tardieu my immense admiration for his immense alertness in protecting France from the peril of invasion, and we parted with quite elaborate politeness.

The reason for the strained relations—to use the proper diplomatic term—was the publication of the secret Anglo-French Treaty two years ago by the Hearst papers, which upset some international "apple carts," but informed the American people; and of course that being the reason, the French government was entirely right in leveling its attack at me and quite wrong in its action toward Mr. Horan, who was only my agent.

I think, however, that the general attitude of the French press toward our opposing the United States' entrance into the League of Nations, or any protective pact to involve our country in the quarrels of European powers, is mainly responsible. Also there might have been some slight irritation at the occasional intimations in our papers that France, now being the richest nation in the world, might use some of the German indemnity to pay her honest debts to America, especially because if it had not been for America she would now be paying indemnity instead of receiving it.

But being a competent journalist and a loyal American makes a man persona non grata in France. I think I can endure the situation without loss of sleep. In fact, the whole affair reminds me of a story of a rather effeminate young man who went to call on his best girl and found her in the arms of another young fellow. The effeminate youth went into the hall, took up his successful young rival's umbrella, broke it, and said, "Now I hope it rains!" You see, for the French national policy of revenge to be entirely successful, we will have to have rain.

The happy vein of humor in this article clearly reflects the joyous mood of the publisher in again having a great nation as his private enemy. Equal to equal, the monarchy of San Simeon against the French Republic. Hearst celebrated by buying the Elizabethan great chamber of Gilling Castle and having it transported from Yorkshire to Wales to become a part of St. Donat's. That done, he sailed on the North German Lloyd liner *Europa* for New York.

His article in the *Evening Standard* had obviously been written for home consumption, with its flattery of American military prowess, its inclusion of the popular American myth about French effeminacy, and its clever injection of the debt issue. His grateful countrymen responded, and Hearst found himself on arrival once more recognized as a distinguished patriot.

The *Europa* was met at Quarantine on September 16, 1930, by the steamboat *Hood Mountain* under the auspices of the disabled American war veterans and with a deputation of congressmen on board, including Senator Robert F. Wagner, and Representatives Black, Bloom, Celler, Dickstein, La Guardia, Lindsay, and Sirovich. Hearst's eyes are said to have filled with tears at seeing so many politicians gathered to greet him.

Two weeks later, the publisher made his first speech over the radio. He was introduced by Mr. Aylesworth, head of the National Broadcasting Company, as "A great editor who fearlessly thinks, writes, and publishes what he believes to be for the best interests of our people and our country."

In reply, Hearst said, in part: "Perhaps, fellow-citizens, some of you will say to me, 'Why did you not sue the French government?' And I say, 'First, because I did not want to magnify the incident, and, second, because I had the simplicity to believe, fellow-citizens, that somewhere among our paid servants at Washington there might be found some public official with backbone enough and American spirit enough to defend the right of law-abiding citizens abroad.'" However little he wished not to "magnify the incident," he could not help going on to contrast the vigorous action which Grover Cleveland or Theodore Roosevelt would have taken, with the supineness of the then occupant of the White House. He was evidently considerably nettled by the silence of Mr. Hoover, who before election had motored all the way from Palo Alto to Los Angeles to see him, whose candidacy he had loyally supported as a Jeffersonian Democrat should, and who yet would not risk even a protest to France on the right of a law-abiding American citizen abroad to publish government documents obtained by good, direct, go-and-get-it American methods. Still, he ventured to hope that "American spirit and American independence and American loyalty to the rights and liberties which we inherited from our fathers" had not really perished with Grover Cleveland and Theodore Roosevelt.

Hearst had had good reason to be happy on the day of his expulsion from France. From New York he went to Boston to be the city's guest of honor at its Tercentennial celebration. Next came an invitation from Mayor Thompson of Chicago, the City Council, and the Cook County Board for him to be the central figure in a Chicago Day celebration which would entirely outdo the attempt in Boston. True, a mass meeting was held in the Auditorium of some 15,000 people, representing the Polish-American veterans, to protest against this honor paid to "an international trouble-maker." But Chicago Day went off successfully, nevertheless, with a parade of 5000 automobiles and fifty bands. Mayor Thompson introduced his old friend and political patron as "one of the foremost patriots in the land." Hearst replied in key: "All that I did . . . was for the best interests of my country. I would do it again tomorrow even if I were to be expelled from every country in Europe for doing it. What does the attitude of foreign countries amount to if a man can find refuge in the hearts of his own people and in the welcoming arms of his native land!"

When he was invited to San Francisco by the Board of Supervisors there was another discordant note. Supervisor Warren Shannon said curtly, "The idea is ridiculous. All it amounts to is Hearst inviting himself to visit the city. The invitation, of course, has been arranged by his representatives. Such a reception would be merely a duplication of the one in New York City where a few lame-duck congressmen waddled down to the dock to welcome him."

Already in St. Louis and elsewhere mysterious buttons had appeared at these meetings, bearing the legend, "Hearst for President." When somewhat belatedly apprised of this fact at a civic banquet in Los Angeles, Hearst said, "If that is so, I know nothing about it and do not approve of it." The reaction to the buttons not being wholly favorable, he ended his triumphant trip across the continent with the words, "Now, I am going to board a train and go down to my ranch and find my little hideaway on my little hilltop at San Simeon."

But after he had traveled a few hundred miles up and down and around his little hilltop, he again became less painfully modest. Realizing anew the greatness of San Simeon as compared with decadent France, he made a generous offer, such as the ruler of an empire might make to some little provincial state, inviting the French government to visit him at San Simeon "to enlarge their experience and broaden their minds," assuring them that "they will not be ordered off the premises for being loyal to their own country." What measures he would take if they tried to steal the silverware he did not announce.

This was all great fun, but unfortunately he might want to go back to France some time. Miss Davies liked to see the Paris fashion displays, and he liked to guide her taste in such matters. Influenced by such wholesome second thoughts, he enrolled as a contributing editor on the Hearst newspapers with name prominently displayed on their mastheads the one-time Progressive, Bainbridge Colby, who had been a member of the American Commission to the Inter-Allied Conference at Paris in 1917 and later secretary of state in Wilson's second term. It would be strange if this well-known friend of France could not sooner or later get the ban removed.

Hearst was the perfect Peer Gynt envisaged by Ibsen's prescient imagination fifty years earlier. He never burned a bridge behind him because, in this tricky world, one never knew when "behind" might turn out to be "before."

But in his happy mood of liberalism at the moment he declared that the pardon of Anita Whitney, convicted of being a member of the Communist Labor Party in 1919, was "a triumph of tolerance and intelligent investigation over political bigotry and hysteria." Anita Whitney was wealthy, a member of his own class; such people surely ought to have the right to freedom of opinion.

Hearst had already come near to breaking with his new friends in the Republican Party by his attitude on prohibition. On that great question his attitude had been as inconsistent as on most others. When the Eighteenth Amendment had been brought forward in 1917, he had vigorously protested on behalf of his beer-drinking German-American clientele, to whom at that time, it will be remembered, he was making a particularly strong appeal. "Prohibition," he said, "would not 'prohibit' any but the milder but relatively harmless stimulants. It would again put this nation on a whisky basis as it was in the days of Jefferson, who advocated encouragement of light beer brewing as the only remedy for the 'poison of whisky.' " But in 1919, when the amendment was actually passed, Hearst was struggling desperately to recover his lost position as a patriot. This necessarily changed the probable effects of prohibition. The passage of the amendment was celebrated by him in language that outdid in extravagance that of the Anti-Saloon League itself. In an editorial in the New York *Journal* of January 17, 1919, he said:

One hundred per cent efficiency has been added at one stroke to the people of America. . . . Half of the misery of half of the people has been abolished. . . . Strong drink has destroyed more each year than the World War destroyed. . . . The suppression of the drink traffic is an expression of the higher morality upon which we are entering.

Henceforth for some years Hearst carried water on one shoulder and beer on the other, outwardly supporting the amendment with great fervor but occasionally voicing discreet questions calculated to raise doubts regarding its success. By 1929 the swing toward repeal was so pronounced that he ventured to come out in the open. The expression of the higher morality, he now discovered, had been "un-American" from the beginning. As he wrote to E. J. Clapp of Durant Motors, Inc., "After four more years of shooting, spying, key-hole peeping and interference with fundamental rights and liberties by fanatics and professional busybodies, the country will be ripe for a revolution against un-American conditions of this oppressive and offensive kind." Publicly he compared prohibition to the "fallen woman" of Victorian tradition. "Everybody knows," he wrote, "that the law ought to be respected; just as everybody knows that women ought to be respected, and that women are respected by every decent man. But occasionally there is a woman who is not respected, who is not respectable, who does not respect herself, and who [sic] no one in his heart can respect, no matter what outward observance of respect he may render. And so occasionally there are laws that cannot be respected."

When in 1930 a young girl died at a drinking party in Gary, Indiana, Hearst raised the question, "Is it not about time for the country to wake up and put an end to prohibition and prohibition parties? . . . Is it not time that the calm conservative portion of our people took stock of prohibition and determined whether

this policy is worth all the trouble and all the evil that it costs?
We have heard enough of fools and fanatics. Let us hear in the
coming election from the sound and sane portion of the American people."

As the panic of 1929 stretched into the depression of 1930,
Hearst came forward with good advice in the New York
American. Wages must not be cut, he insisted; employees must
not be dismissed. "Prosperity must be built from the bottom.
... The wealth which our statesmen burned up in the war and
our high financiers so recklessly threw to the four winds of
Europe must with bent back and strained muscles be laboriously
rebuilt by the workers. The first duty of this government is to
give the workers work. They will give trade to the shops and
orders to industries. They will pay rent, buy shoes and clothing
and put money into circulation."

Having thus done his duty by the workers in general, Hearst
put into effect the first of three wage cuts among his own employees, which were eventually to reduce the Hearst wage scale
far below the average. He also organized, by methods to be
discussed later, a gigantic holding company to protect his interests as a publisher. This done he sailed for England to cement
the new alliance between Hearst and the British Empire.

St. Donat's Castle had by now been fitted up as a summer
residence for the successor of the Stradlings. Many antiques
had been shipped back from America, and many more had been
purchased abroad. The whole castle, in the words of Mrs. Fremont Older, "had been made into a rare museum," filled with
Elizabethan and Jacobean furniture, "priceless" lacquer cabi-
nets, and quaint relics of the past such as a bed in which Charles I
once slept and the very pair of shoes worn by Henry VIII at
the Field of the Cloth of Gold. While in these ways the new
owner "preserved the atmosphere of the place," the comforts
of modernity were not forgotten. The hundred and thirty-five

rooms were equipped, not precisely with a hundred and thirty-five bathrooms, but with a score or so; tennis courts were laid out, and a swimming pool was built.

Full justice to the glories of St. Donat's can be done only by quoting the words of Mrs. Older. "Dinner at St. Donat's is picturesque and like a page out of the time of Elizabeth. . . . The table is ablaze with flowers and silver equal to a king's treasure. When set for guests the silver on the table is worth a quarter of a million dollars. On either side of the centerpiece are delicate nautilus cups, the work of contemporaries of Benvenuto Cellini, one Elizabethan and one Italian. One is worth eight and the other ten thousand dollars. The great Queen Anne monteiths are priceless, and so is the Charles II wine cooler. In order to obtain his collection of Elizabethan and Georgian tankards, Hearst has made new price records. . . ."

As a prospective English squire, Hearst joined all the agricultural and sport clubs in the vicinity and offered prizes at agricultural shows. As owner of a Welsh castle, he invited the most famous of living Welshmen, Lloyd George, to visit him. The latter was delighted with all the improvements in the castle and declared on leaving that St. Donat's when completed would be comparable as a medieval residence with Windsor itself.

After enjoying the companionship of a has-been British prime minister, Hearst returned to America to cultivate the friendship of a would-be American President. This was John Nance Garner of Texas, Hearst's old admirer in the Fifty-Eighth and Fifty-Ninth congresses, who rose rapidly to fame as Speaker of the House of Representatives in the Seventy-Second Congress through sponsoring a billion-dollar public-works bill so loosely drawn that it was essentially a gigantic pork-barrel measure. Hearst was enthusiastic over such a scheme of public works, suggesting that the amount ought to be raised to four or five billions, and he became very enthusiastic for Garner, in whom he detected a greater John Hylan.

Speaking over the radio from Los Angeles on January 2, 1932, Hearst solemnly nominated Garner for the presidency on an "American" platform, declaring that he was "a loyal American citizen, a plain man of the plain people, a sound and sincere Democrat; in fact, another Champ Clark." He admitted that there were other good men in the Democratic Party: Franklin Roosevelt, Al Smith, Owen Young, Newton Baker, and Governor Ritchie of Maryland—but they were all tainted with "Wilson internationalism." Wilson, that fount of evil, he characterized as he had so often other political enemies, in terms remarkably applicable to himself: "He was . . . an unstable thinker and an unreliable performer; an advocate at some time or other in his career of both sides of almost every public question; an opportunist in his support of any principle at any time."

In support of his "American" program, he featured the cry "Buy American" in the Hearst press, which bought all its paper from Canada! Later, when the Canadian price rose, Hearst shifted his purchases to Finland on the ground that the latter was the only nation which had paid its debt to the United States.

John Francis Neylan, once an obscure San Francisco reporter who had been taken up by Hiram Johnson and had become one of San Francisco's leading attorneys, was now Hearst's chief legal counsel and financial adviser. He was placed in charge of Hearst's Garner campaign, but he was shrewd enough to see that the Texan's chances for the presidency were really very slight. The best that could be hoped for would be to drive a bargain, at the most appropriate moment, with the Roosevelt forces, whereby Garner would be assured the vice-presidency in return for his support. The arrangements were made in advance with Roosevelt's manager, James Farley. Also, Hearst had an understanding with Mayor Cermak of Chicago that the Illinois and California delegations should vote together. The publisher had never shown any enthusiasm for Roosevelt, but he was determined at all costs to prevent the election of the dreaded Al Smith.

So when the Chicago convention went to three ballots with Roosevelt still far from the necessary two-thirds majority, Farley telephoned Neylan in San Francisco that the hour had come. Neylan telephoned Hearst in Los Angeles: "Roosevelt must have California and Texas now." Hearst telephoned McAdoo and Garner, and the deed was done. Just like that. It was an instructive example of the way in which American presidents are made.

During the campaign, the Hearst press, of course, labored energetically on behalf of the Democratic ticket. Mrs. Hearst, too, loyally did her bit as head of the Women's Division of the Nassau County Roosevelt-Garner Club by offering ten thousand dollars in prizes to promote the sale of Hearst-Garner medallions. Then, after the election, men waited to see how long it would be before Hearst, as usual, would break with the successful candidate.

The break was long in coming. During the first year of the new administration, the publisher had reason to be fairly well satisfied with its policies. In February 1933 he appeared before the Senate Finance Committee and gave his views as to the proper emergency measures to be adopted: these consisted of moderate inflation, a public-works program, and a sales tax in preference to the much talked of income tax; the latter he denominated a "racket," and the worst form of class legislation, while a sales tax, bearing equally upon rich and poor, was the most democratic of measures possible. When Mr. J. P. Morgan bought a loaf of bread he would have to pay just as heavy a tax upon it as the poorest man in the United States. Though the sales tax was not adopted, the income tax was successfully headed off, and though the public-works program was temporarily subordinated to direct relief, moderate inflation, the most important of Hearst's policies, at least for himself, became the cornerstone of the administration's financial program. As a result, Hearst's mining properties boomed, Homestake alone trebling its earnings between 1932 and 1934.

The year 1934 brought Hearst a new enemy to attack, who was, as usual, an old friend. Senator Hiram Johnson and Hearst had been brought together by their common opposition to the League of Nations in 1919. In 1920, when Hearst was supporting Warren G. Harding for the presidency, he tried at Harding's suggestion to persuade Johnson to run on the same ticket, but the Californian refused to sacrifice his Progressive principles for a mere vice-presidency. From then on, as Johnson and Hearst grew old and conservative together, they maintained relations of the utmost amity. But always the senator was a lap behind the publisher in swinging to the right, and in April 1934 he suddenly kicked over the traces by voting for the Couzens amendment to the revenue bill whereby ten per cent of the 1934 personal income tax would be added to that for 1935. Hearst's wrath was swift to descend. His papers immediately demanded that Johnson be defeated in the next election.

The amendment, however, passed into forgotten history, and Hearst left the next month for Europe in happy mood, accompanied by three of his four sons, their wives, all soon to be divorced, and a party of eleven friends. Before sailing, he had luncheon at the White House, after which he announced that he was "entirely in sympathy" with the President and the New Deal.

The one serious error of the New Deal, from Hearst's viewpoint, was the N.R.A., but as long as the codes were purely voluntary and made by the employers he saw little reason to object. When the Newspaper Guild was formed, he declined to take it seriously, remarking only that he had always supposed journalism to be "a profession," governed by professional ethics, rather than a mere trade. But, he smilingly admitted, perhaps he was "old-fashioned." As to collective bargaining in general, of course he approved of it, as he had always done.

Later, when the Newspaper Guild became a reality in earnest, it was a different story. The *Call-Bulletin* was swift to dismiss the Guild organizer, Dean Jennings, and several others were dismissed by the Hearst papers on the Coast because of their Guild activities. But President Roosevelt came to the publisher's assistance by removing the Jennings case from the jurisdiction of the Biddle Board when it decided against Hearst. The N.R.A. was inconvenient, but it was not greatly to be dreaded by a multi-millionaire.

HOLLYWOOD ENTERTAINS

An "international" studio luncheon. From left to right, the guests are Louis B. Mayer, Baroness Philippe de Rothschild, Assistant Secretary of the Navy Col. Henry Roosevelt, Marion Davies, and Baron Henri de Rothschild. Standing are Hearst, Irving Thalberg, and Hal Wallace.

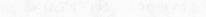

CHAPTER XVII

American Fascist

WHEN Hearst and his party went to Europe in May 1934 they traveled on the *Rex*. The publisher was bound for Italy where, as he announced, he hoped to meet Mussolini; after that, the next country on his itinerary would be Germany, where he hoped to meet Hitler.

Mussolini showed no great interest in his American admirer, but it was different with Hitler. From Bad Nauheim the publisher carried on a voluminous correspondence with the *Fuehrer*, who became so impressed with this septuagenarian student who had crossed the Atlantic to sit at his feet that he invited him to Berlin and received him into the inner Nazi circles. Hearst had his photograph taken in the midst of a group of prominent Nazi officials looking quite like one of them—a photograph which he neglected to reproduce in any of his American newspapers or magazines. He perfected arrangements to secure for the Hearst International News Service a monopoly of all American news published in the government-controlled German press. Most important of all, he himself derived a new political vision from his Nazi contacts—a vision of the power to be obtained by the ruthless use of force in open warfare with the labor unions, by suppression of hostile criticism, and by the use of patriotic propaganda which he himself had early mastered but had never, as he saw now, used with sufficient singleness of purpose for the preservation of that capitalist system on which his own wealth and influence depended. The capitalist system was endangered now in America as it had been in Germany until Hitler saved it. There was one last great rôle left for him, William Randolph Hearst, to play: that of the savior of American capitalism alike from its overt enemies and its timid Rooseveltian friends who would ruin everything with their compromises.

Opportunity for an effective début was immediately at hand. A longshoremen's strike on the Pacific Coast for higher wages, shorter hours, and the control of hiring halls had tied up nearly all the shipping on the coast during the month of June. The San Francisco Chamber of Commerce, aided by the Industrial Association, representing the leading financial interests of the city, then attempted to break the strike by the importation of gun thugs with the result that on July 5, in a clash between the longshoremen pickets and the police and gunmen, two strikers and a sympathizer were killed and over a hundred on both sides were so seriously injured as to require hospital treatment. During the week that followed this "Battle of Rincon Hill," as it was called, a movement for a general strike gained headway which finally went into effect on July 16. On the previous evening a meeting of the five leading Bay publishers (two of them Hearst men) was held, at which an organization was established, headed by John Francis Neylan, for the purpose of starting an old-fashioned vigilante movement against the strikers. Hearst himself was reached by telephone in London, and he promised to cable a news story on the breaking of the general strike in England in 1926. This story was run the next day accompanied by an editorial that set the keynote which all the other papers followed:

> . . . If the small group of Communists, starting with their control of the longshore and maritime unions, extend their power over the community of the bay area—and thence into the whole, or even part of the State—California would be no more fit to live in than Russia.

Overnight the trades unions of San Francisco had been metamorphosed into "Communists" by a simple flick of the Neylan-

Hearst magician's wand! The next day fuel was added to the flames by an incendiary speech of General Hugh Johnson at the University of California (of which Neylan is a regent) in which the former director of the N.R.A. also attributed the strike to "subversive influences" and said that the people should "wipe out this subversive element as you clean off a chalk mark on a blackboard with a wet sponge." Inspired by the general's patriotism, hundreds of students thronged across the Bay from Berkeley, eager to act as vigilantes or as strikebreakers.

Although the strike committee had striven to minimize the difficulties of the general public by allowing the municipal railroad to continue running, food and milk deliveries to be made, small amounts of gasoline to be given out, and fifty restaurants to remain open, still there was unavoidably so much hardship and inconvenience that the newspapers had no difficulty in getting a large following for the reign of terror which they instituted. The strike headquarters were raided along with those of all other organizations suspected of radicalism, furniture and equipment were destroyed, and anybody in the neighborhood who looked like a radical was beaten up. A reign of terror was inaugurated in California during which according to Lew Levenson, writing in the *Nation*, August 29, 1934, "literally thousands" were gassed, shot, trampled on, or had their skulls cracked. The incomplete list of casualties he gave occupied five columns of fine print.

Frightened by the demon he had helped to raise, General Johnson attempted to make a plea for moderation before the newspaper council but was abruptly silenced by Neylan, who said, "I do the shouting in this part of the country, General!" Told by the publishers that they would brook no interference from him and advised that it would be well for him to get out of their city if he didn't like its ways, the general withdrew in the meek manner of a whipped schoolboy and took the first train for Los Angeles.

The strike was broken, but it was far from entirely lost, as in the final settlement by the government's National Longshoremen's Board some months later the strikers were awarded increased pay and shorter hours though they lost their fight on the hiring halls. More important than these immediate issues, however, was the fact that the Hearst papers in California had successfully started a "Red" scare that with sufficient coddling might easily develop into a national movement.

When Hearst first returned to America, he thought to use Hitler as a name to conjure with. Eulogistic "news" articles were run under such headings as "REICH ASKS PEACE, AVERS NAZI CHIEF" and "NAZIS TAKE HIGH ROAD TO AMAZING ECONOMIC RECOVERY." A whole series of syndicated articles from Goering was published. But even Hearst's public, willing to accept almost anything, did not take kindly to these maneuvers. With the appearance of the boycott against Germany because of the persecution of Jews and Catholics, Hearst found it advisable to throw Goering overboard. The persecutions, he maintained, were not by Hitler's orders. "The Nazi ministers," ran an editorial in the Los Angeles *Examiner*, "Dr. Wilhelm Frick and General Goering are said to have got out of hand and to be proceeding on their own without clear authorization from Hitler and according to some reports, in opposition to him." When Hitler insisted on taking the discredit to himself beyond all possibility of denial, Hearst reluctantly ceased to support him openly. It was clear that he would have to be his own Hitler.

One of the first lessons he had learned from his German mentor was the importance of terrorizing the faculties of colleges and universities. Under modern conditions whoever controls the educational system controls the social system. Hearst was in a particularly advantageous position to make the attempt because it was well known that he had always been a "friend" of public education just as he had always been a "friend" of union labor. Actually, his friendship had amounted to no more than a constant clamor for the erection of new school buildings, always productive of fat contracts for local business men. During the depression, when enrollment was falling off and teachers' salaries were cut or left unpaid, Hearst continued to shout that the one educational need was more buildings. Never a word then or ever on the need for better instruction or more adequate recognition of the teachers. On the contrary, Arthur Brisbane and Winifred Black had for years devoted their best witticisms to the impracticality and uselessness of college teaching. Still, Hearst was a well-known "friend" of education and as such was conveniently situated to undermine its fundamental basis of free speech and free discussion.

The great campaign began in November 1934, when a Hearst reporter from the Syracuse *Journal*, disguised as a prospective student, managed to interview Professor John N. Washburne of Syracuse University on the subject of the courses in economics and sociology at the university. The next day he returned, accompanied by another reporter, represented to be a draftsman of the elevated railroad, and the two persuaded the unwary professor to go out to lunch with them. On November 22 the Syracuse *Journal* came out with screaming headlines to the effect that the Syracuse University (one of the most conservative institutions in the country) was infected with "Communism." On the first page it gave "the gist of conversations held with Professor John N. Washburne," so badly garbled that it was quite impossible to tell how much was authentic speech and how much was reportorial imagination. Professor Washburne promptly repudiated most of the statements attributed to him, and the student newspaper of the university printed an editorial condemning the methods of the Syracuse *Journal*. The Hearst organ thereupon defended its tactics, remarking, "When you go after bear you generally take a gun." It failed to note that even when going after bear one doesn't generally send skunks on the trail.

On December 19 the New York *American* published an article on "Red degeneracy" in the schools, written by Richard Washburn Child, the pro-Fascist former minister to Italy. And on the same day the *Evening Journal* attempted to repeat the Syracuse coup at the expense of George S. Counts and William H. Kilpatrick, two of the most distinguished members of Teachers College, Columbia University. But these men took the precaution to have stenographers present at their interviews with the alleged prospective students; as a natural result, Hearst never published the interviews. They were, however, printed in the February issue of the *Social Frontier*, and they make interesting reading.

Both of the reporters broke down and confessed their identity. The one sent to Dr. Counts admitted frankly that "Mr. Hearst is engaged at present in conducting a Red scare. . . . You realize of course that because of my assignment I will have to select the most sensational statements from the interview in order to make out a good case. This is what Mr. Hearst is expecting." The other's confession to Dr. Kilpatrick afforded an illuminating picture of the state of mind of a Hearst reporter:

DR. KILPATRICK: How do you feel about doing this sort of thing?

THE REPORTER: Just about as you think I feel. I don't like it very much. I hope when the Newspaper Guild achieves its complete organization this sort of thing will go.

DR. KILPATRICK: I have a feeling when I read a Hearst paper that the editorial policy is dishonest, that it is not advocating things because it believes them but because it wants to advertise them for some other reason. Almost every appeal is a demagogic appeal. Does that seem true to you?

THE REPORTER: You could find instances of it. Many of them in fact. Say last spring, when Hearst decided he wanted the McLeod Bill to go through. We were instructed that we were in favor of the bill and were to go out and make everyone else in favor of it. We were instructed to get one hundred telegrams from various people sent to Congress saying they favored the bill. I don't think I

found a single person who knew what the bill was or cared, but we
got the telegrams because of the obligations they felt to the paper.

DR. KILPATRICK: So the telegrams were sent just to carry out
the obligation to the paper?

THE REPORTER: Certainly—another instance was when Mr.
Moses came out with the statement that he didn't like the approach
to the Tri-Borough Bridge. The next morning we all got instructions that we were to kill that idea—stir up people, get telegrams,
etc., to the effect that people didn't want the approach changed. Well,
we all knew Hearst had been buying up property around there and
wouldn't hear to having the approach changed.

DR. KILPATRICK: Now tell me, would you not as a newspaper
man rather be with a newspaper that was honestly trying to work
for the good of the country? Would you not work harder and
would you not live a better life? Wouldn't you be on better terms
with yourself? Don't you feel ashamed to come and talk to me in
this way?

THE REPORTER: I'm not ashamed for myself but for the situation that makes it necessary to do this in order to keep alive.

DR. KILPATRICK: You are not ashamed for yourself?

THE REPORTER: I would rather not do it. Probably I am
ashamed, but I won't let myself be. I excuse myself on the basis of
expediency.

DR. KILPATRICK: Wouldn't it be a tremendous relief to you if
that whole situation could be got rid of? Don't you think so?

THE REPORTER: I don't think it, I know it. But after all I have
had periods of being out of work. I've been on three papers that
folded up unexpectedly and it is pretty tough. I wouldn't like working in a slaughter house either, but if that was the only work open,
I would probably do it. There's very little choice.

DR. KILPATRICK: I could do that with a clear conscience. I
could at any rate be honest about that.

THE REPORTER: Certainly your conscience would be clearer.
But it's pretty hard to know what to do. We do get pretty sick of
the things we're asked to do.

Not having any luck at Columbia, Hearst turned his attention to New York University, where it was discovered that Professors Sidney Hook and James Burnham were members of the Workers' Party and so, by inference, must be engaged in "treasonable plotting."

After New York University came Harvard, but by this time the educators' counter-attack was under way, and the Hearst reporters could get no more interviews to garble.

The reply of the professors was spirited. A letter to the McCormack-Dickstein Congressional Committee, engaged in investigating "un-American activities," requesting it to investigate the un-American activities of William Randolph Hearst, was signed by twenty-one of the most prominent educators in America, including John Dewey, Charles Beard, Harry Emerson Fosdick, E. C. Lindeman of the New York School of Social Work, Joseph K. Hart, associate editor of the *Survey,* and Jesse Newlon, former president of the National Education Association. On the other side arose the well-known Red-baiter, Matthew Woll, president of the National Civic Federation and vice president of the American Federation of Labor, who sent a letter to Congressman McCormack advising him not to take "too seriously" the statements of the educators. Protests sent to William Green, president of the A. F. of L., by the Teachers' Unions of New York City and Philadelphia, received one of Mr. Green's customary noncommittal replies.

Practically the entire February issue of the *Social Frontier,* the leading educational journal of the country, was devoted to an exposure of Hearst. Among other able articles was one entitled "Free for What?" by Bruce Bliven, in which the editor of the *New Republic* said:

Mr. Hearst and his reluctant or willing henchmen are trying to "nazify" the colleges on the unspoken but very real argument that nobody who has a chance to hear both sides of the case fairly presented can possibly want to live in a civilization which tolerates Mr. Hearst and approves his ideas. In this case, however, the activity is not in my judgment the result of any direct pressure from conservative capitalist interests, but is just another quaint idea of the old gentleman from San Simeon. It is nevertheless a coincidence, if nothing more, that his campaign should have been tremendously intensified immediately after he had a long private talk with Herr Hitler.

In the February meeting of the Department of Superintendence of the N.E.A. at Atlantic City there was long and vociferous applause for the words of Charles Beard:

In the course of the past fifty years I have talked with presidents of the United States, senators, justices of the Supreme Court, members of the House of Representatives, governors, mayors, bankers, editors, college presidents (including that great scholar and thinker, Charles W. Eliot), leading men of science, Nobel Prize winners in science and letters, and I have never found one single person who for talents and character commands the respect of the American people, who has not agreed with me that William Randolph Hearst has pandered to depraved tastes and has been an enemy of everything that is noblest and best in our American tradition. . . . There is not a cesspool of vice and crime which Hearst has not raked and exploited for money-making purposes. . . . Unless those who represent American scholarship, science, and the right of a free people to discuss public questions freely stand together against his insidious influences he will assassinate them individually by every method known to yellow journalism.

Two resolutions were adopted, one favoring the formation of a nation-wide federation of teachers, clergymen, and newspaper editors to safeguard the freedom of the press, the other calling upon the Nye senatorial committee to investigate various forms of Fascist propaganda. American educators have traditionally been noted for their timidity, but Hearst had roused them. Thinking to squash a caterpillar, he found himself treading on a rattlesnake.

His answer took the familiar form of a fake interview. Willard E. Givens of Oakland, Cal., secretary of the N.E.A., was quoted in the Hearst press as saying, "No man in the United

States has contributed more to the well-being of schools and school teachers than Mr. Hearst." The words were promptly repudiated by Mr. Givens.

But Hearst was not to be left without the support of at least one "educator," John Gabbert Bowman, who in his youth had unsuccessfully attempted to obtain the Columbia Ph.D. but had been since 1921 chancellor of the University of Pittsburgh, where he enjoyed an unpleasant notoriety in his profession because of his dictatorial methods and ruthless dismissals of faculty members who earned the hostility of the Mellon interests behind the university. That of the historian, Dr. Ralph E. Turner, led to an examination by a committee of the American Association of University Professors, whose report was summarized as follows in the New York *Post* of March 6, 1935:

A committee for the association finds that the dismissal of the brilliant Dr. Ralph E. Turner, associate professor of history and noted liberal, was a move to placate wealthy Pittsburgh industrialists.

The university was in the midst of a fund-raising campaign. It threw Turner and academic freedom overboard in order to please the coal, iron, and aluminum nabobs who resented Turner's activities as head of the Pennsylvania Security League.

The committee now unanimously reports that Dr. Turner's dismissal was "an unjustifiable termination of his services." It continues: "Far more significant than any wrong the chancellor may have done Dr. Turner and the other men dismissed is the irreparable damage inflicted on the self-respect of every man and woman on the faculty."

Appropriately enough, Bowman rose to Hearst's defense in a speech before the Daughters of the American Revolution in which he said:

In recent years there has been brought into our schools and colleges a vast amount of propaganda not interested in the truth. . . . If you oppose this propaganda, you are met at once by floods of blather about freedom and liberty. . . . I insist that our teachers be reverent and patriotic. That is just plain duty and common sense. In this connection, and on Washington's Birthday, I want to say a word of appreciation for the recent efforts of William Randolph Hearst both to show the source of the destructive influences in the land and to uphold our ideals of patriotism and reverence.

It was the first time Hearst had ever been praised as an exponent of "reverence," but he doubtless felt that Bowman had read his inner character correctly. Thus encouraged, he resumed his campaign against the colleges with additional vigor. Among those who had spoken out most forcefully on behalf of academic freedom was President Glenn Frank of the University of Wisconsin; hence President Frank was one of the first slated for disciplining. The Hearst press put all its force behind a legislative investigation of Communistic activities at Wisconsin, and when this collapsed through lack of evidence the Hearst papers attempted to revive it by shifting the issue to "free love rampant" at the university—Hearst continuing to be as much opposed as ever to any free love outside of the Kingdom of San Simeon. But this, too, broke down because the gossip collected by the Hearst reporters was found to have been gathered not in 1935 but in 1933 and not at the university but at the Extension Division in Milwaukee eighty-five miles away.

Next came the turn of the University of Chicago. Pursuing his invariable sniping methods, Hearst first opened fire on a single individual, Frederick L. Schuman, assistant professor of political science. In a letter to the *New Republic* of April 17, 1935, Mr. Schuman gave the entire history of the case, showing that the Hearst papers were running true to form.

Sir: Since William Randolph Hearst has publicly demanded that I be dismissed from my academic post, I wish to make public the following sequence of events, which will prove illuminating to all interested in the tactics of the Hearst press.

On November 14, 1934, the Chicago *Herald-Examiner* published a report of a meeting of the University of Chicago Student Union

Against War and Fascism, in which I, as well as several other people, were grossly misquoted. In a letter to the editor, Mr. Watson, I protested against this misrepresentation, and incidentally called attention to the fact that the alleged quotation from Lenin on the dictatorship of the proletariat, which was then appearing at the top of the editorial pages of all the Hearst papers, was nowhere to be found in Lenin's writings. Mr. Watson sent my protest to Mr. Hearst, who asked Mr. Charles Wheeler of the *Herald-Examiner* to "investigate." I received Mr. Wheeler in the presence of a third person and was shown material from his files showing conclusively that I had been "accidentally" misquoted—a fact Mr. Wheeler blandly conceded. He also conceded that the Lenin "quotation" was pure invention. "We just do what the Old Man orders. One week he orders a campaign against rats. The next week he orders a campaign against dope-peddlers. Pretty soon he's going to campaign against college professors. It's all the bunk, but orders are orders."

Shortly afterwards a New York anti-Nazi group requested me to prepare a series of replies to the syndicated articles by Goering appearing periodically in the Sunday issues of the Hearst papers. The International News Service [Hearst] encouraged the group to believe that an opportunity would be given for such replies. Two articles were submitted. Both were refused. . . . Meanwhile the "campaign against professors" materialized. On February 23 I delivered an address on "Communism and Liberalism" before the Cook County League of Women Voters in which I traced the historical relationship between the two ideologies, quoted with approval the Declaration of Independence, and made a plea for a new liberalism adequate to the exigencies of today. Mr. Charles Wheeler attended the lecture. In the *Herald-Examiner* of February 24 it was reported under the headline: "HOPE LIES IN SOVIETS, U. OF C. TEACHER SAYS; DECRIES LIBERALISM OF WASHINGTON." The article contained numerous statements in quotation marks that were purely products of Mr. Wheeler's imagination. In the same issue all the Hearst papers throughout the nation editorially condemned a number of educators as "advisers to Moscow" and "authorized disseminators of communistic propaganda in the United States who deliberately and designedly mislead our fine young people and bring them up to be disloyal to our American ideals and institutions and stupidly to favor the brutal and bloody tyranny of Soviet Russia." The victims of this slanderous attack were all persons who have publicly criticized the Nazi regime in Germany. They included Robert M. Hutchins, Charles H. Judd, John Dewey, George S. Counts, Hallie Flanagan, Susan Kingsbury, I. L. Kandel, William F. Russell, Henry Pratt Fairchild, Frank P. Graham, Howard Odum, *et al.*

On March 16, 1935, the *Herald-Examiner*—with Hearst papers elsewhere copying—published an editorial "Schuman of Chicago," which took out of their contexts two of Mr. Wheeler's misquotations and presented them as evidence that I am making a "direct challenge to American institutions in the name of communism." I was further accused of having "just written a book on Russia which has been approved by Moscow." (I have never written a book on Russia. My doctoral dissertation, "American Policy toward Russia since 1917," was published in 1928 and was rejected for translation by Gosizdat, the Moscow State Publishing House, because it was not written from the Communist viewpoint.) The editorial described me as one of "these American panderers and trap-baiters for the Moscow mafia" who should be investigated by Congress and "gotten rid of" as a "Red."

This is but one of numerous instances of slanderous and libelous attacks upon American educators in the Hearst press. This strategy is exactly comparable to that of the Nazi press in Germany between 1920 and 1933. . . . If American universities and colleges are to be spared the fate that has befallen such institutions in Germany, if American scholars and educators are to be protected from Fascist bludgeoning of this type, if American traditions of freedom are to survive, Mr. Hearst must be recognized as the propagandist and forerunner of American Hitlerism and must be met with a united counter-attack by all Americans who still value their liberties.

FREDERICK L. SCHUMAN
Assistant Professor of Political Science.
The University of Chicago, Chicago, Ill.

On the basis of the same sort of evidence as that in the Schuman case Hearst next demanded the resignation of President Hutchins, Professor Robert Morss Lovett, Professor Charles G. Merriam, and others. Then Charles R. Walgreen, the wealthy head of a national drug store chain and a good friend of Hearst's *American Druggist,* withdrew his niece named Lucille Norton from the university, because, as he testified solemnly before a Senate Investigating Committee, she had been asked to read the *Communist Manifesto, New Russia's Primer* (a Book-of-the-Month Club selection!), and an article by Stuart Chase in which he made the treasonable statement, "It must be more than a little of a bore to be a business man dedicated to a life of unrelenting greed." Walgreen was followed on the stand by Mrs. Albert W. Dilling, author of *The Red Network,* who proved to know nothing about the University of Chicago but talked volubly about Russia until the bored senators dismissed her as having nothing of importance to contribute. Her disappointed husband vented his feelings by punching the face of an irreverent spectator who sat next to him, after which the Dillings withdrew in confusion. The investigation of the University of Chicago collapsed like that of Wisconsin. Throughout, the Hearst papers had given it an enormous amount of space with numerous eulogistic accounts and photographs of Walgreen and Mrs. Dilling. And its collapse, of course, did not halt their attacks on President Hutchins and the exonerated professors.

On the other hand, to show that Hearst was not opposed to universities when devoted to their proper purposes, his papers at this time featured the generous prizes which he offered to university rifle clubs all over the country. "HARVARD TEAM'S PATRIOTISM" read one heading, followed by a long story beginning, "Martial music and the thrill of the colors lent patriotic pageantry yesterday to an impressive ceremony in which the Harvard Military School and its crack cadet riflemen were presented with the William Randolph Hearst awards for marksmanship. The handsome silver trophy for the school and the

It's the Four R's Now

The Board of Education of the District of Columbia has—on the basis of an opinion from Corporation Counsel Prettyman—ordained that teachers shall *teach* Communism in the public schools; this along with a strange proviso that they shall not *advocate* it.

Inasmuch as Congress, which appropriates the money for the District of Columbia, had evidently been forewarned of Communistic influences at work in the schools and had ordained that Communism should be NEITHER taught nor advocated, the Board of Education may have stored up some real trouble for itself.

Disobeying Congress, by servants of Congress, usually calls for CONTEMPT CITATIONS.

And there is another phase of this unusual matter.

Try to find a Communist in a school or college faculty—and they are there—who will ADMIT that he ADVOCATES Communism.

They all say, "WE TEACH—we do not ADVOCATE!"—and part of the later technique of school propaganda is to insist upon the RIGHT to TEACH Communism and then MISUSE that "right" to ADVOCATE Communism, which becomes merely a matter of emphasis.

They call it ACADEMIC FREEDOM!

THE "RED" BOGEYMAN

This editorial cartoon in the Hearst press aims to bar historical reference to communism in the classroom, holding that the desire to mention its place in history is really a desire to advocate it.

beautiful gold medals, etc., etc." Opposite were large pictures of the team and the trophies.

But the unpatriotic educators, as contrasted with the patriotic rifle teams, remained incorrigible. The national convention of the N.E.A. in July 1935 established the committee on academic freedom suggested at the meeting of superintendents. And the next convention of the Department of Superintendence in February 1936 listened to speeches by Charles Beard and—oh sorrow and shame—by Norman Thomas, along with representatives of the Republican and Democratic parties. Emphatically, by both precept and example, American teachers insisted upon their right to discuss controversial issues in spite of all the Hearst edicts to the contrary.

A few verbal victories were nevertheless won by the publisher through the aid of politicians directly under his influence. In New York the Ives Bill, supposed to have been virtually written by him, requiring all teachers to take an oath of allegiance, and the Nunan Bill, making a similar requirement of students, were both passed over the protests of teachers and students who were of course denounced as "traitors" in the Hearst press. And although the Kramer Sedition Bill, introduced by Representative Kramer of California, was defeated in Congress, a rider was successfully smuggled into the Appropriation Bill, making it illegal to "teach or advocate communism" in the District of Columbia. The question at once arose whether this merely forbade indoctrination or also forbade the giving of any information whatsoever about communism. The counsel of the D. of C. Board of Education, E. Barrett Prettyman, took the former view, the Daughters of the American Revolution the latter. Hearst, of course, supported the Daughters and attacked Prettyman. There was no question of interpretation, he insisted. " 'TEACHING OR ADVOCATING OF COMMUNISM,' in the language of the law, means just THAT." This explained many apparent inconsistencies in the Hearst editorials; whatever they might seem to say, they always meant "just THAT," "THAT" meaning whatever Hearst chose to have it mean at the moment of writing or at any time in the future.

When Controller-General McCarl announced that he would require written statements from the teachers every two weeks that they had obeyed the law before he would issue their pay checks, Hearst hailed the edict as another great victory for Americanism. His touching faith in the efficacy of oaths, his naïve belief that teachers engaged in treasonable plotting would still shrink from falsification, might have been interpreted as an infantile regression due to senescence, had it not been in perfect harmony with the childish attitude toward patriotism which he had always had.

Meanwhile, during the entire year 1934–5 the Hearst press conducted a campaign against Russia which was fully as extravagant and mendacious as that against the teachers. A hitherto unknown correspondent, Thomas Walker, introduced in the Hearst press as one "who for several years has toured the Union of Soviet Republics," followed the lead of Hitler's German papers in announcing a wholly non-existent famine in the Ukraine. "SIX MILLION PEASANTS DIE AS SOVIET HOARDS GRAIN" ran the headlines—six million lies in a single sentence. Louis Fischer in the March 13, 1934, issue of the *Nation* showed, from the dates on Walker's passport, that Hearst's correspondent had been in Russia for precisely thirteen days—just long enough to collect a set of photographs of the 1921 famine for reproduction as of 1934. At the same time that Walker's articles and photographs were being run, another Hearst correspondent, Lindesay Parrott, head of the International News Service in Moscow, was reporting that there was no famine but that on the contrary the Ukraine enjoyed two bumper wheat crops.

After Walker had been exposed, one Harry Lang was advanced to tell of a famine in 1932 and to tell of it in such a way that most readers would think he was talking about contemporary conditions. Then when Lang was discredited, Jacob Papin, a Russian immigrant who had not been out of San Francisco since 1906, was put forward to write, under the name of John Slivcoff, on "SIX TERRIBLE YEARS SPENT IN RUSSIA" under the Soviet rule. No matter how many Hearst liars were exposed, he could always find others to take their place.

Furthermore, he was able to discover new Communists every day. One might have thought that an absolute limit was reached when he introduced Dr. Nicholas Murray Butler in that capacity because of his activities as president of the Carnegie Endowment for International Peace, activities which Hearst said threatened the sovereignty of the United States and constituted "the most SEDITIOUS proposition ever laid before the American public." But no, after demanding the suppression of the Carnegie Foundation, Dr. Butler, and most of the leading educators in the country, Hearst went on to investigate the churches. "RED PROPAGANDA IN RELIGIOUS ORGANIZATIONS," "COMMUNISM IN THE CHURCHES," ran the heads of a series which showed the treasonable character of the National Council in the Episcopal Church, the National Council of Methodist Youth, the Methodist Federation for Social Service, the Fellowship of Reconciliation, the Federal Council of Churches of Christ in America, Union Theological Seminary, the Y.M.C.A., and the Y.W.C.A. After this, one half expected to see any morning in the Hearst papers a series headed "RED PROPAGANDA IN THE BANKS" or "COMMUNISM IN THE DUPONT FAMILY."

The logical conclusion toward which he was traveling was evidently that everyone in the United States was a Communist except Hearst himself. Though in his now plainly psychopathic condition of mingled fear and megalomania some such unspoken conviction may well have been present, verbally he went no further than at last to include the whole Roosevelt administration in the class of Communist sympathizers.

CHAPTER XVIII

Business Man Embattled

THE inevitable open break with Roosevelt came at the beginning of 1935 with the President's message to the Seventy-Fourth Congress advising American entrance into the World Court. Hearst's friends, Harding, Coolidge, and Hoover had all previously suggested this course without calling down upon their heads any anathemas from the publisher, although he had always been opposed to the measure. But in his new "Americanism" campaign, the World Court, an appropriate symbol of all the personal slights and snubs he had encountered abroad, quickly became something almost demoniac. He called to his assistance Father Coughlin of Detroit, who had already done yeoman work on behalf of Hearst's inflationary policy. Coughlin had visited the publisher at San Simeon, and on trips to New York was entertained at the Hotel Warwick, the metropolitan residence of Hearst and Miss Davies. His sermons were featured at much greater length in the Hearst press than in other papers. Hearst turned over to this useful demagogue the radio attack on the Court while his editors thundered against it in writing. Congress was overwhelmed with Coughlin and Hearst telegrams—how easily secured we have learned from the confessions of the Hearst reporter in the Kilpatrick interview— and the recommendation of the President was decisively rejected.

As yet, however, the publisher was willing to overlook this single error of judgment on Roosevelt's part, provided his other measures were correct. He rejoiced in the Supreme Court's action on the gold clause, hoped for heavy government subsidies to the aviation companies in which he was financially interested, and even deemed it possible that the President might not veto the Patman Bonus Bill. Support of the latter, on which Hearst and Coughlin now concentrated their political efforts, had the double advantage that the bill if passed would add to inflation and Hearst's mining profits, and whether passed or not the support of it would further strengthen Hearst's standing with the American Legion and the Veterans of Foreign Wars. The President's veto of the measure made Hearst's break with the administration definitive. Outraged by Roosevelt's lack of patriotism, Hearst demanded, "Why merely be penurious toward the veterans?" and replied that there was "absolutely no answer, no explanation except INCONSISTENCY and HYPOCRISY!"

When in May 1935 the N.R.A. was declared unconstitutional, Hearst exclaimed, "THANK GOD FOR THE SUPREME COURT!" And with reason, for the next day the working hours on the Hearst press were increased. Now was the time, Hearst maintained, for the administration to retreat. "TURN TO THE RIGHT, MR. PRESIDENT!" he appealed. "LET AMERICAN INDUSTRY BRING RECOVERY." Having obtained all he wanted from the government, it was now the latter's duty to keep its hands off of business.

Up to this time a favorite object of Hearstian denunciation had been the Power Trust. In season and out of season, his papers had kept up the attack. If there was one form of business which more than any other, in the opinion of the Hearst press, exploited the American people, it was the public utilities. But as soon as the Wheeler-Rayburn bill to regulate them was presented with a chance of passage, the real Hearst revealed himself. As conclusive evidence against the bill, he listed those opposed to it—just such a list as in former years would have been cited in the Hearst press as proof positive that it was the "predatory interests" who were against it:

The Chamber of Commerce of the United States and the State Chambers of Commerce of New York, Ohio, Florida, and Pennsylvania.

Twenty-six insurance companies whose assets would be greatly injured.

Merchants' and manufacturers' organizations, representing virtually the entire trade and industry of the nation.

Almost equally objectionable to Hearst, and presumably to many of the advertisers in the *American Druggist*, was a local California "Pure Food and Drug Act," which Governor Merriam was urged to veto on the ground that "it would be a nuisance both to dealers in drugs and to manufacturers of drugs within and outside the state."

The climax of all came with the President's income-tax bill, which caused the aging millionaire to emit actual howls of agony. The measure, he cried, was an "ADMINISTRATION BLUDGEON," it was "TAXATION FOR INTIMIDATION," it was "BLACKMAIL"; the President's policy was summed up as one to "SOAK THE THRIFTY!—LOOT INDUSTRY! AND SPREAD POVERTY!" Henceforth, the New Deal was always referred to as the "Raw Deal." In a signed article, Hearst recounted the history of the Roosevelt administration under the title, "THE RAKE'S PROGRESS." The period since 1932 was called in the Hearst press "THE ROOSEVELT REPUDIATION ERA." The President virtually deserved impeachment, for:

President Roosevelt has repudiated his oath of office.

He has repudiated the Constitution.

He has repudiated the fundamental Democratic doctrine of state rights.

Above all, the administration was now discovered to be inspired by communistic aims. In an article entitled "AWAKE, AMERICAN PATRIOTS!" published in the Los Angeles *Examiner*, November 24, 1935, Robert H. Hemphill, "financial authority" of the Hearst press, declared,

I do not know what catastrophe will be required to shock this nation into a realization of the enormous consequences which are planned and ARE BEING EXECUTED by the Federal Administration and its little band of fanatic adventurers. . . ,

This band of revolutionary radicals PROPOSE TO OVERTHROW THIS GOVERNMENT.

AND THEY ARE DOING IT!

The government was found to be simply infested with Communists. "AVOWED COMMUNISTS IN PUBLIC OFFICE" ran one heading, "COMMUNISTS ON RELIEF ROLLS" ran another, Hearst insisting that anyone who fed a starving Communist was as good as a Communist himself. Tugwell was an open Communist who ought to be "driven from office." Wallace was a secret Communist who ought to share the same fate.

But the most damning clause in the indictment of Roosevelt's advisers was not that they were Communists but that they were not business men. Wallace "never *created* anything in the way of an industry in his life." Tugwell "NEVER CREATED ANY INDUSTRY OF ANY KIND." What could one expect from such advisers? All that they could do was to create Socialist-Communist undertakings such as the A.A.A. and the T.V.A.

Finally, there appeared a choice article headed "MRS. ROOSEVELT AND COMMUNISM" which read:

Mrs. President Roosevelt has graciously come to the rescue of those puzzled over the difference between "teaching" and "advocating" Communism.

She cites the following example as the way teachers will be "tongue-tied" under the ruling of Controller-General McCarl banning the teaching of Communism in the Washington public schools:

"A child asking, 'What form of government do they (the Russians) live under?,' the teacher having to say, 'My dear child, I can't tell you.' "

Any public school teacher who would answer in that manner would be guilty of an untruth.

Her answer would be as follows, and it is the WHOLE TRUTH:

"CHILDREN, THE RUSSIANS LIVE UNDER A COMMUNISTIC FORM OF GOVERNMENT. IT HAS DESTROYED THE RIGHT TO OWN ANYTHING. EVEN THE CLOTHES ON THE BACKS OF RUSSIAN CHILDREN BELONG TO THE GOVERNMENT. IT HAS DESTROYED ALL FREEDOM TO EXPRESS OPINION OR WRITE WHAT IS FULLY BELIEVED UNDER PENALTY OF DEATH. THE RUSSIANS ARE RULED, CHILDREN, UNDER A DICTATORSHIP, WHICH IS WHAT WE DENOUNCED IN THE DECLARATION OF INDEPENDENCE AND WHICH IS CONTRARY TO THE AMERICAN CONSTITUTION."

That is what any honest teacher in an American school can say to a child who wants to know what kind of a government the Russians live under.

If she should answer, "I can't tell you," she is probably pro-Communist.

If after this the Hearst readers couldn't tell whether Mrs. Roosevelt herself was pro-Communist, they must have been even stupider than usual.

Shortly after the end of Congress, Hearst had come out in a signed article for a revival of "Jeffersonian democracy," saying, "I think definitely that the historic Democratic Party of Jefferson, of Madison, of Monroe, of Jackson, of Cleveland, should nominate candidates who are recognized Democrats; and adopt a platform of sound Democratic principles." As a beginning, he proceeded characteristically to give his support to the presidential candidacy of the Republican governor of Kansas, Alf M. Landon. Day after day, the Hearst headlines and "news" stories extolled Governor Landon's achievements in cutting down taxation (at the expense of education and relief). If they did not mention Landon's friendship for the oil interests and public utilities, some things could be understood between gentlemen.

In all his anti-Roosevelt, anti-Communist campaign, Hearst was greatly hampered by the lack of competent editorial assistance. Most of his once brilliant group of journalists were gone; those who remained were in the sere and yellow leaf. Chamberlain and McEwen were dead; Carvalho was eighty and Goddard seventy; Brisbane at seventy-two was only the shadow of himself; his daily column, save for an occasional feeble paragraph in eulogy of Mussolini or the California vigilantes, had degenerated into sentimental nonsense about Mother's Day and similar inanities. Winifred Sweet Black Bonfils did indeed every now and then give up writing her helpful articles on such topics as "Conceit Has No Place in Life," "Adversity Often Real Blessing," "Prettiness Caused Her Woe," in order to help "the Chief" solve the more profound social problems of the day; but though Winifred was willing, she was rather terrible. The best she could do on even such a promising subject as "Labor Must End Class Warfare" was to string together a series of questions: "What's it all about anyway? Isn't there any such thing as common sense making the best of a bad situation any more? We keep hearing about the millions of people out of work that won't take it. . . . The birds get along without strikes and so do the other animals. Man, they say, is just a little lower than the angels. Well, he seems to be getting a good deal lower than that these days. . . . Have we made ourselves over into a kind of machine, we poor little, feeble, struggling ants? What is it that is leading us so far astray? It makes the head swim even to try to figure it out, doesn't it?"

This plaintive tone didn't get one anywhere. None of all the Chief's ancient staff of writers could really keep up with him; none was really worthy of him; not a single one.

He did, however, have a new source of strength that had been lacking in the old days—his moving picture influence. This had been used effectively at the beginning of his Fascist phase in the defeat of Upton Sinclair for governor of California. In his racy book, *I, Candidate for Governor, and How I Got Licked* (1935), Sinclair tells the story from his own viewpoint:

While I was in New York some reporter asked: "What are you going to do with the unemployed motion picture actors?" I answered: "Why should not the State of California rent one of the idle studios and let unemployed actors make a few pictures of their own?" That word was flashed to Hollywood, and the war was on.

Louis B. Mayer, president of Metro-Goldwyn-Mayer, was vacationing in Europe when he got this dreadful news, and he dropped everything and came home to take charge of the campaign to "stop Sinclair." You see, he is chairman of the State Committee of the Republican Party, so he had a double responsibility.

Also Mr. Hearst was summoned from his vacation. Mr. Hearst belongs to the movie section on account of Miss Marion Davies. Hearst had been staying at Bad Nauheim, and Marion, through a coincidence, was there also. They were hobnobbing with Hanfstaengl, Nazi agent to the United States. You see, Hearst wants to know how the Reds are to be put down in America; so "Huffy," as they call him, flew with Hearst to interview Hitler.

As soon as Hearst learned of my nomination, he gave out an interview comparing me with the Pied Piper of Hamelin; and then he and Marion came back to New York and gave another interview, and from there to California, where he called me "an unbalanced and unscrupulous political speculator." His newspapers began a campaign of editorials and cartoons denouncing me as a Communist. I didn't see any denouncing me as a free-lover, and a menace to the purity and sanctity of the American home.

Hearst, Mayer, the Warners, headed the fight to save California from the Epics and Sinclair. They produced fake news reels. They threatened to move to Florida if Sinclair was elected. They assessed all their players and screen writers for funds with which to defeat him.

The trade magazine, *Hollywood Reporter*, exclaimed with delight:

When the picture business gets aroused, it becomes AROUSED, and, boy, how they go to it! . . . Never before in the history of the picture business has the screen been used in direct support of a candidate. . . . And this activity may reach much farther than the ultimate defeat of Mr. Sinclair. It will undoubtedly give the big wigs in Washington and politicians all over the country an idea of the real POWER that is in the hands of the picture industry.

The *Hollywood Reporter* was quite right. The movies occupied the position which the "yellow journals" had held at the· beginning of the century, and had Hearst been what he once was he would undoubtedly have made a mighty effort to capture them for a patriotic movement under his exclusive leadership. But even the best of old dogs cannot learn tricks indefinitely. In militaristic propaganda he suffered the disgrace of being outdone by the *Fox Movietone News* which devoted 13.30 per cent of all its items to the cause whereas the Hearst Metrotone News lagged behind with a paltry 10.60 per cent. Though to be sure, the Warner Brothers–First National partly atoned for this by their three militaristic feature films, *Here Comes the Navy*, *Flirtation Walk*, and *Devil Dogs of the Air*.

Yet even the movies had to be watched for "communism." When the film *Oil for the Lamps of China*, based upon Alice Tisdale Hobart's novel, was produced in 1935, Louella O. Parsons declared, "The few necessary liberties . . . taken have not in the least hampered the drama nor robbed the story of its important situations." What had actually happened was that the screening had been held up for weeks while an entirely new ending, actually inverting the significance of the work, was being written at the command of Hearst.

The owner of the Hearst press was still more incensed at the production of the film, *The President Vanishes*, in which the publisher of a chain of newspapers figured as one of the villains in the piece. There came an edict from Joseph Willicombe, Hearst's private secretary, in the usual form, "The Chief says

. . .," ordering that no publicity whatsoever should be given to this film.

When *Five-Star Final* appeared, Hearst looked upon it as an attack upon his papers (though the New York *Graphic* was the actual model taken, he recognized that he and Bernarr McFadden were twins under the skin), so the command was sent out to give no publicity and accept no advertising. Then, since business was business, he changed his mind and ordered the acceptance of advertising, coupling this, however, with the information that a "sample review" would be sent from Hollywood upon which all his editors were expected to base their own reviews.

Yes, Hearst was primarily a newspaper man and did well to stick to his last. If his "Red" scare had aroused chiefly ridicule in the rest of the country, it had brought results in California where the merchants and large land-owners had given it good support. The leaders of the share-cropper and tenant-farmer strike of 1934 in the San Joaquin Valley had been held in jail for many months while the Hearst papers labored to create the atmosphere of hysteria necessary for their condemnation under the criminal syndicalism law. By the beginning of 1935 this was accomplished. Then during the summer—the season of strikes—the Hearst press fostered a renewed terrorist drive against "communism."

"Six reds flee patriot fury" ran the Los Angeles *Examiner's* heading of its account of a vigilante raid. "Six additional Communists on the 'tar-and-feather' list of the Sonoma County Vigilante 'night riders' who early this morning punished two radical leaders, today were believed to have hastily fled from this vicinity. With sunset this evening set as the new deadline for Red chieftains to get out of the county, citizens here tensely awaited new vigilante raids. Sheriff Harry Patteson, militant foe of Communists, announced he had received 'no complaints' from the two radicals tarred and feathered by a mob of 300 early today. 'I plan no action unless a complaint is made,' the Sheriff said. 'And I don't anticipate any complaints.'"

Sheriff Harry Patteson's sentiments were perhaps reserved for the benefit of Communists alone, but not so the aged publisher's. His papers apologized for the lynching of a twenty-four-year-old gunman named Clyde Johnson at Yreka, California, on the old vigilante plea of speedy justice. "This lynching and others that have occurred in recent months can all be attributed to the law's delay, and to the corruption of some of the machinery of justice; and while lynchings are deplorable, still more deplorable are the conditions that precipitate them. If the machinery of the law is not sufficient to deal justice to the criminal, the public can hardly be blamed for taking the situation into their own hands." Johnson had been captured only a few days before the lynching but the *Examiner* attributed it to resentment over the fact that a policeman had been killed in Yreka two years before by another gunman named George Hall and that Hall had not yet been executed. "Hall still lives," it said pointedly, "in Folsom prison's death row, while the United States Supreme Court reviews his case." The whole attitude of the paper was a distinct incitement to further violence, and why not? The *Examiner* featured to sales advantage numerous photographs of the lynching, an especially gruesome one showing Johnson hanging from his rope, and the same type of people who stripped the bark from the lynching tree for souvenirs would welcome accounts of bigger and better lynchings in the future.

But the Hearst press and Hearst himself would certainly have denied that their two years' campaign of violence against "the Reds" had had anything to do with the "deplorable" recrudescence of lynchings in California. They did not believe in violence in general any more than in war in general. Hearst had recently said that war ought never to be declared without a popular referendum—if that didn't prove his hostility to war, what could? They believed in violence and war only when some great principle was involved, such as justice or Americanism or the preservation of the Hearst fortune.

In October 1935 Hearst suddenly made a grandiose gesture calculated to attract the attention of the whole country. He was leaving California because of the income tax. "The house at San Simeon will be closed before the end of the year," he announced. "Of course I hope that it may be opened again some day, but I cannot tell when—if at all. . . . New York is my legal and voting residence and has been for over thirty years. I simply cannot afford to be a resident of California as well as a resident of New York, nor can anybody else. The California law would make me a resident if I spent over six months in California. Then I would have to pay a fifteen per cent income tax in California, in addition to the lesser income tax in New York, and the extremely heavy Federal taxes. . . . No, the cattle ranch at San Simeon will certainly not be closed. The cows are a little more fortunate than we humans are in this respect. They can continue to enjoy the glorious climate of California without being subjected to quite confiscatory taxation. . . ."

Within a very few days after this defiant declaration, the Hearst press was able to announce, "THREE STATES INVITE MR. HEARST AS RESIDENT." The invitations came from Governor David Scholz of Florida, seconded by the Florida Chamber of Commerce, the Mayor of Jacksonville, the owner of the Hotel George Washington at Palm Beach, and the Lions Club of Tallahassee; from the Chamber of Commerce of Reno, Nevada; and from the president of the Seattle Real Estate Board.

Then Miss Louella O. Parsons, just back from New York, brought further good news. "New York," she said, "is delighted that Mr. Hearst plans to spend most of his time there—and is jubilant because it is generally believed that scores of important motion picture persons and wealthy people generally will follow his example."

The threat to California in all this was plain. But Hearst miscalculated his influence over the people of the state in imagining that they would come crawling to his feet, begging him not to leave. Manchester Boddy, editor of the *Illustrated Daily News*, expressed the general sentiment toward Hearst's attempt to scare the state into submission:

> Mr. Hearst has challenged millions of citizens up to their necks in troubles as difficult as his own, to call his bluff.
> And call it they will!
> That Mr. Hearst should imagine that his insolent "rebuke" to the state of California should cause a sympathetic uprising in his behalf betrays a degree of egotism of which not even he has hitherto been suspected.

Hearst took five days to reply to the invitation from Governor Scholz of Florida, and when his answer came it indicated that his gesture had been just what Boddy called it—a bluff.

"I would be honored," he said, "as anyone would be, by citizenship in so delightful and so notable a state. Indeed, I would accept the invitation with pleasure and gratitude did I not feel that I had many obligations to the state of my present citizenship and to the state of my birth. Unnecessary and unreasonable taxes are grievous things to pay. Still, while it is humanly possible, we must strive to pay what the state imposes. . . ."

But he took advantage of the opportunity to explain in some detail the final political and economic philosophy which he had reached:

> In the last analysis, we have got to live by our own honest labor and earn our bread in the sweat of our brow. . . .
> For prosperity, therefore, we must have active industry, and for successful industry we must have competent and experienced leaders.
> Leaders who are qualified by intelligence and experience are as important to industry as generals are to armies, as captains are to ships, as conductors are to orchestras.
> We cannot win battles if we dismiss our generals.

We cannot sail to safe harbors if we throw our captains overboard.

We cannot get sweet symphony if the orchestra is led by the iceman; and we cannot again head the world in industry and enterprise if we drive out our experienced managers and allow the trade, the commerce, the industry, the wealth-creating and distributing agencies of this great business nation to be burdened and bullied and hampered and harassed by cranks and college professors, dunces and demagogues.

The long overdue explicit announcement of the alliance between Hearst and Big Business was here made.

His withdrawal from California having already secured the desired amount of attention, it was no longer necessary to carry it out except in form. He did indeed spend a few weeks in New York during November, when its inhabitants succeeded remarkably well in concealing the delight and jubilance that Louella O. Parsons had observed. But easterners were notoriously given to hiding their real feelings. Hearst definitely preferred the frank and open West where he was born.

December 1935 found him safely at home again in San Simeon.

CHAPTER XIX

The Hearst Business Empire

IF ON his seventy-second birthday William Randolph Hearst looked back over his long career he must have admitted that in all but one respect he had been a supreme failure. With greater initial opportunities than had fallen to the lot of any other leader of public opinion in America, he had so terribly misused them that at the end he had sunk to be a follower of the D.A.R. and Mrs. Dilling of *The Red Network*. As a reformer, he was discredited even by himself. As a journalist, he owned twenty-nine papers, but not one of them was a *news*paper in the proper meaning of the word. As a politician, he had been defeated in every movement he had undertaken. As a man, he was, as Professor Beard had said, held in universal contempt by the thinking people of the country. It was not a pleasant record to survey. To be considered, as he was, a trickster in reform, a liar in journalism, a charlatan in politics, a hypocrite in morals—what was there left? The greatest of all: for according to the authorized biography of Mrs. Fremont Older, likely to be authentic on this point at least, he had accumulated the second largest fortune in America. This single claim could not be denied even by his worst enemies; he was one of the mightiest of all American captains of industry. This alone amply entitled him, according to his final political philosophy, to his position as a leader of public opinion.

Again and again his fortune had come to his rescue to save him from the worst effects of the schizophrenia that had wrecked his personality at the beginning. Though his neuroticism had manifested itself in an inferiority attitude that almost invariably drove him to attack his own candidates as soon as they were successful, and in a constant habit of attributing his own peculiar faults of character to his enemies—known in psychiatry by the technical name of "projection"—nevertheless, his wealth had enabled him to gratify his instinctive defensive substitution of new interests when the old ones failed and so survive a series of defeats that would have crushed anyone of lesser means. It, and it alone, had enabled him to defy public opinion and live his private life exactly as he pleased. It had kept him physically hale and hearty into the seventies where many an honest reformer had died of heartbreak long before. Hearst indeed had reason to be grateful to his wealth.

The realization that at last seems to have come over him—so far as he was capable of seeing himself at all—that he was primarily an industrialist interested in his own financial ventures meant the abandonment of all his pretended schemes of social reform. The old Hearst was now dead. But he had never been really alive. There had been only, as one of his intimate acquaintances has described it to the authors, "a shell encasing a curious kind of emptiness." But at the very end of his career the inner Hearst came forth, threw off the masks, and almost achieved the reality of an honest robber baron.

Hitherto, the past tense has been used in our account of deeds that already belong to history—the history of American charlatanism. But Hearst the industrialist is still with us. In the remaining sections of the book it will be more fitting to treat its subject as a living being, not the pseudo reformer and fake journalist but the real Hearst, the owner, the buyer, and the seller. Even at the cost of some repetition and the inevitable dullness of statistics it is necessary now to summarize rather fully the activities of Hearst as multi-millionaire.

For many years the story had been carefully cultivated that it was a mere accident that Hearst happened to be a millionaire.

"I didn't care about making money," he said to Lincoln Steffens in 1906, "at least not just to make money, and I don't care anything about that now. If money was what I was after, I could get that—now—more easily, more surely, and with less trouble and less labor, in some other way." No doubt Hearst told the literal truth when he said that he "did not care *just* to make money." Few men do. They usually care for money as the necessary means to security, comfort, leisure, travel, pleasure, or power. It has meant all these things to Hearst, and above all the rest it has meant power. He has been a lone wolf much of the time. He has fought, and fought bitterly other capitalist groupings—but that was essential to the success of his type of enterprise. To imagine him as unidentified with the capitalist system as such and uncontrolled by the demands of his vast capital investments outside his newspapers would be absurd. That the millions invested in the Hearst publishing enterprises represent less than half of his total wealth; that these publishing enterprises are not self-perpetuating but rest upon a solid foundation of more valuable and more typical capital investments; that Hearst's policies as a publisher are largely determined by his other interests; that, in a word, his newspaper career is only the most interesting phase of his career as a capitalist—all this is what his own actions have been telling us with increasing clearness ever since 1929, and it becomes perfectly clear as we trace his entire life.

Money has made Hearst in the sense that without it he could not have become any of the things which he has become. It was the unstinted backing of his father's millions which made it possible for him to experiment wildly and recklessly with the San Francisco *Examiner*. Without the fourteen millions derived from his mother through the sale of Anaconda stock, he could not have afforded to lose $7,000,000 on the New York *Journal* before it began to pay. No other newspaperman in the country ever started out with a fraction of the money and valuable investments that Hearst had when he began. His immediate predecessors in yellow journalism, James Gordon Bennett and Joseph Pulitzer, started from scratch and had to make money from the start. Hearst did not, so he was free to make much more money in the end.

The vast and profitable estate built up by George Hearst found its way to William Randolph Hearst—some directly at the time of his father's death in 1891, some during the following quarter century, and the balance after his mother's death in 1919.

The parental nest-egg included a vast empire of mining properties, valuable forests, tremendous holdings of agricultural and grazing lands, and city real estate. The mines form the basis of the empire, and William Randolph Hearst is, in the first instance, a mining magnate of substantial dimensions. He owns the Ontario mine in Utah, the Ophir mine in Nevada, the San Luis and Guanacevi gold and silver mines of Mexico; 51,000 shares of the Cerro de Pasco in Peru and in the Homestake mine in South Dakota. He likewise has extensive interests in the Eureka Mining Company and the Santa Eulalia Mining Company.

The Cerro de Pasco Copper Company owns 730 mineral claims comprising 5900 acres, as well as other extensive land holdings, railroads, brickyards, mining equipment, smelters, and considerable other property. According to *Moody's Manual* "the Cerro de Pasco mineral district, situated about 220 miles by rail from Lima, is one of the oldest and richest in the world." The company's assets are listed at $40,000,000. It has no funded debt, and is a heavy producer of copper, silver, and gold. Edward H. Clark is president of this corporation, which has on its board of directors Ogden L. Mills, whom, it will be recalled, Hearst supported for governor of New York. Hearst inherited Mr. Clark also, for he has been the financial director and adviser of the Hearst estate for decades.

The Homestake Mining Company was for many years the largest gold mine in the world, and is still ranked as one of the largest. The long lean years of depression didn't affect Homestake. In 1933 it had a net operating profit of $8,735,225. Its earnings per share in recent years tells an interesting tale:

1928	1929	1930	1931	1932	1933	1934	1935
$5.86	$4.16	$8.00	$8.45	$10.60	$15.00	$30	$44

Directly connected with the mining ventures is Hearst's interest in the American Metals Company, with Mr. Clark on the board of directors. This corporation, with assets of $77,-771,443 at the beginning of 1934, has extensive holdings in northern Rhodesia, Mexico, Cuba, New Mexico, Oklahoma, and Pennsylvania. It is an importer and exporter of non-ferrous and precious metals, ores, and acids, and employs about 6000 people.

The internal workings of Hearst-controlled enterprises have always been kept secret. Private Investors, Inc., a New York investment trust, which held 100 shares of Homestake stock, sued the mining corporation, demanding the right to examine its books in order to make an analysis of the company's 1934 annual report. Private Investors, Inc., claimed that Homestake listed the value of its property and equipment at $4,295,000 when in reality it should be $86,000,000. Judge Griffin of the Superior Court of San Francisco on January 5, 1936, upheld the plaintiff—but the officials of Homestake announced they would appeal the decision to a higher court and fight to the limit to prevent their books from being examined.

Measured in square miles, Hearst's agricultural holdings are even larger than his mining properties. These, too, with the exception of smaller bits, were likewise inherited. His 270,000-acre estate at San Simeon puts to shame the holdings of the great barons of the Middle Ages. It covers more than 420 square miles. But San Simeon is only one of his many vast estates. There is Wyntoon, nestling in the shadow of Mount

Shasta, 50,000 acres of northern California's finest timberland. And there are numerous "smaller ranches" such as the 6000-acre bit on the outskirts of Los Angeles. On his Babicora Ranch in Chihuahua, Mexico, Mr. Hearst must travel seventy-three miles to reach his own house, and beyond it he can still travel sixty miles without leaving his own land. Babicora contains 900,000 acres or over 1400 square miles of land. Down in Vera Cruz lie his hardwood holdings—260,000 acres, and adjacent thereto is his 350,000-acre Campeche ranch, which supplies about five per cent of all the chicle imported into the United States. And at Ojinaga, Mexico, he owns some 70,000 acres of valuable oil lands. All in all, he claims title to between 1,900,-000 and 2,000,000 acres—more than 3000 square miles of land —more than the combined areas of Delaware and Rhode Island.

Hearst also received the San Francisco *Examiner* in 1887, and from then on began to add to the accumulations of the Hearst domain. In 1895 he bought, for $180,000, the New York *Morning Journal,* later renamed the *American,* and *Das Morgen Journal.* In 1896 he started the New York *Evening Journal* and the following year bought (and killed) the New York *Morning Advertiser* so as to obtain an Associated Press franchise. In 1900 he launched the Chicago *American* followed by the Chicago *Examiner* in 1902. At the request of leading trade unionists of Los Angeles, who wanted a paper "friendly to the working man and organized labor" Hearst established the Los Angeles *Examiner* in 1903. In 1904 he invaded New England with his Boston *American.*

Hearst's entry into the magazine field began in 1903 when he began the publication of *Motor.* Two years later he bought the *Cosmopolitan,* one of the first of the illustrated monthlies. In 1911 he purchased the *World Today,* whose name he soon changed to *Hearst's International.* This was consolidated with the *Cosmopolitan* in 1925. *Harper's Bazaar* was added to the growing list of Hearst magazines in 1913. Meanwhile he had made his incursion into British journalism by obtaining possession of *Nash's Magazine* and the *London Budget*. In June 1914 he purchased *Pall Mall*, which was immediately amalgamated with *Nash's Magazine*.

Only one other paper was added to the Hearst chain prior to the World War. That was the Atlanta *Georgian*, purchased in 1912. A two-column editorial on the front page of Hearst's new organ told the skeptical and worried bourbons of Atlanta:

In extending his newspaper chain into the center of this great Southern country, Mr. Hearst is simply enlarging his capacity to help the great people who live here, and to do his full share of work in the greater future which is before them. . . .

The Hearst newspapers always go to stay. They can be neither bullied, bribed, nor broken. They never die because their principles are founded upon the things, which, being vital to the people, ought to endure, and will endure.

For a short time it appeared that Hearst's entry into Dixie journalism was about to repeat the successes of San Francisco and New York. "He shot the doddering and decrepit *Georgian* full of comic strips, headlines, and syndicate features," says Herbert Asbury, "and for a little while Atlanta took him to her bosom and fawned upon him; journalistically he soon had the town by the tail and was swinging her high, wide and handsome, to the extreme distress of the *Constitution* and the *Journal*, whose editors had never before known the terrors of competition with America's journalistic wild-cat." But the South wearied of sensationalism quicker than the North and West, and in the end remained unconquered.

Boston was again invaded in 1917 when Hearst purchased the *Advertiser*. The Chicago *Herald* was bought in 1918 and combined with the *Examiner*. The immediate post-war period was one of feverish expansion for the Hearst chain. The year 1919 saw the *Wisconsin News* and the Washington, D. C., *Times* added to the empire. The Boston *Record*, acquired in 1920, was

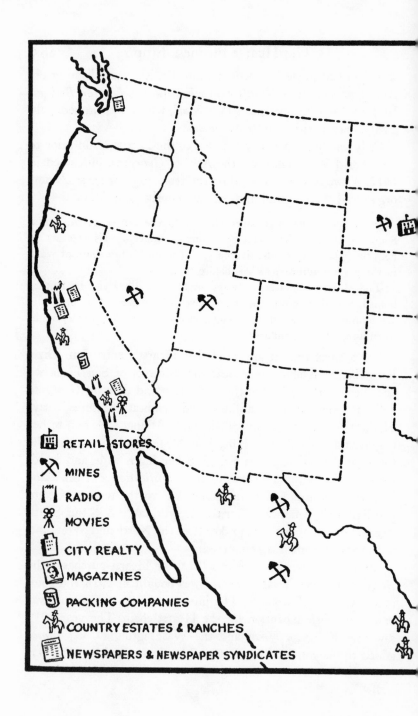

RETAIL STORES

MINES

RADIO

MOVIES

CITY REALTY

MAGAZINES

PACKING COMPANIES

COUNTRY ESTATES & RANCHES

NEWSPAPERS & NEWSPAPER SYNDICATES

THE HEARST BUSINESS EMPIRE
Showing the chief holdings in North America.

combined with the *Advertiser*. The Detroit invasion took place in 1921 when the decrepit *Times* was taken over and remade to the Hearst-Brisbane pattern. The following year, 1922, brought seven new acquisitions in several new territories. These were the Syracuse *Evening Telegram* and the Rochester *Evening Journal*, in upstate New York; the Washington, D. C., *Herald;* the Seattle *Post-Intelligencer;* and three California papers, the San Francisco *Call*, the Oakland *Post-Enquirer*, and the Los Angeles *Herald*.

Baltimore tempted Hearst in 1923. He bought two papers there, the *American* and the *News*. Then he tried his luck in Texas, buying the Fort Worth *Record*. Here he was given a stiff battle, and did a most unusual thing for Hearst—he sold the paper. It is the only one he has ever disposed of in that fashion, and he is reported to have said on many occasions that he is sorry he did it. He made one more try at Texas the following year, 1924, when he bought the San Antonio *Light*. That year he also purchased the Albany (N. Y.) *Times-Union* and started his first tabloid, the New York *Mirror*.

In reply to a series of questions submitted to him by *Editor and Publisher* in the summer of 1924, when the newspaper world was buzzing with rumors about Hearst's expansionist policies, he said: "I have no intention to possess any given number of newspapers nor any plan to possess any more newspapers or to take on any more work or trouble . . ."

Nevertheless, the past ten years have seen the following added to Hearst's imposing array of papers: the Milwaukee *Sentinel;* the Pittsburgh *Sun-Telegraph*, the Pittsburgh *Post-Gazette*, the San Francisco *Bulletin* (subsequently merged with the *Call*); the Omaha *Bee-News*, and the Los Angeles *Express* (merged with the *Herald*). Then, too, he has added to his magazine chain with *Good Housekeeping*, *Motor Boating*, *Pictorial Review*, *Town and Country*, *House Beautiful* (combined with *Home and Field*), the *American Druggist*, and the *Ameri-*

ican Architect. In England he publishes an English edition of *Good Housekeeping,* and *The Connoisseur.* Thrifty housewives also have the privilege of buying *Pictorial Patterns* and *Excella Patterns* from the Hearst enterprises.

The American Weekly, which is "welcomed into the homes of 5,770,066 families throughout the United States," is the sensational Sunday magazine section carried by every Hearst Sunday paper. Fathered by Brisbane, it has been built up by A. J. Kobler and Morrill Goddard into the largest weekly periodical in the world, which may account for the yearly salaries of $80,000 and $161,222 respectively.

Back of the newspapers and the magazines are to be found Hearst's various news and feature syndicates which include International News Service (1906), International Feature Service and Newspaper Feature Service (1912), King Features Syndicate (1914), Universal Service, the Premier Syndicate, and International News Photos. King Features, founded by Moses Koenigsberg, is without doubt the world's largest organization of its kind. Its services are bought by no less than 2200 newspapers in the United States alone. They go out to ninety countries, and as *Fortune* puts it, "In thirty-two languages, including the Arabic—Jiggs and Popeye are homely U. S. Ambassadors all over the world." King Features, we are told, "sells comics, serials, editorials, puzzles, patterns, fashion hints, advice to the lovelorn, sports comment, poems, health talks, bridge problems, Broadway gossip, book reviews, Wall Street comment, Bible stories, articles on etiquette, child raising, radio, movies, crime, etc."

It should be evident by this time that the enormous Hearst press is not a newsgathering agency so much as it is a personal organ of propaganda. But it is also, and perhaps mainly, a medium for the advertising which brings in its chief income. Since the great advertisers in the newspapers today are the large retail establishments, Hearst decided early in the game not to antagonize them willingly. When the bubonic plague broke out in San Francisco in 1901, the business interests felt that the newspapers had to prevent word of this from spreading broadcast lest tourists and customers shun the city. The work of the government experts who were fighting the deadly plague was effectively hampered by the papers, and the quarantine was rendered ineffective. The Hearst press worked hand in hand with the others in giving misleading information to the public about this serious situation. They joined in a similar campaign to play down the extent of the dysentery epidemic during the Chicago Century of Progress Exposition in 1934.

It has long been observed that Hearst editorials are slanted to endorse and support such business enterprises as Hearst happens to be interested in—but never in the history of American newspapers has there been the outright sale of editorials to buyers of advertising space as occurred in the New York *Journal* during 1908 and 1909.

The *Journal*, despite its immense circulation, didn't reach the class of people who constitute the Broadway audiences, so managers and theatrical producers carried very little advertising in the paper. Hearst and Brisbane decided to get some of their advertising. On December 13, 1907, appeared the announcement of a change in editorial policy. The *Journal*, thereafter, announced Brisbane, would follow a system of "constructive criticism" of plays, books, and actors. It desired "to tell the public about those that are GOOD AND WORTH SEEING, and leave the others to their natural fate WITHOUT KICKING AN UNHAPPY FAILING MAN OR WOMAN. . . . We want [our readers] to know that if they read extended criticism of a play in this newspaper IT IS ONLY BECAUSE IT IS A GOOD PLAY AND ONE THAT, FOR REASONS STATED, WOULD AMUSE OR INSTRUCT THEM. Why do we not imitate the sun that warms, develops, and brings out what is good?"

With the next theatrical season, the "constructive criticism" also began. Brisbane on November 6, 1908, headed his leading editorial: "A Great Play—Two Powerful Men Collaborate." "Go see it," he advised. "It will make you think. . . . It contains a lesson for husbands and wives and others." The play was William Gillette's *Samson*. On the following day there appeared a full-page ad in the *Journal* for that play. On December 30 Brisbane had an editorial: "*The Battle*—Ingenious Play Ingeniously Advertised." Three days later there appeared a full-page ad for *The Battle*. On January 29, 1909, came an editorial: "*A Gentleman from Mississippi*—This is one of the plays that has a PURPOSE—may its success breed imitators." The full-page ad appeared on the thirtieth. Again and again during that season Brisbane would write a piece of "constructive criticism," and as surely as night follows day there would appear a full-page advertisement for the play so criticized. The scheme was somewhat reversed in the case of *The Girl from Rector's*, whose full-page advertisement was run on February 6—to be followed two days later by a seven-column illustration and story from the pen of Nell Brinkley entitled "Mighty Scrumptious Frocks in *The Girl from Rector's*." Stars like Stella Mayhew, Eva Tanguay, and Annette Kellerman were drawn by Nell Brinkley for the *Journal*—always preceded or followed by a half-page ad. This policy was continued through 1910, and "Tad," Merle Johnson, and Beatrice Fairfax were also used for this type of work.

Will Irwin tellingly exposed this procedure of the Hearst-Brisbane combination in his article in the June 3, 1911, issue of *Collier's Weekly*, in which he said:

The new advertising policy of the *Journal* was public property in the theatrical district, where gossip travels as in a little village. Every manager knew that the *Journal* offered a page advertisement and a Brisbane editorial for a thousand dollars. It was remarked that Brisbane would not "boost" under this arrangement, any play which he did not like—but his tastes are catholic. Just as well was it understood that for five hundred dollars the *Journal* would give a half page advertisement and a "special" with illustrations by Nell Brinkley, together with liberal "news notices."

The *Journal* generally signed no contract for these transactions; it was just a gentleman's agreement between solicitor and manager. Of course, what the managers really wanted for their thousand dollars was not the advertisement, but the editorial.

According to Irwin, when a great circus came to Madison Square Garden and refused to buy the required space in the *Journal,* it was told that it would get no publicity whatsoever. During its month's stay at the Garden it drew story after story from all the other papers. Only one appeared in the *Journal,* announcing that the circus had opened and that a trapeze performer had broken his wrist.

When Hearst first learned that a series by Will Irwin on "The American Newspaper" was to be published, and long before it began to appear, he threatened *Collier's* with both criminal and civil libel. After the articles had come out he did bring suit—for $500,000. Robert J. Collier upon receipt of the summons and complaint declared: "I was greatly pleased to receive it. I had practically invited such a suit, and my only anxiety is that it shall be brought to trial. I have no idea that it will. In fact I am quite positive it will not." Editorially his magazine stated on June 17, 1911, that Hearst, in bringing the suit, had been shrewd enough not to bring the threatened criminal action but merely the civil, "so he can safely circulate his $500,000 bluff, knowing that he can wait three or four years and then drop his case. Probably he suspects that, following our custom, we have not discharged all of our ammunition in the first engagement."

Collier's was right. Hearst made a lot of noise in his papers about bringing the libel suit. Then, after the public had forgotten the case he quietly let it drop.

The methods employed by the Hearst papers in getting advertisers have been many and varied, but most colorful, perhaps, were those developed by his Chicago papers, which, within a few years after their establishment, were extremely successful in this line—so successful in fact, that some of their best solicitors were later transferred to New York and other centers to show the more backward regions how such things were done.

When, for example, a score of years ago one of Chicago's great merchant princes died in a house of questionable virtue, the Hearst press did a front-page layout of the whole story, sent it to the manager of the dead man's firm, and asked for more details. The story never appeared—but an ample supply of advertising space was bought by the company. Though such happy chances as this were unusual, an alert manager could often find grounds for pressure in the most harmless matters. In Los Angeles, for instance, the Hearst press opened a legal fight against one of the largest department stores (which had withdrawn its advertising during the war), because it had built an enclosed bridge across a public alley. Before the case was settled it had cost that concern a great many thousands of dollars. It, too, learned that it pays to advertise in the Hearst papers.

Another method successfully developed—though since copied by other papers—has been to make all newsboys buy more copies of a paper than they can sell, thus raising the listed circulation figures. This method of swindling the poor newsboys is referred to in the trade as "eating sheets." The Hearst managers are particularly effective in forcing their thousands of newsboys to "eat" scores of thousands of copies every day. A definite ratio is established—usually 10% of the copies actually sold. Of course it cuts down the earnings of the boys—but it makes circulation figures mount, and this in turn means that a higher advertising rate can be charged.

The Los Angeles *Times*, long the bitter foe of Hearst, at the end of September 1934 ran a four-page supplement on the latest trick of the Los Angeles *Examiner* in creating fake advertisements:

The Los Angeles *Examiner* in an effort to cheat its way to classified leadership is now filling its classified columns with hundreds of fake "box-number" advertisements.

Whereas the *Examiner* on week days normally prints approximately 45 "box-number" advertisements, compare this with the *Examiner's* classified pages of Monday, September 24, reproduced herein in full size, in which appear 713 "box-number" ads.

On Sunday, September 23, the *Examiner's* "box number"—or blind ads—totaled 476 against a normal run of 100 to 140.

Tuesday, September 25, these blind ads increased more than 500% over the total number.

This flagrant padding has become a regular practice on the part of the Los Angeles *Examiner*, and, growing bolder of late, it is now padding its columns at the rate of 10,000 to 15,000 fake advertisements per month.

The *Examiner* replied with a series of attacks on the *Times* but never denied the charges.

If Hearst has been wary about suing others—and he has—he has been equally wary in suppressing information about the numerous suits for both criminal and civil libel that have been filed against him or his papers. His batteries of highly paid attorneys are kept busy keeping cases from going to court, or in dragging them out for years on end until the plaintiff gives up for lack of funds or through sheer exhaustion. But despite all this, many damage suits have been won against the Hearst press —some of them breaking all previous records in the amounts awarded.

Perhaps the first was a suit brought years ago by Bardina Wittlevein against the New York *Journal*. Trusting to a head-line in the *Journal* which read, "Girls in Trouble Urged to Confide in Mrs. Humiston—She Promises to Keep Stories Se-

Hearst at the age of eight.

BROWN BROS.

KEYSTONE

Hearst at the age of seventy-two, telling reporters high taxes had determined him to move from California.

cret," Miss Wittlevein had told her story—only to see the whole thing blazoned sensationally in the *Journal* a few days later.

A news item from Chicago of May 5, 1918, read:

William Randolph Hearst's Chicago *Examiner* was assessed $75,000 today for libel of Superior Court Judge William F. Cooper by a jury in the Circuit Court.

The suit was based upon editorial attacks by the Hearst paper in June 1913, in attempts to get Judge Cooper to cease his investigation into alleged frauds in a previously held election. It was also charged that reporters were sent to the judge with stories dealing with his actions in dismissing cases against men charged with serious offences against young girls.

Judge Cooper said he understood the stories were to be printed unless he desisted in his efforts to uncover the election frauds.

In October 1930 Bishop James Cannon, Jr., of the Methodist Episcopal Church South, sued Hearst for libel to the amount of $5,000,000. The New York *Journal* and other Hearst papers were charged with having circulated stories to the effect that the Bishop had been "guilty of improper, unseemly and immoral conduct in that he was at the apartment of Mrs. McCallum [his present wife]" on the night before the death of his first wife. Hearst was charged with having said that the most important duty of his papers all over the country, next to World Court matters, was the destruction of the influence of the group that Bishop Cannon represented, "and that this can best be done by constant, though careful, insults upon the plaintiff." Hearst's attorneys finally settled the case out of court for a substantial sum.

In California more recently a suit was won by a Mr. Davis against Hearst, costing the latter $35,000. Hearst's Star Company was sued by one Mr. Evans in 1925—and the award to the plaintiff amounted to $125,000. Edwin C. Dinwiddie sued the Los Angeles *Examiner* for libel on July 13, 1927, and a jury in 1930 awarded him $40,000 compensatory and $100,000 exemplary damages.

Most sensational of all however, are the amounts that have been received by Frank E. Bonner and F. W. Griffith on account of a clever but unfortunately libelous parody of "The House That Jack Built" written by Hearst himself in 1930, which clearly implied that these officials of the Federal Power Commission were in the pay of the Power Trust. This excursion into poetry has the unique distinction of being by far the costliest bit of versification in the world. Hearst, as the modest writer of the parody, also has the unique distinction of having paid more for the privilege of seeing his bit of verse in print than has any other known writer.

The record to date, stated chronologically, reveals that the following awards were made:

Date	Place	Recipient	Amount
Jan. 1933	Boston	Mr. Griffith	$ 4,200
May 1933	Washington, D. C.	Mr. Griffith	1,000
June 1933	Washington, D. C.	Mr. Bonner	45,000
Nov. 1934	Boston	Mr. Bonner	40,000
May 1935	Chicago	Mr. Bonner	3,140
Jan. 1936	Los Angeles	Mr. Bonner	75,000

The total awards by the juries amount to $168,340, which, plus court costs and legal fees, will raise the sum to about $200,000.

The verdict for Mr. Bonner in Washington was the highest ever awarded in a libel suit in the District of Columbia. The Boston verdict likewise shattered all known libel awards there and the recent Los Angeles decision sets an amount for Hearst to pay which is twice as large as any other ever authorized in that city.

It is rather ironical, in view of Hearst's present attitude, that this costly parody was written to show how the Federal Power Commission was in the pay of the iniquitous Power Trust!

"Hearst believes that all men are rascals, more or less," writes a former employee, "and that the secret of all loyalties is money. Pay a man enough money and you can spit in his face as a part of your daily exercise."

His treatment of men in this respect is well illustrated by Cornelius Vanderbilt, Jr., who relates in his book *Farewell to Fifth Avenue* how he sought out Hearst at the Ambassador Hotel in Los Angeles to ask his advice about starting a paper in that city.

After the young aristocrat had explained the purpose of his mission, Hearst replied: "Los Angeles is not the place for you. Here's what I want you to do. I am about to start a tabloid in New York. I will hire you as editor. You know nothing about editing a newspaper but your name is worth thirty thousand dollars a year to me. You will leave tonight for New York and report to Arthur Brisbane. My secretary will attend to your transportation. Good-by and good luck."

Hearst's decisions are usually reached like that—in a moment's time. To him it didn't matter that young Vanderbilt had come with the idea of seeking advice on starting a paper of his own—nor did it ever enter Hearst's mind that his visitor would fail to respond at once to his offer of a job. That, too, is a part of the Hearst technique. He hires and he fires at a moment's notice—nor can he understand all the fuss people make about such things.

All the important people on the Hearst press are employed under long-term contracts—from two to five years. But there are always methods by which Hearst can oust someone undesirable. The contracts are so drawn that the person employed can be made to do anything in the way of work about the establishment—or for that matter—anywhere the organization wants him to be. This part of the contract, if explained at all to the employee, is said to be "just one of those things which are written into all contracts, but it doesn't really mean anything." Under this clause, one editor who refused to tear up his contract when Hearst got tired of him (it had four more years to run) was shifted out of his regular work and put on a delivery truck. He was obliged to get up at two in the morning and start his rounds at four. Sixty days of that kind of life finished him. He gave up the contract. Another known instance is of an editor's being required to report to his office every day and sit there for eight hours without being permitted to talk to anyone, to read, to write, or to do anything except sit. A few weeks of such torture is likely to bring the desired result.

Under such circumstances there is naturally no such thing as loyalty on the Hearst press. Quarrels, intrigues for place and position, and constant sneers at the publisher characterize to an extraordinary degree every Hearst office. But this does not mean that Hearst's editors and reporters will ever fail to do his bidding. They will always say, "Orders are orders," meaning pay checks are pay checks. His army is sullen, but it is not mutinous.

Hearst is not only a mining magnate, a lord of vast estates, and the greatest owner of newspapers, magazines, and feature services in the world. He has become, in the course of two score years, a realtor second to none in America. In New York City his real estate holdings top the list of men like Morgan, the Rockefellers, the Astors, and the Vanderbilts.

From the modest beginning, nearly forty years ago, of the purchase of a house at Twenty-eighth Street and Lexington Avenue in Manhattan, Hearst has gone on accumulating larger and larger properties. He bought a small block fronting Broadway, Eighth Avenue, and Fifty-eighth Street in 1895, and with that as a base began to acquire more and more property around Columbus Circle, which he hoped to make into a glorified Hearst Plaza that would supersede Times Square as the hub of

New York City. He paid over $2,000,000 for the block bounded by Broadway, Central Park West, and Sixty-first Street in 1911. In 1913 he bought the Clarendon apartment house at Riverside Drive and Eighty-sixth Street for $950,000. As late as 1930 he was still buying Columbus Circle property. In April of that year he paid $1,500,000 for a 175-foot frontage on Fifty-seventh Street.

Three large New York hotels belong to Hearst: the Ritz Tower, the Warwick, and the Lombardy. He owns the Zieg-feld Theatre, the 471 Park Avenue building, the Sherwood Studios, and innumerable other properties. These are held under a wide variety of corporations, such as the Apperson Realty Company, Hearst Tower Realty Company, the Parkav Corporation, the Park-Fifty-Seventh Realty Corporation, the Randolph Realty Corporation, the Veronica Realty Corporation, the W.A.R. Corporation, the Mad-Park Holding Corporation, the Maha Realty Corporation, the 24 East 67th Street Corporation, the Bainbridge Building Corporation, and the H.A.B. Realty Corporation. *Fortune's* estimate of $41,000,000 as the value of Mr. Hearst's Manhattan realty holdings, is based only upon *assessed* valuation so that the real value exclusive of mortgages may be anywhere from 60 to 75 millions of dollars.

In the field of motion pictures, Cosmopolitan Productions belongs entirely to Hearst, and he has a 50% interest in the Hearst Metrotone News. The former is valued by *Fortune* (October 1935) at $3,000,000 and the latter at $1,000,000.

Hearst's Piedmont Land & Cattle Company, as the name implies, devotes itself to land and cattle. His Sunical Packing Company, at Oroville, California, raises and markets fruits from the Hearst orchards, and the Hearst Mercantile Company, of Lead, South Dakota is the company store from which the employees of Homestake are expected to do their buying.

The radio has been the last of all fields into which Hearst has ventured (unless it be aviation, in which his holdings are

considerable, but cannot be checked). The income is just beginning to show itself—but as an additional medium to sell Hearst
and the things he stands for to millions of radio fans all over
the country, these stations have been eminently successful. From
east to west, the Hearst Radio chain spans the nation. There is
WINS in New York, WBAL in Baltimore, WCAE and
WWSW in Pittsburgh, KYA in San Francisco, KTM in Los
Angeles, KELW in Burbank, and KEWE in Santa Monica. On
August 20, 1935, appeared the announcement of the creation
of a special organization, Hearst Radio, to unify and co-ordinate
the activities of these various stations. There are good reasons
for believing that this indicates the beginning of a period of
rapid expansion in the field of broadcasting. When Hearst took
over KTM and KELW late in 1934, all the liberal groups who
had been buying time over these stations were immediately
cut off.

If at times Hearst has tossed money away in reckless aban-
don, he has more often sought ways and means to hold on to
what he had. While shouting for honest government and
cheaper government, he has constantly resorted to methods of
political pressure and wire-pulling, as well as to the use of holding companies in order to keep down his taxes and hide his
real income. A memorandum by the Couzens Senate committee,
which was studying the operation of the Internal Revenue Bureau administered by Secretary of Treasury, Andrew W. Mellon, states: "It is to be noted that no records are kept by Mr.
Hearst in spite of the various ramifications of his interests."
According to this same report, Hearst's Star Publishing Company received reductions in tax liabilities over a period of three
years totaling about $1,750,000. (Is it to be wondered at that
Hearst supported Mellon!) And in 1919, Mrs. Phebe Hearst
lent a cool million dollars to the New York *American*, for
which she took interest-bearing notes, and then "for no apparent
consideration" assigned them to her son.

L. C. Manson, counsel for the Senate investigation committee, contended before that committee that Hearst had escaped
"$151,000 in taxation for the year 1918 by deducting from his
personal income a loss of $301,232 sustained in supplying roto-
gravure sections for his Sunday newspapers in New York, Boston, and Chicago." The Bureau of Revenue Agent, Harry
Herskowitz, declared, "As a matter of fact that section was a
losing proposition to all newspapers. Here we have a shrewd,
successful, far-visioned newspaperman of vast experience, entering into a contract which in advance he must have known to be
a losing venture. . . . The inference is simple. Why not experiment with his personal income, of which the government would
get 56% (under the surtax rates), and develop his newspaper
enterprise? At best, this money was a loan, an advance, a capital
outlay."

Hearst's first big bond flotation took place in December 1925,
when a $15,000,000 loan was secured with which to erect new
buildings for his New York papers and magazines. Less than
five years later, he found it necessary to attempt another, and
greater flotation. This time, he determined to "let the public
and faithful employees" in on the deal. Hearst Consolidated
Publications, Inc., was organized in June 1930 as a Delaware
corporation, selling 2,000,000 shares of Class A stock at $25 per
share. Another 2,000,000 shares of common stock at no par
were issued and given to Mr. Hearst for the assets of the Star
Publishing Company which he turned over to the new organization. Two hundred thousand shares of "A" stock were set
aside to be sold to officers and employees of the Hearst organization on the installment plan. All Class A stock is non-voting;
it can only assume the right to vote for a majority of the Board
of Directors of the corporation if and when dividends on Class
A shall be in arrears for four consecutive quarters.

This gigantic holding company holds the common stock of
the following corporations: (1) Hearst Publications, Inc. (own-

ing in turn the American Newsprint Corporation, the Examiner Printing Company and the Call Publishing Company of San Francisco, the Post-Enquirer Publishing Company of Oakland, the Los Angeles Evening Herald Company, the Post-Intelligencer Company; (2) the New York Evening Journal, Inc.; (3) Evening American Publishing Company (owning in turn the Chicago Evening American, again owning in turn the Cosmopolitan Newspaper Corporation); (4) Times Publishing Company of Detroit; (5) Pitt Publishing Company of Pittsburgh; (6) Pitt Building Company; (7) American Weekly, Inc. (owning in turn the Comic Weekly Corporation).

While engaged in this Insull-like pyramiding, Hearst also took a leaf out of the Insulls' notebook in his methods of promoting the sale of stock for the new corporation. Just as Insull's employees were compelled to buy public utilities stock or lose their jobs, so throughout the length of Hearst's newspaper chain, reaching from the Atlantic to the Pacific, editors, reporters, everyone down to the office boys, received the necessary tip that it would be well for them to hold some stock in Hearst Consolidated. This is what is known as "profit-sharing," a well-known form of capitalist benevolence.

A strenuous campaign has been carried on among readers of the Hearst papers as well as in smaller communities to build up a mass of stockholders in the corporation. This has been achieved. On July 1, 1935, a total of 1,947,532 shares had been sold to some 58,975 stockholders, and of these 42,572 own from one to twenty shares. Only 2353 investors, or 4 per cent, own in excess of 100 shares. To date, these stockholders have received a 7% annual return on their investment.

As head of his Consolidated Publications, Hearst draws a salary of $500,000 per year. But this is only a fraction of his yearly income, which has been estimated as somewhere between $4,000,000 and $5,000,000. To his chief executives he also pays liberal salaries. Brisbane tops the list with $265,000 per year. T. J.

White gets $88,648; J. F. Neylan $88,000; Frank Barham, publisher of the Los Angeles *Herald-Express*, $68,039; H. M. Bitner, $52,000; Walter Winchell, $52,000; and Jack Lait, $52,000. At least another three-score executives get anywhere from $15,000 to $60,000 per year. Paul Block, the publisher who has so often served as a stooge for Hearst when he wanted to acquire a newspaper in a community where he was not liked, has now been given the job of handling all the national advertising that appears in the Hearst press. The Paul Block Associates, as the organization is called through which Mr. Block handles all this work, gets a 15% commission for this, and has taken over into his own organization many of the key men on the Hearst advertising staffs throughout the country.

The great Hearst empire, estimated by *Fortune* as worth approximately $220,000,000, is unique in that a very considerable portion is so organized as to function not only as a source of additional profits to himself but also as a great fleet of convertible merchant ships carrying concealed guns. Governments have to pay for their battleships; only private citizens like Hearst can make their battleships pay them.

The first line of defense, let us say, consists of the newspapers, twenty-nine of them, located in eighteen of the largest cities in the United States. In the great industrial centers of the country his papers are read by nearly half the population. In Boston, Pittsburgh, and Los Angeles they have more readers than all others combined. And in such centers as Seattle, Baltimore, and Milwaukee (Socialist Milwaukee!) he almost holds his own against the field. Chicago, San Francisco, and New York have been Hearst strongholds for decades. Taking these eighteen cities together, in them, on an average, out of every five newspaper readers two will be reading the journals which comprise the front line of the Hearst fleet for defending and enlarging the Hearst empire.

His second line of defense consists of his eight news and film services. They not only supplement the work of the fleet itself in the major urban centers, but penetrate to the smallest towns and hamlets.

Hearst's third line of defense consists of Hearst's Magazines, Inc., with assets listed in 1935 as more than $20,000,000, supplemented by others worth an additional $5,000,000. These magazines, to the amount of 6,000,000 copies, monthly pour out upon the American public. The most successful, like *Good Housekeeping, Pictorial Review,* and *Harper's Bazaar* make their special appeal to women—and women, as Hearst well knows, are potent in American politics and business.

The last of these defenses consists of his air fleet—the strategically scattered radio broadcasting stations. Hearst is very much air-minded at present, so this part of his force will undoubtedly be enlarged and expanded as rapidly as conditions permit.

It will be admitted that as an armed capitalist, able to do battle with all the weapons of propaganda in defense of himself and his class, Hearst is inferior to no one in the world.

THE BATTLE FLEET OF THE LORD OF SAN SIMEON *

NEWSPAPERS

City	No. of Papers	Circulation Daily	Circulation Sunday
New York	3	1,464,576	1,766,192
Chicago	2	740,551	860,565
Boston	3	543,576	429,476
Los Angeles	2	456,136	429,187
Pittsburgh	2	308,752	306,056
San Francisco	2	289,522	368,674
Detroit	1	281,019	372,424
Baltimore	2	223,153	201,396
Washington, D. C.	2	196,003	145,249
Milwaukee	2	168,376	143,764
Omaha	1	91,989	101,658

Seattle	1	86,853	148,932
Atlanta	1	76,410	144,865
Syracuse	1	60,342	94,125
Oakland	1	53,072	....
Rochester	1	46,037	65,547
San Antonio	1	45,877	63,644
Albany	1	38,085	49,227
18 Cities	29	5,180,329	5,690,981

The *American Weekly,* which is also sold as a Sunday supplement to other than Hearst papers throughout the country, claims a circulation of 5,077,066.

MAGAZINES

Title	Circulation
Good Housekeeping	1,915,676
Hearst's International Cosmopolitan	1,665,127
Harper's Bazaar	104,415
Pictorial Review	2,061,736
Motor	54,679
Motor Boating	20,744
American Druggist	39,314
Town and Country	17,681
House Beautiful	101,221
American Architect	8,913
Total for American magazines	5,989,506

BRITISH MAGAZINES

Good Housekeeping	(The figures for British publications are not available.)
Nash's Pall Mall Magazine	
The Connoisseur & International Studio	

---

* All figures taken from **N. W.** Ayer & Son's *Directory of Newspapers & Periodicals.*

CHAPTER XX

Lord of San Simeon

ALONG the sea and mountains, symbolically almost midway between the middle-class paradise of Los Angeles and half-Fascist San Francisco lies the already legendary estate of San Simeon. In the days of Hearst *père* it was an ordinary ranch of a mere 40,000 acres undistinguished from others save by its beauty of location—a part, together with the Santa Rosa and Piedra Blanca ranches, of George Hearst's large cattle range. On those hills William Randolph Hearst as a boy was bred to the saddle; he hunted in the forests and fished in the coves; his cold blue eyes appraised his father's possessions and saw that they were good; but during the years of active manhood his interests lay elsewhere. San Simeon, though its acreage was many times enlarged, was not treated as a place of permanent habitation, was not developed; it was allowed to remain a pleasant wilderness to which its owner could retire from the world occasionally and, aided by a moderately luxurious camping outfit, renew his childhood's early intercourse with "nature." Not until the twenties, when his increasing interest in Hollywood led him to recognize in the meretricious charms of the cinema the perfect realization of his own pseudo-æsthetic ideals, did the notion come to him of converting honest San Simeon into a fabulously extravagant moving-picture realm, a magical but ultra-modern Venusberg.

The spacious, cleanly beauty of distances, of wind-swept hills and soughing pines, of green meadows and tinkling water— these are the inherited treasures of San Simeon. And into this setting, capable of developing even under private property at least as harmonious a life as that of England's landed gentry, the great American tendency toward neuroticism was introduced in the person of the present owner. With the power that moves mountains, which is not faith but wealth, he has raised, as with the touch of some mad enchanter's wand, a castle that looks like a Spanish mission with a dining hall that looks like a monk's refectory, "cottages" that look like châteaux, everything looking like something else than what it is except the flying-field, tennis courts, and swimming pools, which themselves have an unreal air on this aloof hilltop, set cheek-by-jowl with so many relics and imitations of medievalism.

The lord of the manor has the finest collection of armor in the world, having far outstripped his nearest competitors, Henry Ford and Andrew Mellon. He also has the finest collection of old silver, the finest collection of old furniture, the finest collection of stained glass, the finest collection of Gothic mantels, the finest collection of Mexican saddles. He has collected pottery and paintings—the choicest one at San Simeon is a Madonna which hangs in the "Celestial Suite," Miss Davies's bedroom— he has collected tapestries and hangings and costumes, he has collected choir stalls and ceilings and fireplaces, he has collected mummies, he has collected Cardinal Richelieu's bed, he has collected—the Lord knows what he hasn't collected! Loot from all the world is gathered at San Simeon. And the end is not yet. At the foot of "La Cuesta Encantada" (The Enchanted Hill—everything here has a Spanish name: "La Casa Grande," "La Casa·del Sol," "La Casa del Monte," "La Casa del Mar" —no vulgar American nomenclature permitted), strewn along the valley for half a mile are packing boxes full of more treasures for which no appropriate place has yet been found. Underneath La Casa Grande is a two-acre store-room devoted to the same purpose. And in New York City, near Southern Boulevard and One Hundred and Forty-third Street, is an entire block of Hearst warehouses, containing among other acquisitions a Spanish castle, taken down stone by stone, each lettered and numbered, on its way to join some time the marvels of San Simeon. And then there are the Egyptian, Etruscan, Roman, Spanish, and Italian pieces and the great English library still in the old Hearst home at Riverside Drive and Eighty-sixth Street—though these may perhaps be deemed more suitable for "St. Joan," the French château purchased by Hearst from Mrs. Belmont at Sands Point, Long Island; or perhaps the owner may take a notion to transport St. Joan, too, to San Simeon so as further to diversify the scenery of California.

While Hearst's sense of ensemble seems a little defective, there is no doubt that he is a connoisseur of details and particularly of *objets d'art*. Hand him an unknown vase or figurine and he can tell you its school and period as infallibly as any antique dealer in Paris or London. He loves to look at them; he loves to pat them and caress them; he loves, above all, to *own* them.

This is probably the reason for the confinement of his æsthetic interest to dead art. Living art, aside from its simulacrum in the cinema, has always left him cold. He has never shown the slightest concern over any contemporary movement in painting, sculpture, architecture, music, or literature; so far as is known, he has never lifted a finger to befriend a single living artist. And living art cannot be torn from its roots and appropriated in the Hearstian manner as dead art can be. The æsthetic impulse throughout Hearst's life has been wholly subordinated to the impulse to *acquire* and *exhibit*.

In fact, the collecting mania has developed in him to the point of "magpieism." Countless knickknacks keep arriving at San Simeon which must be worked into the general scheme of things by his architect or the servants irrespective of whether they fit into the surroundings or not. At one time he bought about two dozen electric clocks for installation in La Casa Grande; at another, dozens and dozens of floor and table lamps; at another, almost innumerable cigarette lighters to scatter about the place—these he would try every day and if he found one that did not work there would be trouble for the servants. The latter regard their master as very childish in such matters. When things do not work, "Out with them!"—whether the things be furniture or antiques or people.

One of the large fireplaces in La Casa Grande smoked when first lighted unless a door on the opposite side of the room was left slightly ajar to create the necessary draft. Hearst, not knowing of this trait of his fireplace, one day touched a match to the logs and kindling when the door was closed, and he was immediately enshrouded in smoke. Loudly he called for help, shouting that he "had never seen such a —— fireplace"; when told that all that was necessary was to leave the door ajar, he exclaimed, "I don't want a —— fireplace if I have to leave a door open. Send for Miss Morgan [his architect]. Tear it out. Rebuild it." Miss Morgan was summoned post-haste to San Simeon, and at great expense the fireplace was entirely rebuilt.

It was shortly after this that Joseph Willicombe, finding the private elevator stuck one day, summoned all hands to repair it, saying, "If W. R. comes in and finds the elevator stuck he will have it torn out."

There is a fair collection of helpers at Hearst's "little hideaway": from four to six waiters, a head butler, a head housekeeper, a chef, a first assistant chef, a pastry cook, a Filipino cook for the servants, three maids, two houseboys, ten gardeners, a telegrapher, a ticker man, an electrician, and three telephone operators working in shifts of eight hours each so that there is continuous twenty-four-hour service. The help is paid the current wage, but miserably housed in mere shacks out of sight down the hill. At one time they did not receive their wages for several months until complaint was lodged with the Department of Labor and an investigator looked into the matter. Such small economies assist in making great acquisitions possible.

The desire for exhibition is almost as strong with Hearst as the desire for accumulation. Were Veblen's *Theory of the Leisure Class* to be edited today, it could be adequately documented from the life at San Simeon alone. "Conspicuous waste" is there seen in its perfection, ostentatious extravagance at a height elsewhere unachieved. Hearst's personal expenses have been estimated at fifteen million a year, and a generous share goes into the hospitalities of San Simeon. For the same man who, as newspaper owner, cuts the wages of his employees to the bone and is a ruthless tyrant in the matter of dismissals, in the rôle of lord of the manor is the most courteous and munificent of hosts.

There are usually from fifty to sixty guests at San Simeon, many of them occupying units in one or another of the magnificent "cottages." In the closets of each suite are complete outfits, for male and female, for every occasion: riding habits, sport suits, lounging robes, dinner and evening dress. The visitor enjoys all the advantages of a club or great hotel: he may drink at the bar, loiter in the sunrooms, stroll over the park-like grounds, play pool or billiards or ping-pong between the choir-stalls in the great medieval hall, go hunting or fishing or use the tennis courts (where the master of the estate still puts up a good game at the age of seventy-two), and end the afternoon, if he desires, with a plunge in either of the two outdoor swimming pools, one of fresh water, the other of warmed sea water—or, if he prefers, in still another under the tennis courts where floodlights bring out the radiance of gold-quartz walls. If interested in agriculture, the guest may visit the poultry and dairy farms; if in horticulture, the grove of young sequoias or those of imported exotics; if in biology, the private zoo including at last enumeration four lions, four zebras, four llamas, three casso-

THE FEUDAL DOMAIN AT SAN SIMEON

Showing glimpses of three of the various "*casas*" that Hearst and his guests inhabit.

waries, two emus, two pumas, one leopard, and one yak, besides several elephants, bears of every variety, all kinds of monkeys, cockatoos, and eagles, and whole herds of bison, gazelles, antelopes, giraffes, and kangaroos. If the visitor is a person of no importance, when his stay is out he is merely taken in an automobile forty miles to San Luis Obispo; but if he chances to be a Bernard Shaw or a Fred Perry he is taken to and from San Simeon in the great silver-topped aeroplane. The even larger and finer red aeroplane, however, is reserved for the use of Hearst's personal entourage; perhaps he feels that no one else could be safely trusted in a plane of so dangerous a color; or perhaps he but waits the hour to transform it suitably into a red-white-and-blue plane. But with the slight exception of a greater deference naturally paid to the more distinguished, Hearst's hospitality knows no limits. Such is San Simeon and such its owner—in his relation to those who have chanced, for any one of a hundred reasons, to obtain access to its precincts.

But, on the other hand, no castle could be more strongly defended against those who, also for any one a hundred reasons, happen to be in disfavor, permanent or momentary. Triple gates, a few miles apart, guard the entrance to the estate. Sentries are on duty, though probably more for show than service, since the porter's lodge at the outermost gate and a porter as inflexible as Macbeth's own are sufficient to deter the unwelcome from further advance. Should a telephone call from the lodge to La Casa Grande bring a negative answer from the lord of San Simeon miles away, the case is closed, no matter who the aspirant. That lodge has been the scene of bitter moments for many a man. Rumor has it that even Arthur Brisbane has known the sting of rejection there. Certain it is that Hearst's private secretary and sometime tutor to his children by Mrs. Hearst, being after many years of faithful service summarily dismissed while on duty in France, journeyed from Paris to San Simeon to plead his cause but got no further than the porter's lodge. Hearst's courtesy ends at the boundary of his estate; it belongs to San Simeon rather than to him.

Even within this modern abbey of Thélème there are four restraints upon the principle of *"Fay ce que vouldras"*—four rules not to be violated on pain of instant expulsion.

The first rule is "no drinking in the guests' suites." Not that the life at San Simeon could be called exactly ascetic: the bar is always open, and the amount of liquor dispensed by the opulent host from a thirty by forty foot cellar is apparently unlimited. But Hearst knows human nature and particularly Hollywood human nature. Fifty people gathered together in the open are more likely to remain within the bounds of law and order than the same fifty people divided into groups of five or ten behind closed doors.

The second rule is a trifle more authoritarian. It is that everyone must come to the great hall of La Casa Grande every evening. First, there is the cocktail hour when guests are, if necessary, introduced to each other by an active and efficient major-domo. Sooner or later, Hearst appears, accompanied by Miss Davies, after which there follows something like the grand march in *Aïda* to the monks' refectory beyond, where the guests are duly seated in the order of their wealth or importance, the two, of course, usually coinciding. Hearst sits in the center and Miss Davies opposite; behind the latter stands a special servant throughout the meal, holding her powder, rouge, and lipstick; beside her sits her dog, "Gandhi," who also has a special servant to bring him his sliced ham or turkey on a silver platter. The china and glassware are varied from meal to meal to produce different color combinations, white, or red, or gold. Menu cards are at every place as in a hotel or restaurant.

Hearst's well-known democratic spirit is shown in several ways. Formal evening dress is not required. San Simeon must always be referred to as "the ranch." No tablecloths are ever put on the table, and paper napkins are always served. Home-made preserves (for which Hearst has a veritable passion), sauces, and condiments are put upon the table in their native bottles. As Mrs. Older would say, the "atmosphere" of a ranch is maintained as far as possible.

After an enjoyable time is had by everyone at this rustic banquet, the third rule comes into play.

This is distinctly tyrannical in character: namely, that all guests must attend the nightly moving picture performance in the private theater. Hearst himself boasts that he has not missed an evening of moving pictures in the last ten years, and for some mysterious reason feels it to be a duty to impose his own taste in this matter on all who come under his power.

The fourth and last rule is the most significant: that no one shall, under any circumstance, mention in Hearst's presence the subject of death. What more complete self-revelation could anyone give, what more open confession of neuroticism and abject spiritual bankruptcy? The hard-headed realistic journalist who for half a century has featured in his papers the most horrible crimes of murder, the blatant super-patriot who has tried again and again on the slightest pretext to force his country into war and send millions of her sons to slaughter—this man dares not face the thought that the common fate of humanity will some day touch him, too. The megalomaniac madness to be wholly different from other men and rule them according as the whim may take him, while remaining himself untouched by the evils that he can inflict upon them, this madness, the driving force of his whole tempestuous career, has found its suitable symbol in the raising of San Simeon, and its final epitaph in the rule "Never mention Death."

Men say that Hearst does not seem happy at San Simeon. The guests are not his friends, if indeed he has any friends; they are those of Miss Davies. The laughter is theirs, not his, and as the evening passes he is likely to be almost forgotten, an old man with stooped shoulders and sagging cheeks, seated somewhere in a corner—but in his hand is a pad, and he is writing editorials. There he wrote, perhaps with Miss Davies's assistance, that famous one of October 5, 1933, signed "An American Husband," pleading for the sanctities of the home now threatened by the licentiousness of the movies. There he writes his fulminations against Soviet Russia and American college professors. And during the small hours of the night he will call up his San Francisco or Los Angeles or New York offices to mention some petty fault, not for the fault's sake but to remind himself that he owns papers in San Francisco, Los Angeles, and New York, that he is not as other men, but William Randolph Hearst, that he has met the great Hitler and may still himself become the Hitler of America. But in his heart he knows that this will never be. What though the stockades are ready, loop-holed and barb-wired, at Salinas and San Mateo? Concentration camps for California—but he will not be there to choose the inmates. The unmentioned and unmentionable word booms through San Simeon louder than the hubbub of all its coming and departing guests. The hour inevitably approaches, swiftly or slowly, when Hearst, too, will be a departing, a departed guest. Unknowingly, all his life he has worked on behalf of death—the death of personal integrity, the death of decent journalism, the death of honest patriotism —and now ultimately death will take its own. The meanest victim of his pen who then still treads the earth will be more powerful than William Randolph Hearst. Therefore, and again therefore:

"Never dare to mention Death in his presence."

APPENDIX

BIBLIOGRAPHY

Books and Pamphlets

Allen, Robert S., and Drew Pearson: Washington Merry-Go-Round (1931)

Atherton, Gertrude: California; an Intimate History (1927)

Ayer, N. W., & Sons: Directory of Newspapers and Periodicals (1933–4)

Baker, Ray Stannard: Life and Letters of Woodrow Wilson (1927)

Bancroft, Hubert Howe: Chronicles of the Builders of the Commonwealth (1891–2)

Beals, Carleton: Porfirio Diaz (1932)

Beard, Charles: Rise of American Civilization (1927)

Beck, James M.: The Enemy within Our Gates (1917)

Beer, Thomas: Hanna (1929)

Bent, Silas: Strange Bedfellows (1928), Ballyhoo—The Voice of the Press (1927)

Bleyer, Willard G.: Main Currents in the History of American Journalism (1927), Newspaper Writing and Editing (1923)

Bonfils, Winifred Black: Life and Personality of Phebe Apperson Hearst (1928)

Brisbane, Arthur: The Book of Today (1924), Editorials from Hearst Newspapers (1906)

Byington, L. F., and Oscar Lewis: History of San Francisco (1931)

Cary, Edward: Journalism and International Affairs (1909)

Clarke, George T.: Leland Stanford (1931)

Cleland, R. G.: History of California (1922), Pathfinders (1928)

Commons, John R., and associates: History of Labor in the United States (1918)

Creelman, James: On the Great Highway (1901)

Cross, Ira B.: A History of the Labor Movement of California (1935), Financing an Empire—a History of Banking in California (1927)

Davis, Winfield J.: History of Political Conventions in California from 1849–1892 (1893)

Dewey, Squire Pierce: Bonanza Mines and Bonanza Kings (1879)
Dickinson, Burrus S.: The Newspaper and Labor (1930)
Dobie, Edith: Political Career of Stephen M. White (1927)
Dobyns, F.: The Underworld of American Politics (1932)
Downie, Major William: Hunting for Gold (1893)
Duffy, Herbert S.: William Howard Taft (1930)

Eldridge, Z. S.: History of California (1914)

Fenton, Francis: The Influence of Newspaper Presentation upon the
    Growth of Crime and Anti-Social Activity (1911)
Flint, Leon Nelson: The Conscience of the Newspaper (1925)
Fowler, Gene: The Great Mouthpiece (1931)

Gladden, Washington: Tainted Newspapers (1914)
Glasscock, G. B.: The Big Bonanza (1931)
Goldman, Emma: Living My Life (1931)

Hapgood, Norman: The Changing Years (1930)
Harvey, Rowland H.: Samuel Gompers (1935)
Hearst, William R.: Brief to the Public Service Commission (1931), Let
    Us Promote the World's Peace (1915), Obligations and Opportuni-
    ties of the United States in Mexico and the Philippines (1916), On
    the Foreign War Debts (1931), Truths about the Trusts (1916)
Hibben, Captain Paxton: The Peerless Leader, William Jennings Bryan
    (1929)
Howe, Winifred C.: Putting the Poison into Columbia's Cup (1916)
Hunt, Richwell D.: California and Californians (1930)

Leach, Frank A.: Recollections of a Newspaperman (1917)
Lee, Ivy L.: The Press Today (1929)
Lee, James M.: History of American Journalism (1917)
Lippmann, Walter: Liberty and the News (1920)
Lyman, George D.: The Saga of the Comstock (1934)
Lynch, Denis T.: Grover Cleveland (1932)

MacGowan, Kenneth: Coiled in the Flag—Hears-s-s-t (1918)
Millis, Walter: The Martial Spirit (1931)
Morgan, W. H.: History of Kern County (1877)
Moskowitz, Henry: Alfred E. Smith (1924)

Older, Fremont: My Own Story (1919), Life of George Hearst (1934)
Older, Mrs. Fremont: William Randolph Hearst—American (1936)

Paxson, Fred L.: History of the American Frontier (1924)
Payne, George H.: History of Journalism in the United States (1920)

Pearson, Drew, and Constantine Brown: American Diplomatic Game
(1935)
Pringle, Henry F.: Theodore Roosevelt (1931)

Russell, Charles Edward: These Shifting Scenes (1914), Stories of the
Great Railroads (1912)

Seldes, Gilbert: Years of the Locust (1933)
Sherover, Max: Fakes in American Journalism (1916)
Sinclair, Upton: The Brass Check (1920), I, Candidate for Governor, and
How I Got Licked (1935)
Smith, Alfred E.: Up to Now (1929)
Steffens, Lincoln: Autobiography of Lincoln Steffens (1931)
Stewart, William M.: Reminiscences (1908)
Sullivan, Mark: Our Times, vols. I and II (1926)
Swasey, William F.: Early Days and Men in California (1891)
Swing, Raymond Gram: Forerunners of American Fascism (1935)

Thompson, C. W.: Party Leaders of the Time (1905)

U. S. Senate: Memorial Addresses on the Life and Character of George
Hearst (1894), Propaganda or Money alleged to have been used by
foreign governments to influence U. S. Senators (1928)

Vanderbilt, Cornelius, Jr.: Farewell to Fifth Avenue (1935)
Villard, Oswald Garrison: Prophets False and True (1928), Some Newspapers and Newspapermen (1926), The Press Today (1930)

Walker, Stanley: City Editor (1934)
Weeks, George F.: California Copy (1928)
Werner, M. R.: Tammany Hall (1928), Bryan (1929)
Wilkerson, Marcus M.: Public Opinion and the Spanish-American War
(1932)
Williams, Mary F.: History of the San Francisco Committee of Vigilance
of 1851 (1921)
Winkler, J. K.: W. R. Hearst—An American Phenomenon (1928)
Woodward, Julian L.: Foreign News in American Morning Papers (1930)

Young, John P.: Journalism in California (1915), San Francisco, a History (1912)

ADDITIONAL SOURCES

California Corporations (1934)
Contemporary Biography of California's Representative Men (1881)
Moody's Manual of Industrial Securities (1929–30–1–2–3–4)
Poor's Manual of Industrial Securities (1931–2–3–4–5)
Walker's Manual of California (1927–8)

Who's Who Among the Women of California (1921–2)

MAGAZINE ARTICLES

American Mercury, Jan. 1926; May 1927; Nov. 1930
Arena, June 1904; Jan. 1906; Oct. 1908
Arts and Decoration, Feb. 1918
Atlantic Monthly, Dec. 1931
Canadian Monthly, Feb. 1904
Christian Century, Oct. 15, 1930; May 10, 1933
Collier's Weekly, Feb. 18, 1908; March 4, 1908; March 11, 1908; Oct. 24, 1908; June 22, 1912; Oct. 5, 1912; Dec. 30, 1922
Common Sense, March, April, May, June, July, Aug 1935
Cosmopolitan, May 1902
Current Literature, April 1904; Sept. 1906; Dec. 1906; May 1907; Oct. 1907; Dec. 1909
Delineator, Sept. 1927
Fortnightly, Dec. 1907
Fortune, Aug. 1931; Oct. 1935
Good Housekeeping, June 1919
Harper's Weekly, May 21, 1904; April 26, 1913; July 5, 1914; Aug. 22, 1914; Sept. 19, 1914; Oct. 9, 1915; Nov. 6, 1915
Hearst's Magazine, March 1912; April 1912; Oct. 1912; Nov. 1912; Dec. 1912; April 1913
Independent, May 12, 1904; May 26, 1904; June 9, 1904; Oct. 25, 1906
Literary Digest, May 25, 1918; Dec. 28, 1918; Nov. 15, 1919; Dec. 30, 1922; Nov. 17, 1923; May 10, 1924; Sept. 26, 1925; Sept. 13, 1930
Living Age, Jan. 1908; Nov. 1930
Nation, Feb. 22, 1906; July 15, 1918; March 28, 1923; April 25, 1923; Dec. 28, 1927
New Republic, July 14, 1920; Sept. 8, 1926; Jan. 14, 1928; Aug. 10, 1932; Sept. 14, 1932; Sept. 28, 1932; Oct. 5, 1932
New Theater, Oct., Nov. 1935
News Week, Nov. 4, 1933; May 12, 1934; Aug. 25, 1934; June 16, 1934
North American Review, Sept. 1906
Overland, Dec. 1907; Jan. 1918; Sept. 1918
Outlook, Oct. 6, 1906; Oct. 20, 1906; Oct. 27, 1906; Nov. 3, 1915; Jan. 18, 1928; March 21, 1928
Review of Reviews, Nov. 1906; May 1907; April 1908; May 1908; March 1932
World Today, Nov. 1911; Dec. 1912; June 1913
World's Work, April 1906; Oct. 1906; Oct. 1922

INDEX

319

Index

Index

Evans vs. Star Publishing Co., 293

Evening American Publishing Co., 300

Evening Examiner (San Francisco), 24-25; *see also* San Francisco *Examiner*

Evening Journal (New York), 87, 89, 112, 145, 149, 254, 284; *see also* New York *Journal*

Evening Journal (Rochester), 286

Evening Post (New York), 41, 44-5, 104; *see also* New York *Post*

Evening Standard (London), 236, 238

Evening Sun (New York), 79

Evening Telegram (Syracuse), 286

Evening World (New York), 84-5

Examiner (Chicago), 285, 293; *see also* Chicago *Herald-Examiner*

Examiner (Los Angeles), 197-8, 252, 269, 274-5, 284, 292-3

Examiner (Oakland), 181

Examiner (San Francisco), xi, 21, 25-7, 29-32, 34, 44, 46-7, chap. IV *passim*, 63-7, 72, 74-6, 78, 89, 93, 141, 162, 180-3, 281, 284

Examiner Printing Co. (San Francisco), 300

Excella Patterns, 287

Express (Los Angeles), 286; *see also* Los Angeles *Herald*; Los Angeles *Herald-Express*

F

Fair, Senator James, 10, 23

Fairbanks, Douglas, 199

Fairchild, Prof. Henry Pratt, 261

Fairfax, Beatrice, 88, 289

Fall, Albert, 212

Fallon, William J., 211-2

Farewell to Fifth Avenue (Vanderbilt), 295

Farley, James, 245-6

Farrelly, Richard A., 78-9

Fascism, xiv, 135-6, chap. XVII *passim*, 271, 304

Federal Council of Churches of Christ in America, 265

Federalism, 178

Federal Power Commission, 294-5

Fellowship of Reconciliation, 265

Ferber, Nat J., 211

Fischer, Henry W., 87

Fischer, Louis, 264

Fisher, "Bud," 50

Fisher, Harrison, 50

Fitzsimmons, Bob, 87

Five-Star Final (film), 274

Flanagan, Hallie, 261

Flint, Grover, 41, 98

Flirtation Walk (film), 273

Flournoy, Judge, 29

Foley, "Big Tom," 205, 211

Folsom Prison, 275

Food and Drug Act, 130

Foote, W. W., 58

Foraker, Hon. J. B., 165, 167-8, 171

Ford, Henry, 305

Ford, James L., 87

Ford, John, 145

Foreign Press Association, 186

Fortune, 287, 297

Fosdick, Rev. Harry Emerson, 256

"Foster, John C.," 186

Fox Movietone News, 273

Frank, President Glenn, 259

Frankfurter Zeitung, 236

Franklin, Benjamin, 89

Frazier, Charles, 50

Frémiet, 149

Frémont, 149

Frick, Dr. Wilhelm, 252

Frye, Senator, 98

Fuggers, ix

Fuller, Edward Markle, 211

Fuller, E. M., & Co. (bucket shop), 211

Fusion-Republican campaign of 1903, 142

G

Gallinger, Senator, 98

"Gandhi" (dog), 310

Garner, John Nance, 121, 244-6

Garrigues, John, 199

Gaynor, Mayor William J., 160-5, 177

Geary Street Grammar School, 39

Gentleman from Mississippi, A, 289

George, King of Greece, 87

George Washington Hotel (Palm Beach), 276

Georgian (Atlanta), 285

Geronimo, 13-4

Getting Mary Married (film), 196

Gillette, William, 289

Gilling Castle, 238

Girl from Paris, The, 119

Girl from Rector's, The, 289

Givens, Willard E., 257-8

Gladstone, William E., 79

Glasgow, Dr. Ida Cowan, 198

Gleason, Arthur, 172

Globe (Boston), 44

Glyn, Elinor, 198

Goddard, Morrill, 76-81, 85, 138, 271, 287